Congratulations

It is not easy
given to awaken to the
fact that most of us
are asleep. It is a task
of no small portion, but

*ARISING

strive and effort we
must to awaken and
*arise - the times demand
it. Kevin and I have
some syncronistic synergies
of intrigue that I will
share at some point. If
it works out, I will
try to let you know when
he's in the TC's next or
before too long - not much
travel now.
                              John
                              4/10/20

MW00561740

ARISING

—— KEVIN LOCKE ——

AS TOLD TO KIM DOUGLAS & ALEAH DOUGLAS-KHAVARI

BAHÁ'Í
PUBLISHING
WILMETTE, ILLINOIS

Bahá'í Publishing, Wilmette, Illinois

401 Greenleaf Ave, Wilmette, Illinois 60091
Copyright © 2018 by the National Spiritual Assembly
of the Bahá'ís of the United States
All rights reserved. Published 2018
Printed in the United States of America ∞

22   21   20   19   6   5   4   3

Library of Congress Cataloging-in-Publication Data
Names: Locke, Kevin, author. | Douglas, Kim. | Douglas-Khavari,
    Aleah.
Title: Arising / by Kevin Locke, as told to Kim Douglas & Aleah
    Douglas-Khavari.
Description: Wilmette, Illinois : Baha'i Publishing, [2018]
Identifiers: LCCN 2018015663 | ISBN 9781618511300 (pbk.)
Subjects: LCSH: Locke, Kevin. | Flute players—United States—
    Biography. | Lakota Indians—Biography. | Lakota Indians—
    Religion. | Bahais—United States—Biography.
Classification: LCC ML419.L63 A3 2018 | DDC 297.9/3092
    [B]—dc23
LC record available at https://lccn.loc.gov/2018015663

Cover design by Jamie Hanrahan
Book design by Patrick Falso
Cover photo by Adib Roy

Referring to the Indigenous people of this hemisphere in his Tablets of the Divine Plan, 'Abdu'l-Bahá, the son of Bahá'u'lláh, the Prophet-Founder of the Bahá'í Faith, has written, "Attach great importance to the indigenous population of America . . . these Indians, should they be educated and guided, there can be no doubt that they will become so illumined as to enlighten the whole world" (*Tablets of the Divine Plan,* no. 6.8).

This book is dedicated to these promised ones who are destined to fulfill the words of 'Abdu'l-Bahá, who are laboring to illuminate the world, and who are journeying on their own red road.

CONTENTS

CONTENTS

ACKNOWLEDGMENTS

As we come to a close on the writing and editing process for "Arising"—a book I did not anticipate creating, I am sitting on the deck of our home at the confluence of the Missouri and Grand Rivers. The earth is bursting with fragrances and hues on this perfect spring day. Swallows swoop and dart while meadowlarks and mockingbirds lead an intoxicating symphony of intonations. It is as if the earth is celebrating these propitious times when the ancestors and all of creation are alive to the significance of this Day of God.

I feel gratitude for the many people involved in the creation of this book, which was truly a collaborative effort. I want to especially thank my mother, the late Patricia Locke, for inspiring Kim Douglas to launch this wonderful writing endeavor. Kim's perspective, open-ended questions, and persistence were the driving force behind shaping, providing direction to, and developing the narrative.

Kim and I are enormously grateful to Aleah Khavari, who joined us when we realized our full work schedules and travels required another collaborator. Aleah's curiosity, attention to detail, and capacity to transcribe hours of conversations advanced the project in ways Kim and I could not have achieved alone.

Thank you also to Anisa Everett, who supported us to read through the page proofs to catch those common errors that become so invisible to those of us who have lived with a manuscript for a few years.

Ceylan Isgor, my wife, also contributed to many discussions and provided vital input, especially for the last part of the manuscript. Not only is

Ceylan my wife, she is also my incredible life coach / personal trainer who gives her all to take great care of our daughter and me. She is the only one in her family on this side of the Atlantic who speaks English and who is a Bahá'í. I thank God for bringing her into my life and want to acknowledge her with love and gratitude for how she balances her role as a mother with her passion for her profession. Since I travel the world with my work and continue to devote much of my time to preserving traditional culture, she—much like a single parent—faces the superhuman challenge of this constant juggling act. Thank you, Ceylan. You are one of the greatest rock stars in my world.

I was moved by Ken Bowers's thoughtful and insightful introduction to the book. Not all European-Americans have the knowledge and sensitivity to the historical atrocities Indigenous communities have endured. Not all respect their traditional beliefs. His words demonstrate his solidarity with and humility before the many communities that have been oppressed and continue to be oppressed. His words have me pondering the life of Abraham End of Horn, my mom's uncle. He impressed upon me the singular importance to Lakota identity of the spiritual teachings of the White Buffalo Calf Maiden. Even though he professed Christianity, he stressed to me that the Maiden foretold the coming of the "Grandfather" and that I had to be vigilant in watching for His promised appearance.

Just a few weeks ago in Rapid City, I visited with the famous Leonard Crow Dog, who is now in gravely perilous health. In his youth, he was a noted promulgator of the traditional Lakota style of hoop dancing. Knowing his preference for conversing in Lakota, I asked him during our visit, "čhaŋgléška wačhípi kiŋ he eháŋni oyáte kiŋ tuktétaŋhaŋ ičúpi he?" ("From where did the ancestors obtain the hoop dance?")

"This dance comes from the universe—the holy world of light, the real world, the eternal world, the same place we all come from," he responded. "You are especially blessed because you can be with children and use Lakȟól wičhóȟ'aŋ—the Lakota way—the way of the covenant to keep them connected to their place of origin."

I am so grateful for what may have been my final conversation with Leonard Crow Dog, who reminded me that through the heavenly ways, even adults can be rescued and brought back from this shadowy dark world that we attach to and falsely believe to be reality. Leonard is one of the many elders throughout my life who spoke to me with the ancestral voice of this land summoning us all to that universal place that transcends race, gender, language, culture, and place.

This is the same place, the universal place to which Black Elk summoned us:

> I was standing on the highest mountain of them all, and round about beneath me was the whole hoop of the world. And while I stood there I saw more than I can tell and I understood more than I saw; for I was seeing in a sacred manner the shapes of all things in the spirit, and the shape of all shapes as they must live together like one being. And I saw that the sacred hoop of my people was one of many hoops that made one circle, wide as daylight and as starlight, and in the center grew one mighty flowering tree to shelter all the children of one mother and one father. And I saw that it was holy.*

Today we are blessed to witness this in-gathering of the hoops of humanity into the one hoop that Black Elk foretold.

Thank you, dear reader, for journeying through the pages ahead. My sincere hope is that you will feel inspired to join those of us who—diverse as we may be—believe in the one hoop and are working to dismantle the outworn dogmas, traditions, and practices that divide us, and that you will find your path to contribute to the all-important challenging work of creating an ever-advancing civilization that upholds the oneness of humankind.

KEVIN LOCKE
Standing Rock, SD
May 2018

---

* Black Elk, quoted in Neihardt, *Black Elk Speaks*, p. 33.

INTRODUCTION

When Kevin Locke and Kim Douglas invited me to write an introductory section to this book, my surprise at this invitation was exceeded only by the fact that the book had been written in the first place. I had known and admired Kevin for many years for his services in sharing and preserving Lakota culture, which he pursued seamlessly with the goal of advancing unity and understanding among people of all backgrounds. More fundamentally, in our personal interactions, I had come to know him as a man of deep spirituality, with his most attractive quality being freedom from the kind of self-absorption that is so rampant in modern society. He and I had conversed about many issues over the years, but rarely had we talked about his own spiritual path—how he had come to be the person he is, and how his sense of place in the world had been formed.

The following pages bear out—in unforgettable fashion—a personality so spiritually attuned, so deeply interested in justice for the oppressed, so interested in all of humanity while remaining a passionate advocate for his own heritage, that it must have been forged as the result of a remarkable personal journey. On the one hand, *Arising* is the story of a struggle all too common in American history—the struggle for identity, for dignity, and for an authentic spirituality in the face of prejudices that have been horrific and nearly all-consuming in their consequences. Yet Kevin's journey also takes a unique and deeply consequential turn in his discovery of a world religion, the Bahá'í Faith, which he sees as the fulfillment of his traditional beliefs and as offering a renewed sense of the destiny of his people and hope for the future of the world.

Bahá'ís believe that Bahá'u'lláh is the latest in a series of Messengers of God to humanity Who have guided our spiritual and social evolution down through the ages. The Messengers are part of one divine plan, the ultimate goal of which is the unification of the entire world and the creation of a new civilization based upon the principles of divine justice. Bahá'u'lláh taught respect for the spiritual heritage of the entire human race, in all its vastness and diversity. He stated categorically that no nation or people have been deprived by the all-loving Creator of their share of divine knowledge and that none are to be condemned or disdained: "Unto the cities of all nations He hath sent His Messengers, Whom He hath commissioned to announce unto men tidings of the Paradise of His good pleasure, and to draw them nigh unto the Haven of abiding security, the Seat of eternal holiness and transcendent glory."*

Kevin found in this message a welcome contrast to the demands from various quarters to reject the beliefs of his ancestors. For the first time, he was able to link his ancestors to the history of humanity's encounter with God in all its forms. Virtually all cultures revere certain great spiritual visionaries whose teachings have provided the moral foundations for their respective societies. Bahá'u'lláh, Who lived in the Middle East in the nineteenth century, mentioned some of these Messengers by name, especially those known to the people of His place and time. Given the vast number of tribes and nations in the world, He did not specifically name all those sent by God for the spiritual education of His children. Yet a person of any particular background might well consider certain souls to have been among such spiritual teachers. White Buffalo Calf Maiden, for example, figures prominently in Lakota tradition and was a source of inspiration and guidance in Kevin's life. She ranks in his heart among these great spiritual luminaries.

Just as all have had access to the divine Source, all religious traditions anticipate a time of convergence and the establishment in the world of an era of peace and unity. All tribes and nations therefore have a legitimate

---

* Bahá'u'lláh, *Gleanings from the Writings of Bahá'u'lláh*, no. 76.1.

contribution to make to the advancement of life on this planet. This does not imply uniformity of thought, however—the watchword is unity in diversity:

> Consider the flowers of a garden. Though differing in kind, color, form and shape, yet, inasmuch as they are refreshed by the waters of one spring, revived by the breath of one wind, invigorated by the rays of one sun, this diversity increaseth their charm, and addeth unto their beauty. . . . How unpleasing to the eye if all the flowers and plants, the leaves and blossoms, the fruits, the branches and the trees of that garden were all of the same shape and color! Diversity of hues, form and shape, enricheth and adorneth the garden, and heighteneth the effect thereof. In like manner, when divers shades of thought, temperament and character, are brought together under the power and influence of one central agency, the beauty and glory of human perfection will be revealed and made manifest.*

The essentials of Bahá'í teachings demonstrate a remarkable harmony with the fundamental beliefs of Indigenous peoples all over the world. Among them are the organic connection of human beings with all creation; the belief in our essentially spiritual nature; the immortality of the soul and the possibility of communion with those who have passed on; worship of the Creator; the importance of consultation and collective action; adherence to justice and uprightness of conduct; and wise stewardship of the environment and reverence for all things. The Bahá'í teachings also present insights relevant to a new age in history—one that will witness the social and spiritual maturation of humanity on a global scale. These teachings are explored within the pages of this book.

Moreover, the Bahá'í Faith places special emphasis on the contribution that the Indigenous peoples of the Americas are destined to make toward the establishment of world peace, and the Faith assures us that as Indigenous peoples encounter and embrace this new revelation from God, ". . . there can be no doubt that they will become so illumined as to enlighten the

---

* 'Abdu'l-Bahá, *Selections from the Writings of 'Abdu'l-Bahá*, no. 225.24–25.

whole world."* Kevin understood that his decision to become a Bahá'í was not a break from his Lakota past but was rather the natural consummation of that ancient heritage and all that it promised—now to merge, together with countless other tributaries, in the creation of a new, united river of human advancement.

The story that unfolds in this volume is exactly what I would have expected from Kevin—not an exercise in self-promotion, but a labor of love in service to others. Although deeply personal, it is universal in the insights it offers. May readers of all backgrounds take inspiration from this story of discovery and connect the journey of an individual with that of a great people, and of that people with the future of us all.

KENNETH E. BOWERS
Wilmette, Illinois
June 1, 2018

---

* 'Abdu'l-Bahá, *Tablets of the Divine Plan*, no. 6.8.

PART I

AYÁŊPA WAČHÍŊ YO
(TO ENDURE UNTIL DAWN)

When my mom presented me the pipe, a family heirloom, in 1972, I was only eighteen and did not pay much attention. Two years later, my curiosity grew. I was living in Fort Yates, North Dakota, on the Standing Rock Reservation. As a student at the University of North Dakota-Grand Forks, I was studying for my degree through distance learning. Employed by the Teacher Corps, I was assigned to teach at the Standing Rock Elementary School in Fort Yates, and even though the program was an innovative and successful program to train teachers for rural reservation areas, I had the uneasy sense that I was not doing what I was supposed to be doing. Throughout college, I tried numbing this feeling with alcohol and distracting myself with the university social scene. I contemplated law school or moving to another city and another job. Perhaps my soul had something of value to produce. Perhaps I could contribute something of meaning to the world. But what? What was I supposed to be doing with my life?

No human being could give me the answers, a few different elders taught me. The elders were wise and experienced members of our tribe who provided counsel and mentoring to younger members of the tribe. They shared with me that the only way I could discover the mystery of the pipe was to engage in *haŋbléčheyapi*, the traditional law of fasting.

Lakota tradition views the pipe as an analogy of a staff that aids us to advance along our path in life. The pipe had been in our family for a long time, and my ancestors had used the pipe for fasting. Before Christian clergy initiated and government edict reinforced the ban of feasts, dances, and the use of the pipe, the Lakota had practiced the traditional Lakota fast to draw nearer to God.

3

As the ninth keeper of my family's pipe, I was determined to engage in the fast to better understand its significance. I had learned from the elders that four days and nights without food and water can push a body to the brink of death. During the first twenty-four hours of fasting, hunger pains invade the stomach. In the days that remain, the parched throat burns with thirst. As the body separates from the physical demands of life, the mind is transported from despair to epiphany. We draw closer to the spiritual worlds, unlocking truths that we could have never otherwise perceived.

In 1975, while still in the teacher corp program at the University of North Dakota, my first daughter was born, and I became a father. When I cradled my daughter and looked into her dark, bright eyes, fear surged through me. How could I provide the guidance she needed when I felt so lost? I pictured her growing up rootless in a tumultuous world and suffering as I had. The weight of her life reminded me of the knowledge I craved—the spiritual knowledge of the pipe, knowledge that would aid me to discover my spiritual and vocational calling.

I found hope and intrigue in the traditional devotional practices and mannerisms of my Lakota elders. They had a vision of something real, as opposed to what is rooted in the shadow world in which we live. They had grounded themselves in a deep, spiritual purpose, and they embodied the way of life I longed for. I sought their mentorship to learn the Lakota language and engage in traditional practices

Even though I proceeded under their tutelage and engaged in a few fasts, I continued to feel an undercurrent of deep dissatisfaction that ran beneath my professional veneer. I had moved from classroom teaching to nonprofit work. I taught a semester at Standing Rock Community College, now known as Sitting Bull College. Though I fulfilled my responsibilities, I felt severed from a sense of purpose. Even upon completing a master's program, with a degree in hand, I felt no more content than before I had started the program.

In 1978, my mentor, Charles Kills Enemy, and I were planning for my fifth fast, to be held the following year. Whenever I spoke to my mentor, I called him "Uncle Charles" since we refer to people by a term of kinship in Lakota traditional society; calling anyone by his or her first name is considered impolite. Charles asked me what I wanted to achieve through this fast.

"Well, I'm not sure what I accomplished in the other fasts," I told him. "I didn't receive the guidance I desired."

"The reason is because you weren't focused on your prayers," Charles said. "Your thoughts and your attention were scattered." He looked firmly at me. "Focus your prayers during this fast on a specific goal. When you do that, you'll find the answers you need."

That year, as I prepared for the fast, I thought about Charles' advice. I began to listen to elders when they prayed. I realized a recurring theme in these prayers: finding the road of life, *čhaŋkú lúta,* the red road. Red is the color of holiness. The red road is the goal of life, the path leading to God.

My elders prayed, "God, look down upon Your poor grandchildren here on this Earth. See how we suffer—lost on paths that are crooked and dark, twisted and convoluted. See how we are blind, dazed, distracted. See our state of depression. From generation to generation, humanity worsens. Yet, You have promised that You will give us a road here on this Earth and that this road will be good and sacred and straight and red. You will lead us upon this road. This road will take us to beauty and harmony, color, movement, and fragrance—to all things holy in Your good pleasure."

I realized that this road was what I wanted. I was among the lost—foundationless and afraid. I was seeking direction and meaning in my life. I wanted to find the straight road foretold in prayers and the tradition of the pipe for my children's sake as well as my own.

So I had decided I would fast again for the fifth time. I would go four days and four nights without food or water. The days would be filled with consecrated prayer, where I would supplicate God for His assistance in finding my purpose. I hoped that this time, by focusing my prayers during the fast, I would be guided to my path. I would discover what I could contribute to this world and who I could become.

* * *

In Indigenous North America, fasting is one of the foundations for all systems of knowledge and understanding, such as pharmacological, food, or art traditions. However, the practice of fasting is not unique to Indigenous people. God's commandment to fast has reached the hearts of people of many diverse cultures and religions. In Christianity, one finds the practice of Lent; in Islam, the period of fasting is called Ramadan; and in Judaism, the period of fasting and atonement is called Yom Kippur. Fasting also occurs in Indigenous traditions around the world, such as the Walkabout, a rite of passage practiced among the Australian Aborigines.

In pre-Christian times, fasting was binding among men in North American tribal communities. Men fasted by abstaining from both food and water for four, five, or even six days. Depending on a person's physical condition, the fast could sometimes be life-threatening; however, Native people knew that life without the guidance and spiritual direction of fasting was purposeless. One who participates in the fast steps into a sacred reality, timeless and placeless. Fasting opens a special dimension of a soul's commitment to his Creator and to the Creator's commitment to the progress of a soul.

My first encounter with this most basic and holy law was within the Teachings and Covenant of the White Buffalo Maiden, the single most important figure to appear to the Lakota. This Maiden is considered by the Lakota to be a holy being and an emissary from God. She delivered the Lakota from despair, remoteness from God, and poverty. She summoned them to arise to their true station as noble grandchildren of God and brought heavenly laws and ceremonies to aid them to do so. Of the seven laws of her dispensation, fasting was the most foundational.

Charles Kills Enemy deepened my understanding, knowledge, and practice of traditional fasting. While I had had great mentoring and tutelage during my previous fasts, I discovered that every fast was a totally different experience due to my stage in life, the obstacles I was facing at the time, and the particular elder accompanying me. Charles was born on the Yankton Reservation. After losing his parents to an outbreak of Spanish influenza, he was brought up by his grandparents on the Rosebud Reservation near St. Francis. They gave him their name, Kills Enemy, signifying someone who has the determination to overcome adversity and the negative forces that hold the people back from moving closer to the Creator.

Charles always had the deep desire to learn more about the mysteries of life, so he turned to the traditional teachings of the Lakota prophet, the White Buffalo Calf Maiden. As a teenager, he started going out in the wilderness to fast and continued to do so for nineteen consecutive years. He received guidance through an avalanche of visions from various spirit-helpers, entities from the spiritual world who assist us in this world. The spiritual world, from an Indigenous viewpoint, encompasses all of creation—the visible and invisible; the past, present, and future. This world, this earth, is only a shadow of the next world and worlds beyond. The spirit-helpers from the spiritual world gifted Charles with insight into ceremonial ways.

Charles' mentors were well-known spiritual leaders—Good Lance, Horn Chips, and Hare—all of whom were born in the nineteenth century pre-reservation era. Under their tutelage, he became qualified to perform different healing ceremonies. He was an expert in ethnobotany and traditional pharmacology. He offered herbal treatments to men with ulcers and to women in labor, and these remedies were often more effective than any modern medicine. Charles also specialized in faith healing—summoning ancestral spirits and forces of creation—to heal patients. His healing often addressed the spiritual reality of both an individual and their community. If a grandmother were ailing, for example, Charles would instruct her to offer special prayers daily at sunrise, alongside her family and grandchildren. Her family's unified prayers would unleash insights from the spiritual realms that would uplift the grandmother and inspire the various members of her family to offer their assistance to her.

When I explained to Charles that during this fast, I wanted to pray for God to help me discover where I should be going in my life, he asked, "How are you going to pray?"

"From my heart," I said.

"Of course, that's good," he replied, pausing. "But the main way that we pray is through song. What kind of songs are you going to use?"

I didn't know what to say.

"Well, God can't help you if you're standing there during your fast and all you can sing is *Mary had a little lamb*."

Right then and there, I understood. He wanted me to commit myself to learn his teachings and songs—songs that he had absorbed from his mentors who were the bearers of ancient traditions. These songs would constitute the foundation of my fasting prayers.

To pass rich cultural and spiritual knowledge from generation to generation, the Lakota rely on oral tradition and song rather than the written word.

Similar to the way the doctrines of the Old Testament were recorded first in song and the way devout Muslims memorize the Qur'án through chanting, songs have enabled the Lakota to preserve this history and knowledge. A complex sequence of songs passes—verbatim—the teachings of one generation to the next. For example, the sequence of the Thunder Songs track the Thunder Beings, from the first appearance of the cumulus clouds, to the lightning that slashes through the sky, to the resounding thunderclaps at the end. The Thunder Beings are symbolic of the power of regeneration in life since the first thunder occurs in March when spring arrives.

Whether a Thunder song, Buffalo song, or Eagle song, each song is sung in strict order and is a spiritual manifestation of a physical reality. The Eagle songs tell about the journey of the eagle throughout creation. The eagle is symbolic of the ascendant nature of people. The Buffalo songs symbolize strength. All the songs affirm the covenant between mankind and the spiritual world. The sequences are prayers that carry inner significances of the Covenant, the sacred relationship that the White Buffalo Calf Maiden established between the Lakota and God. Ceremonial specialists, such as Charles and his mentors, have carried this hallowed Covenant forward through their staunch dedication to ensure the integrity of the passing of wisdom down through the generations. Fortunately, Charles had also discovered the wonders of recording technology, which he used to preserve this system of knowledge.

Charles was eager to methodically and conscientiously share his encyclopedic knowledge of all the sequences of prayer songs. I consecrated myself to the task, and with the help of my first tape recorder, I started documenting his songs, stories, and narratives to use during my fast. As I engaged in my everyday tasks and activities, I played the recordings and eventually memorized them.

My first mentor in the law of fasting was Pete Catches, Sr., who was influenced by the great nineteenth-century traditionalist Good Lance. Good Lance's vision was the Eagle Way, a ceremonial practice for healing that restored harmony and balance. Pete, like Charles, was instrumental in preserving Native traditions and ceremonies at a time when the government and religious leaders condemned them as satanic and outlawed. Despite government restrictions, Pete found a way to maintain Native knowledge. Frank Fools Crow, a spiritual leader and medicine man born in the late nineteenth century, and nephew of the renowned Black Elk, mentored Pete. Other elders also taught Pete how to make bows and arrows. This enabled Pete to secretly hunt for his own food. Since I was connected with Pete and curious about the significance of the pipe, he graciously shared his knowledge and offered to guide me in the traditional practice of the fast.

Back in September of 1974, outside Pete's rustic cabin on a hill above White Clay Creek, I had fasted for the first time. The only traces of modern civilization were the occasional jet trails high above me. No buildings, no people, and no technology connected me to the outside world. I was alone with God's natural creation. An expanse of pines, as far as my eyes could see, housed me. Hard frost clung to the ground. Only two buffalo skins protected me from the grueling cold. As harsh as the physical environment was, the isolation was a greater challenge for me. I persevered, however, spurred on by the desire to participate fully in this sacred tradition.

After the first twenty-four hours, the sensation of hunger disappeared. Everything took on a heightened dimension in this state of uncommon reality. The flitting of the birds, the pungent aroma of the pine trees, the quiet, and the stillness took on added meaning. I looked to the clouds, as I did when I was a child and saw stories unfold. When a leaf drifted to the ground, I meditated on the purpose of its movement.

I had heard from others how elaborate, technicolor visions sometimes occurred during fasting and affected both mind and body. I did not receive any such visions; instead, I began to perceive how all of creation reflected the power and beauty of the Creator. To find order in the universe, I realized, was my duty. The connectedness of creation filled me with a sense of grace. Fasting deepened my thirst for this grace—a thirst that would never die.

Pete came to check on me once during my fast because when his wife had stepped outside to retrieve water, she had glanced toward the hills and had seen hundreds of people surrounding me. Curious, Pete had hiked up the hill to investigate. When he arrived, he found me alone. He realized that his wife had seen the ancestors, those who provided guidance from the spiritual realms. Pete didn't mention this to me until after the fast. Even though I didn't realize it at the time, I was not alone.

* * *

Four years later, in September of 1978, I selected the location for my fifth fast, which I would observe the following June. I chose *Waŋblí Oyúspa Pahá*, Catch Eagle Butte: a flat-top hill nestled between several other geographically isolated and remote hills close to my home in the Wakpala District of Standing Rock Reservation. The buttes rise 2200 feet above sea level. Alongside them, deep ravines and valleys wind down to the confluence of the Grand River and Missouri River. Long ago, the torrential meltdown from thawing glaciers sculpted and carved the landscape, flattened the east river country, and punctuated the land west of the Missouri with valleys and rivers. For hundreds of thousands of years, the land surrounding the buttes eroded, causing the structures of compacted sediment to rise higher and higher.

Standing at the top of Catch Eagle Butte, I traced the rippling waves of ancient seas imprinted upon the sandstone pressed together in tight formation. Embedded in the stone were mollusk shells and ancient petroglyphs—messages sent from prophets of old, Indigenous people believed. Autumnal prairies cascaded from the base of the butte outward. Green grasses had faded to gold. An array of trees—oak, ash, elm and cottonwood—sported branches heavy with multi-colored leaves. The clear blue sky extended as far as I could see.

Now known as the Rattlesnake Buttes in English, these hills were called Catch Eagle Butte because, long ago, eagles perched and hunted from there. The Native people who had prayed there had also fasted before attempting to catch the eagles. To capture the eagles, the Natives dug a pit on the hilltop, camouflaged the top of the hole with twigs and grass, and had someone crouch down in the hole. Then they tied a live rabbit on top of the camouflage. When an eagle swooped down to devour the rabbit, the person in the pit reached up and grabbed the eagle. The bird clawed and bit his captor as this person attempted to remove the two king feathers—the two center tail feathers—from the bird. When this was accomplished, the caught bird was released.

The eagle symbolizes the ascendant nature of the human spirit. Its feathers represent virtuous qualities such as truthfulness, honesty, wisdom, kindness, and justice. As humans, we come equipped with a full set of these qualities that remain inert until activated through service to the greater good. When we use these God-given virtues in selfless service, we attain our true station. We soar as eagles in spiritual realms.

I chose Catch Eagle Butte because I had been inspired by the analogy of the eagle. I hoped that during my fast, I might come to recognize the qualities I had been given—the qualities that would carry me through my path in life.

When June of '79 arrived, several days before I observed my pledge to fast, I drove two hundred miles to the border between South Dakota and Nebraska to pick up Charles. We had much to do to continue preparing for the fast according to traditional ways. Together, we would construct the *inipi,* the sweat lodge, for the fasting ceremonies and the *owáŋka,* the altar, on Catch Eagle Butte, where I would spend the four days of my fast.

Charles required that everyone he mentored procure various items during the year leading into their fast. To represent new beginnings, everything—the tools we would use to build the inipi, the bucket and dipper for the ceremonies, and the offerings for the altar—had to be brand new. Most of the offerings except for the center tail eagle feather were easily obtained. I gathered the supplies before Charles came, and I also bought tobacco, string, and cotton cloths in the traditional colors for the *čhaŋlí wapháhta*—tobacco ties—necessary for the construction of the *owáŋka.*

I had learned this art from an elder, Mrs. Tobacco, who was living in Pine Ridge during my first fast. She and I piled into my little red Datsun 510, nicknamed *uŋkčé pagmíyaŋ,* which translated into English means "dung beetle" or "turd roller." We drove to a couple of nearby stores that were familiar with our list of necessities: cloth, tobacco, and string for the 405 tobacco ties that would mark the sacred space. Mrs. Tobacco then tutored me in the fine art of tying tobacco ties. Before us were hundreds of small squares of cloths in the ceremonial colors. Each color represented a cardinal direction: black represented west, red represented north, yellow represented east, and white represented south. We filled each tiny square of cloth with a pinch of tobacco in the center. Then we bunched up the cloths and double-half-hitch tied them together.

I admired that Mrs. Tobacco was a true syncretist: a devout Catholic with no qualms about practicing the Lakota ways. She blended her Catholic faith with the traditions of Native people, and she saw no conflict between Lakota Traditions and Christianity. She taught me to continually beg the Great Spirit to have pity upon and help me.

Now, several years later, as I made my tobacco ties alone in preparation for my fifth fast, I remembered her tutelage. I repeated her prayer—a prayer asking God to have mercy upon me and to assist me during this fast. Hope brimmed within me. That night, I found myself anticipating what the coming four days would bring.

Before dawn on the day of the fast, Charles and I went to the *inipi*, the sweat lodge. We had constructed the waist-high domed structure the day before with ten- to twelve-foot stalks and stems from willow saplings. We built the lodge to hold the opening ceremony before my fast.

The time was approaching. The re-creation of life would occur symbolically during this ceremony using the four elements: fire, water, rock, and air. Both my mother and my aunt, Margaret One Bull, came to participate. I was among the first people to fast in Standing Rock in a few generations. Though traditions such as the Sundance and fasting reemerged on other reservations, few had participated in these practices here. My mother's generation had seen these sacred practices made illegal—condemned as "satanic" and outlawed. I knew the move back to traditional practices brought her great joy because she saw it as a sign of the people awakening and taking charge of their spiritual well-being.

To prepare for the inipi, Charles stacked wood for a fire and lined up seven rocks running from west to east on the woodpile. I had prepared a rendering of buffalo heart fat. Charles dipped his finger into the fat, then into some red clay powder. As he drew circles the size of silver dollars on each rock, he uttered a prayer. The circles represented the mark of creation. Charles consecrated each rock to one of the seven directions—west, north, east, south, the heavens, the earth, and the center—and placed the rocks in their proper position in the fire pit where they would blacken.

We lit a fire on the woodpile to signal the beginning of the fast and the limiting of all interaction to the uttering and chanting of prayers. The flames enveloped the stones. I sang songs of the White Buffalo Calf Maiden while Charles, also praying, began to fill the pipe.

Kȟolá, léčhel ečhúŋ wo!
Kȟolá, léčhel eečhúŋ wo!
Kȟolá, léčhel ečhúŋ wo!
aéj Héčhanuŋ kiŋ, nithúŋkašila waŋníyaŋg ú kte ló. aéj új
Friend, do it in this way.

Friend, do it in this way.
Friend, do it in this way.

When (if) you do that, your Grandfather will come to see you.

Hóčhoka waŋží ogná ílotake čiŋ, míksuya opági yo!
aéj Héčhanuŋ kiŋ,
táku ehé kiŋ,
iyéčhetu kte ló. aéj új

If you sit down inside the sacred circle/altar.
Remember me.
When you do that,
then the things you say will come true.

Čhaŋnúŋpa waŋží yuhá ílotake čiŋ, míksuya opági yo!
aéj Héčhanuŋ kiŋ,
táku yačhíŋ kiŋ,
iyéčhetu kte ló. aéj új

If you sit down with a pipe.
Remember me.
When you do that,
then the things you want will come true.

Kȟolá, léčhel ečhúŋ wo!
Kȟolá, léčhel ečhúŋ wo!
Kȟolá, léčhel ečhúŋ wo!
aéj Héčhanuŋ kiŋ, nitȟúŋkašila waŋníyaŋg ú kte ló. aéj új

Friend, do it in this way.
Friend, do it in this way.
Friend, do it in this way.
When (if) you do that, your Grandfather will come to see you.

With each pinch of the mixture of red willow bark and tobacco, Charles continued to pray. He sealed several pinches of tobacco with the buffalo's heart fat. At the end of my fast, the spiritual energy sealed within the pipe would be released to the Creator in the form of smoke.

As the flames died down, the rocks began to char. Our sweat before the fast would not be as hot or as long as other sweats—only fifteen to twenty minutes, with each minute sacred. When the rocks blackened, we lifted them from the embers with pitchforks and carried them inside the lodge to the center pit. A trail of ashes speckled the air above the rocks, and we used a dipper to pour the first waters. Steam billowed from the pit, sweeping the specks of ash from midair. The lodge became the *wakíŋyaŋ wahóȟpi*: the Thunder Being nest. The rocks represented the eggs of the Thunder Being, the power that animates creation.

I joined my mother and aunt around the rocks and sat at the place of honor, the *čhatkú*, opposite the door on the east side of the lodge. Charles dropped down the *inipi* door, and complete darkness engulfed us. Charles sang the opening song to announce our desire to draw closer to the spiritual worlds. Already droplets of steam clung to my skin. My family and I began to sing to the four cardinal directions. Our song lifted me from the realm of this earth to the realm of the ancestors.

Then Charles opened the door, and cool air, symbolizing the Holy Spirit, rushed in. Lakota belief holds the Holy Spirit as the spiritual thread between the Holy Stone Woman, the Beautiful Flower Woman, and the White Buffalo Calf Maiden—the women who ushered in different dispensations of Lakota belief. Years later, I would learn of the Maiden of Heaven, the fourth woman, who was a direct fulfillment of prophecy to bring to creation the new world.

Charles once again lowered the lodge door, and we began chanting our prayers and songs in the dark. We meditated on the Holy Spirit. I took in deep breaths of hot, damp air and felt the steam cleanse me. After twenty minutes, Charles raised the door. We had completed the first two doors and had symbolically cleansed ourselves.

* * *

After the *inipi* ceremony, Charles, my mother, and my aunt and I made our procession from the sweat lodge to the fasting site, carrying with us the offerings for the *owáŋka*. Charles led the procession and stopped four times along our route to offer prayers and songs at every stop. Carrying the buffalo skull, I followed behind him. My mother and aunt carried the offerings— the cherry saplings, tobacco ties, center tail eagle feather, and conch shell. All the offerings had been purified during the *inipi* ceremony when Charles used the dipper and poured water on the rocks. I held each item, one at a time, over the steam to purify the objects, according to ancient ritual.

We arrived at a site I had already identified as the one where I would complete my fast. Burrowed between two peaks, the space I chose was a natural amphitheater of sorts. It provided seclusion, a feeling of being nestled in the bosom of Grandmother Earth. The area surrounding the butte was still lush from the snowmelt earlier in the season and the spring rain. Purple bouquets accentuated infinite shades of green. Birds cried from up above, vying with each other to herald the glory of the day. None could rival the virtuosic intonations of the western meadowlark, whose call sank deep into my heart.

I took in a deep breath. This was my spot, the altar where I would remain for the four days and four nights of the fast.

Charles and I marked out a square space roughly seven feet by seven feet for the *owáŋka*. Shoving a crowbar into the soft earth, we made holes at each corner for the altar. We thrust four cherry saplings into the soil until they stood strong and stable. After the saplings were positioned, we hung four flags, each with a large pinch of tobacco, at the four corners of the altar. Each flag faced one of the four directions: the black flag faced west, the red flag faced north, the yellow flag faced east, and the white flag faced south. We worked in silent reverence.

"This is the center," Charles instructed, continuing to mentor me. I remained silent, taking in his instruction. The only words I could utter would come later in the form of prayer and song. We placed a fifth cherry sapling between the south and west corners of the altar. "This is where all the powers of heaven and earth converge. This is where you will face during your fast."

I nodded. Lakota tradition does not have one point of adoration as most religious traditions do. Our practice establishes any place sanctified by prayer as the center of the universe.

We attached the blue and green offering cloths at this fifth sapling. Charles stood at its base and tied the offerings onto the tree: the strip of

15

red felt represented God's color, the conch shell symbolized the lowest form of creation, the eagle king feather portrayed the highest form of creation, and the small pipe signified the Covenant and the link that ties everything together. Charles then placed the buffalo skull in front of the sapling, its horns and the back of the skull facing west and its face facing east. The buffalo skull would be used as the pipe rack during the fast.

Then he and I took big bundles of sage and spread out their dry leaves to create a thick carpet inside the altar. The crisp fragrance hung in the air. We tied the strings of tobacco ties around each of the corner saplings and once again paired each color with its matching cardinal direction. For the fifth sapling, we had tied the blue offering cloth on the top of the tree and the green around the trunk. Charles tied the pink cloth in between the blue and green on the sapling in homage to one of his own personal spir-it-helpers, who had the interesting name of "Scotty." This ancestral spirit had doctored and resuscitated a young patient named Scotty (at the time a small boy about four or five years old) and exchanged his own personal name with Scotty's name. In former times individuals often acquired several names over their lifetime and would often give their names away as the occasion demanded, sacrificing even their personal identity to accomplish a devotional goal or purpose.

Charles and I completed our preparations. This sacred space was the *owáŋka*, the altar, my place of vigil, where I would fulfill my vow to fast and pray for four days before *Tȟuŋkášila Wakȟáŋ Tȟáŋka*—Grandfather Great Spirit.

When I situated myself in the altar, Charles sang a prayer. He, my mother and aunt then formed a procession and left before high noon. Buoyed by the songs and prayers I had shared with my family in the *inipi*, I felt invincible in the wake of this fast, even though the temperatures were abnormally high for June. I was filled with the vigor and optimism of youth. I had focused my prayers, as Charles had instructed, on finding direction and meaning in my life. I would no doubt discover the path that God intended for me over the course of these next four days.

After a vibrant sunset, chill of night settled over the butte. Birds called back and forth, celebrating the relinquishment of another hot summer day. Crickets clicked, and mosquitoes hummed. Tranquility prevailed through-out the night.

The second day, I rose with the morning star. The symbol of a new day, with its promise of color and beauty, transmuted the darkness. My hunger had faded, replaced by an electric hum of euphoria. I sang the songs Charles had admonished me to learn. I sang to the sun, the moon, and the morning star. I sang to the winged nations and the heavenly concourse. *With this pipe, I send my voice out. That which is sacred, hear me.*

The Lakota word for prayer is *čhékiya*, which translates literally as "to cry within oneself." In the same way a young child cries out for his parent's assistance, we pray to God, our Creator, the one who knows our every need. As I beseeched the Creator for direction and guidance, I recalled how the word for the law of fasting, also *čhékiya*, stems from the same word as prayer; it means "to cry for vision," indicating a yearning for divine guidance and assistance.

As Charles had taught me, I prayed to each of the cardinal directions—the west, the north, the east, the south. *Toward the four directions I stand, sending out my voice.* As I offered prayers, I visualized all the people I had met who lived and moved in that particular direction. I cast wide the net of my compassion. Love carried me, as I thanked God for all He had created.

But soon the brilliant sun became stern and vengeful. Throughout that long day—and the days are long in South Dakota—the heat seemed to relentlessly pound on my body. It wore me to nothing. I stood in the altar in over one hundred degree temperatures, aching with thirst. I had fasted before, but never in this kind of heat. The fervor of my prayers intensified with my desperation; these prayers were my only threads of hope.

That second evening, when the sun had sunk below the hilltop, I thanked God. I felt new kinship with the coyotes, the nighthawks, and other nocturnal creatures; I, too, welcomed the night season.

On the third day, the sun continued to punish and torment me. I watched an ant crawling toward its hill with such determination, such focus. I became envious. The ant had meaning in its life. It had direction. But I didn't. I had talents and abilities that I didn't know how to develop and use to better the world. I was lost, purposeless. The heat drained me of energy. Thirst pained my every move. I was certain that I would perish there in the hills. *But then again*, I thought, *a life such as this, without any substance or meaning, is pointless.*

17

Shadows passed over my head. Perhaps eagles were soaring high above me, reminding me of my potential. I looked up and saw buzzards. Those buzzards were surely awaiting a good meal once I had dropped dead from the heat.

I remembered how, as a child, before the days of cable TV, I would overturn large rocks to observe the insects living underneath. I would wedge a thick stick under the base of a huge rock and turn the stone on its belly. Once the stone was overturned, I would see that the earth, where the rock once rested, squirmed with life. When exposed to the radiance of daylight, the worms and pill bugs scrambled to re-submerge themselves in the cool darkness of the dirt.

On the final day of my fast, I realized that maybe I was like those insects. I, too, loved complacency. Did I really have it in me to change my ways? The heat burrowed through me. I felt physically exhausted. How could I possibly change my ways? I wanted to scurry back to the darkness of my former life. I wept uncontrollably. I knew that I was born an insignificant being and that I would live and die and return to the dust, perhaps having done nothing of consequence with my life. Anguish and unworthiness overwhelmed me. I was weak, lost, and alone.

Though the last day was an ordeal, I didn't want it to end. I had no answers to my prayers. What did I want to do with myself? What direction did I want to take with my life? The sun was approaching high noon, and the end of my fast was drawing near. I had committed to this fast hoping to receive guidance, and I had received none.

* * *

Returning for me as the sun reached its full height, Charles and two of my uncles found me on the ground of the altar. I could barely raise my eyes. I was reduced to a state of nothingness. They lifted me to my feet and wrapped my arms around their shoulders. We did not speak. Together, we hobbled out of the hills.

As we grew farther from the *owáŋka*, I reflected on the fast, on my condition, on the goal of my quest—to discover my path. Nothing had come to me. I saw myself back there at the altar wailing. Why had God not answered?

We arrived at the sweat lodge and entered. My mom and aunt were there. I sat at the *čhatkú*, and Charles closed the door of the lodge. He poured water on the rocks and sang. In the dark, he blessed the fast, thanking the Creator for the abilities I had been given during this time, abilities that would become apparent in the future. His prayers offered hope that I could not feel.

Then Charles lifted and lowered the sweat lodge door and gave me a braid of sweetgrass that had been soaked in water. I held it and managed to sip. Beads of water trickled down my bone-dry throat. I felt a hint of relief. He closed the door the final time. During that second round, I recounted the vision of my experience, *haŋblóglaka*. I shared that I was grateful to fast and to observe all the different animals and other signs of creation. Even though I felt deep discouragement, I simply shared with my relatives that I felt I was at the beginning of my search.

At the end of the second door, I lit the pipe that we had sealed in buffalo heart fat before the opening ceremonies and passed it around. Everyone smoked the pipe, and I finished it. Charles offered special prayers to accompany the smoking of the pipe. *Here at the center of creation, the eagles have convened and are smoking the pipe that belongs to God.* The eagles, in this prayer, represented us.

When the ceremony at the sweat lodge concluded, Charles gave me the bucket and dipper we had used for pouring the water on the rocks. "I ordain you," he said in English, "to conduct the inipi ceremony."

I took his offerings, struck by the word he used. *Ordain.* A holy order. Charles wasn't a native English speaker; he had learned much of the English language from the Catholic Church. This was an authorization from my mentor, who had been consecrated by his own mentors, that someday I would carry out this hallowed practice on my own. I would use this same bucket and dipper in the years to come. I, too, would become a mentor for others.

* * *

That evening, Charles conducted a final ceremony at my home, calling upon spirit helpers to bless my fast and to make my prayers more potent. Before the prayers, we had a special feast. A puppy had been ceremoniously killed, cleaned, and served as part of the meal. Dogs, in Native culture, have always been more than merely pets; the Indigenous people's survival depended on these creatures. They were used for transportation, hunting, protection, and companionship. The puppy, offered as a sacrifice, concluded the traditional fast. The reason why a puppy is offered, rather than a dog, is because a puppy is imbued with potential and value, making the sacrifice greater.

My family, along with a few members of the Wakpala community, had all gathered for the Puppy Feast. My aunt had carried out the proper preparations, and Charles beatified our meal with the appropriate traditional songs. The atmosphere during the feast, though solemn, radiated support for what I had just accomplished.

For them, for all of us, this space was a refuge—an extension of the sacred space of the fast, a way of honoring our culture and traditions. We lived in a society where Lakota culture was deemed irrelevant. We came from a past where our ancestors were forced into total subjugation. It was not often that we could gather together in a space that embodied the dignity of our heritage. This meal affirmed the traditions we held close to our hearts.

After the meal, Charles conducted a final ceremony. He invited the spirit-helpers to join us and thanked the spiritual worlds for the completion of the fast. As he offered prayers and thanks, a newfound realization dawned. I had suffered through the fast and survived. The final ceremony was not the resolution; the final ceremony was the beginning.

I remembered a song that Charles had shared before my fast. From the voice of a heavenly intermediary, the song speaks to the one who is fasting about their purpose. I did not know if Charles had learned it from one of his mentors or if he had received it as inspiration from the dream world.

Hokšila táku yakȟá huwó?
Boy what is the matter?
Hokšila thehíya mayáni kte lo.
Boy your journey will be difficult.
Ni-Tȟúŋkašila thehíya waníčuŋzape lo.
Your Grandfathers have assigned you a difficult decree.
Hokšila čhaŋnúŋpa kiŋ thehíya yuhá mayáni kte lo.
Boy your journey with the pipe will be difficult.

From here on, I had to take something meaningful from my experience. I spent the upcoming days meditating on my experience and future calling. I had to find my path, my purpose, the reason for my being. During those days of deep contemplation, I did not have an inkling of the unexpected blessings and assistance that would come to me.

PART II

ÇHEKPÁ OKÍLE
(TO SEARCH FOR ONE'S BIRTH TIES)

1

My family lived near the ocean in California for the first five years of my childhood. I remember when I was a child, my mother often took my younger sister and me to the beach. No matter where we lived, my mother always found a lake, swimming hole, nearby river, or irrigation ditch for us to play in. A former surfer and excellent swimmer who even taught swimming lessons, Mom loved the beach. Often, she read with one eye and kept the other on Winona and me, playing along the water's edge. We splashed in the waves and dug our fingers through the sand, sculpting towers and carving moats. We collected shells and polished glass that had washed up on shore.

On several occasions, Mom invited her dear friend, Francis Makepeace, and her children to spend a day at the beach with us. A survivor of polio, Francis had restricted movement and couldn't traverse the steps from the parking lot down to the beach. To get Francis to the waterfront, my mother scooped Francis out of her chair, slung her over one shoulder, and carried her down nearly one hundred steps to the water's edge and then back up again when it was time to leave.

During our beach days, I waded in the surf, although my mother's watchful eye ensured that I never went in too deep. The power of the ocean—the force that pulled the tide and let it loose—always fascinated me. Wave after wave curled in on itself and crashed on the shore. There is nothing in this contingent world more superlative than the ocean. Though I had not yet become a strong swimmer, I was not afraid of those mighty, mystical waters.

* * *

I was born on June 23, 1954 in Los Angeles, California. My parents, Patricia Locke and Charles Edward Locke III, met when they were both students at the University of California in Los Angeles. My mother received her bachelor's degree and had been teaching elementary school before I was born. My father studied Psychology at UCLA and worked as a handyman installing furnaces in those early years.

My father's father, Charles Edward Locke II, was one of the first brain surgeons in the late 1920s to work at a hospital in Cleveland. When my father was only three years old, his father died from toxic smoke inhalation while rescuing patients during a fire at the hospital. My grandmother, grief-stricken, struggled to care for her children. As a result, my father and his brother went to boarding school. Because he was born with one leg shorter than the other, my uncle walked with a cane. Other students ridiculed him for his disability, but my father always stood up for him. My father was his brother's greatest defender, ever protective and watchful.

My mother's parents met in Minneapolis; my grandfather, John McGillis, served in World War I, and my grandmother was a nurse at the hospital where he was sent after the war. A member of the Chippewa tribe from northern Minnesota, John was born in 1887 and spent his childhood living a traditional subsistence life. He grew up at a time and in a region entirely populated by Indigenous people; folks would move from one area to another in a regular pattern depending on the cycle of subsistence living. This kind of subsistence living had evolved over millennia in sync with the abundance provided by Grandmother Earth. My grandfather moved from camp to camp—from wild rice camp, to hunting camp, to maple sugar harvest camp and other such camps depending on the season.

Eva Flying Earth McGillis, my grandmother, was from the Standing Rock Reservation, Wakpala District. Her parents were born in pre-reservation days, prior to the mass EuroAmerican immigration. Her father, originally from tribal homelands around what is now the Minneapolis-St. Paul metroplex, then known as Imníža Ska, was one of the Bdewákhaŋthuŋwaŋ Dakhóta or Spirit Lake Village people, while her mother was a member of the Húŋkpapȟa Oyate. The name *Húŋkpapȟa* refers to their people's assigned position at the *tip of the horn*, the traditional semicircular configuration made when all the disparate camps of one tribe assemble for ceremonial / official / state occasions.

As a young man, my grandfather had tried to enlist in the army but was denied because he wasn't a legal American citizen. American Indians were not considered citizens until the passing of the Indian Citizen Act of 1924, which granted them full citizenship. My grandfather wrote letters to appeal the Army's decision. The letters reached the highest ranks of the War Department, and eventually he was allowed to enlist in the military. My grandfather became the first American Indian to serve legally as a non-citizen in the Armed Forces in World War I, and he served in France and Belgium.

After the war, my grandfather and grandmother were married, and my grandfather, after surviving the trenches of the frontline and finishing his service in World War I, began a career with the Bureau of Indian Affairs. The BIA was initially under the War Department. Created to deal with the "Indian problem," the BIA had a policy of Indian extermination, or ethnic cleansing. When it was transferred over to the Department of the Interior, the BIA's new focus became managing trust lands. My grandfather worked with this focus as a clerk, managing land leases and repayments.

My mother was born near the Shoshone Bannock Reservation in Pocatello, Idaho in 1928. As she was growing up, she moved every three to four years when the government reassigned my grandfather. The Klamath Agency in Oregon, the Colorado River Tribes Agency in Parker, Arizona, and the Riverside Indian School serving several "Mission" Tribes in California were among the localities where she resided with her family. In each place, my mother and her family could have been penalized for participating in underground traditional activities, such as speaking their respective Native languages whenever possible, attending Sun Dance and other ceremonies, and participating in the tribal sunrise ceremony.

Being skilled syncretists, my grandparents developed the ability to conceal their true Indigenous identity when participating in the Euro-American world. My grandparents had grown up during a time of mass immigration to the United States from Europe. These immigrants were escaping unbearable conditions of despotism, corruption, disease, and poverty. They came here to start a new life to fulfill their dreams. Tragically, in order to fulfill their dreams, they destroyed the paradise of the Indigenous population, whose future they usurped. My grandparents lived in those tumultuous times when their world was being overtaken by waves of immigrants bent on claiming the paradise of North America for themselves.

My grandparents wanted to spare their children the pain they had experienced growing up. Even though they were impoverished and relegated to the lowest tiers of society, they attempted to raise my mother and her sister as best they could. My mom and aunt have made only positive comments regarding the strength and dignity of their parents. They have shared stories of how their dad used his skills as an expert hunter to put food on the table and how both parents sacrificed for their girls and avoided backing down from tough decisions for the sake of expediency. Their parents stood for what was right and true and avoided compromising their ancestral teachings and culture.

Similarly, my childhood was shaped by the loving attention of my parents. Every night, my mother sang to Winona and me, and the ebb and flow of her deep voice lulled us to sleep. *Hush little baby, don't say a word, Mama's going to buy you a mockingbird.*

My father's passion for music also influenced me. Dad was a percussionist, and he often played Glenn Miller records and tapped his drumsticks along to "Tuxedo Junction" while my sister and I listened. I enjoyed singing, and though I didn't think I had great vocal talent, I joined the school choir. My father and I also played baseball and Frisbee together, and we occasionally watched baseball, though I found it quite boring. I learned, however, to appreciate and love what the natural world provided. I spent most of my time outside, engaged in physical activity and exploring my environment, regardless of the weather. I found something to enjoy in each of the seasons, and anything strenuous and intensely physical captivated me. I swam, I ran, I bicycled, and I cross-country skied.

My family moved to Great Falls, Montana when I was five. My dad had accepted a position with a company who provided training for military installations for the Cold War. At the time, Great Falls was a small town. We had a place on the outskirts of town near Hill 57, a cascading hill perfect for sledding and biking. Beyond it, the prairies spanned far and wide. One of my favorite artists, Charlie Russell, has depicted the majesty and beauty of this part of Montana. His paintings show the vast skies in purples and blues, the golden plains and the misty mountain ranges, and how the high buttes and hills add texture to the horizon.

I first learned to ride a bike on those Montana hills. Some bigger kids from the neighborhood lifted me up on one of their bikes positioned near the top of Hill 57, and they took a running start and pushed me. I flew down the hill, with the weeds and grasses blurring on both sides of me. The wind bolstered me and kept me from wobbling. All too soon, I saw that a dead end awaited me at the bottom of the hill. I hit the curb and crash-landed, thankfully, on a neighbor's lawn. That's when I learned that when you fall, you have to pick yourself up and get back on the bike.

My neighborhood friends and I had other ways of entertaining ourselves. Some afternoons, we ran out past the hill to the grasslands to see who could catch a prairie dog. Prairie dogs leave small craters in the pile of earth where they dig their dens; the land behind the hill was speckled with these mounds. I would position a loop of twine in the hole and then add twenty to thirty feet of rope. Then I would wait, with my eyes fixed on the hole, heart pumping. When a prairie dog poked his head out of a den, I would yank on the snare. Often, I missed, but sometimes the twine closed around the prairie dog. I had a few moments to hold the wriggling animal before I released its neck from the snare and it disappeared back down its hole.

My friends and I also tried to catch rattlesnakes. We found sticks with forked ends and scoured the grasses for the shifting striped body, the tight coil of a rattle. When I found one, with a swift thrust of the arm, I tried to pin the snake's head with the stick. I grabbed its body and threw it in a gunny sack. We did this until one of my buddies got bit. His arm swelled up horrifically, a reaction to the neurotoxin released through the snake's fangs. Before that happened, we weren't aware of the danger; we were just excited by the adrenaline rush of catching a snake. Thankfully, my friend didn't die but was hospitalized and had a swollen arm for some time.

Kids grow up in front of the TV nowadays, but back then, the entertainment most readily accessible to me was the world outside—the prairies and the hilltops. My friends and I invented all sorts of things to do outdoors. We climbed trees and held pinecone wars. We scooped up black and red ants, tossed the ants on each other, and watched them battle. In the winter, we took sides and had snowball fights.

When I found myself indoors, I loved to draw, mostly cars and dinosaurs, even from an early age. My mother often recounted a story of me, at the age of three, giving her a drawing of a Volkswagen Beetle. The picture captured the curved shape of the car, complete with wheels and windows. "Where did you get this, Kevin?" she asked, not believing that I could have made the drawing on my own. According to her, I promptly sat down in front of her, took out a piece of paper, and drew another Beetle that was a carbon-copy of the first. I was a nonstop artist. Once, when I ran out of paper, my parents caught me drawing on the walls. They quickly realized that I always needed to have paper on hand.

After we moved back to California when I was seven years old, I became a connoisseur of comic books. Marvel's comics were my favorite because of their dynamic illustrations and interesting storylines. I bought the latest issues to study the visuals and entertain myself with the exploits of Spider-man, Ironman, and the Fantastic Four. Each comic was ten cents; to earn this, I would drag my wagon along the side of the road and collect bottles that had been thrown away. At the grocery store, I exchanged each bottle for a few cents. Once I had my ten cents, I bought a new comic.

As a family, we often took weekend trips. Some of my parents' close friends had a place in the Belt Mountains in Montana, and on weekends, we drove up there to stay in the cabin and go swimming in swift-flowing Belt Creek. Moss grew along the rocks, so I made my own waterpark. I used the rocks as a natural water slide and slid across them into the moving waters.

We also visited Glacier National Park. My parents especially loved the resort town of Apgar. We stayed at the Village Inn near Lake McDonald, and the scenery outside of the Inn looked as if it had come right off a post-card: snow-capped mountains and giant coniferous trees surrounding a vast pool of clear blue. We inhaled the intoxicating scent of pine, felt small beneath the mountain peaks, and hiked the trails of the biggest glacier field in the United States. During one of our stays at the Village Inn, I found a turtle in the lake and fancied keeping him as a pet; I carried him around with me for a few days, but when I tried to take him swimming, he escaped my clutches and swam away.

The first time I flew on a plane was on a trip with my dad. We took a DC-10 from southern to northern California. The pilot invited me, the only child on the flight, to sit in the cockpit and pinned a pair of wings on me. The rumble of the engine beneath my feet and the jolt as the plane first separated from the earth and ascended into the air, exhilarated me. From my new, lofty perspective, I watched as the land I knew grew small and the clouds drew closer. What a miracle to be transported into the sky!

2

When Winona's children, my niece and nephews, were young, my mom bought a satellite dish for them. One day while visiting, I noticed my nephew scrolling through different channels. He decided, as always, to watch an old samurai movie, entirely in Japanese and without subtitles.

"Why do you want to watch this?" I asked him.

He shrugged. "I don't know? There's something about these guys that I like."

I realized then that he had searched through the TV channels for a program that showcased characters that looked like him and that the Japanese films had come closest to providing a sense of belonging for him.

We all need to feel a sense of belonging, to affirm our place in the world. As a child in the early 1960s, I was one of the only children with brown skin at my school in Great Falls, Montana. I never told my parents that I was picked on incessantly and ostracized. I knew I was different because of my dark complexion; still, I did not completely understand at that young age why other students treated me as an outsider.

In elementary school, during English class, my teachers taught us to read from the *Dick and Jane* readers. These books showcased an ideal nuclear family, blonde and fair-skinned, in a tidy home with a glowing green lawn and white picket fence. *See Dick run. See Jane run. See Spot run.* I already knew the basic vocabulary in these stories because I had been reading far beyond that level for years. My mother was an avid reader, and she loved mystery novels and articles from *The New Yorker*. She read many nonfiction books as well and was always buried in some sort of research project. My father, too, was well-read. Books lined the shelves of our home, and with my parents' example, I learned to read at an early age. I would read any book I could get my hands on, from stories about dinosaurs to Greek and Roman mythology to Dr. Seuss books. While at home, I was reading far beyond my age level, but at school, my teachers always placed me in the lowest reading group, based on the assumption that I couldn't read well, if at all.

When class let out for recess, a few kids in my class would deliberately wait for me on the playground. They teased me, shouted that my mother was ugly, and usually beat me up. Those first years in elementary school, I accepted their tormenting, never uttering a word about it to the teachers or my parents. I was naturally introverted and withdrawn. Only once—fed up with being beat up yet again—I hit one of my bullies back. As I lashed out at him, my first grade teacher spotted me. She marched over, her face stern. She told the two bullies to pin my arms behind my back and gave one of them permission to hit me. The bully punched me in the stomach. I doubled over, my body constricting in pain.

From then on, my teachers and peers considered me the classroom dunce. My teacher often made me sit on a chair facing the corner of the classroom, while she taught the lesson behind my back. I never saw this happen to any other kids. I felt singled out, isolated, and powerless, and I began to master the art of avoidance. I retreated into my own interior world—my coping mechanism. I took back-routes to school and avoided the playground where my tormentors lurked. I escaped into my books at home and in my outdoor activities.

Today, I do not dwell on these unpleasant memories from childhood, but I do remember them. I have been told that this would never have happened to White children. I try not to give it much thought; it is too painful. Later, with guidance from wise elders and in my journey with faith, I would discover a new worldview, one that has enabled me to comprehend these events. I have come to understand that many peoples of the world both then and now encountered and still encounter prejudice, materialism, and the denial of fundamental human equality—and not just from schoolyard bullies. Though this was not a part of the general, collective American consciousness during the late 60s and 70s, the struggle for equality and recognition of our inherent oneness would emerge as a pressing collective concern—along with greater awareness of the sufferings of others.

With this, I realized that the energy we expend in enduring intolerance and injustice in our communities is not lost. We can allow these trials to build within us greater fortitude and magnanimity. Our struggles do not have to be in vain.

As I advanced through elementary school, we read books about the Oregon Trail and about how settlers moved across the western states in covered wagons. Along the way, the settlers would fight Indians because the settlers were fixed in their belief that they were a superior race and had divine authority to conquer inferior people. At home, I watched western dramas, such as the Lone Ranger. These shows illustrated the same theme of manifest destiny, that it was God's will for the American settlers to have dominance over the entire continent. Indigenous cultures were exaggerated and distorted. Native characters were shallow and emphasized the stereotype of the ignorant, monosyllabic savage. I accepted what I saw without question, and I didn't think about the power of these images and the messages they were conveying until later in life.

When my skin tanned quite dark in the summer, I would go to the beach, and people would ask: "What are *you* doing here?" They saw the same programs I did—and they had internalized the same message of the savage Native impeding manifest destiny. They saw Natives like me as a group that deserved to be confined to the fringe and to eventually disappear. This was the whole hope: the vanishing red man.

The lack of representation of Indian people meant that I had to discover who I was for myself. I was not deeply connected with my Native American roots during my early childhood. I attended powwows with my parents in Browning, Montana, outside of Great Falls. The Native culture was not integrated into our local community. My father had also never learned of his Native roots in the same way my mother had. He was European-American, with a small fraction of Indigenous heritage. Many of the connections to his roots were lost after his father died.

During her childhood, with both parents working for the Bureau of Indian Affairs, my mother was exposed to numerous tribes. Her parents took great joy in sharing their Native languages with her—Lakota, from the side of my grandmother and Ojibwe from the side of my grandfather—though English was the primary language of the home. Her parents transmitted basic universal human values, which they had obtained from being raised in their traditional cultures. Their subsistence life had required hard work, punctuality and precision, and they applied those universal values to every aspect of their lives. Though my mother was close to her roots, during my childhood years, she accepted the mindset of the times and adopted an "American" identity, relegating our Native heritage to the margins.

Our family moved to Anchorage, Alaska in 1966. My father had accepted a new position with a Cold War subsidiary firm called Systems Development Corporation, which took him to the Elmendorf Air Force Base in Anchorage. Here, my mother would begin to experience an awakening, a shift in her consciousness that led to a deeper understanding of our culture.

We packed our bright yellow Volkswagen van for the move. Anchorage lay 3500 miles away, and nearly one hundred hours of driving lay in store for us. Before making our way to Canada, we headed south through the Dakotas and to Standing Rock Reservation to visit family. The prairies, the drizzle, and the love and hospitality of the people attracted me to the Reservation and made our visit fond and memorable. We stayed only a short while, then retraced our path through Montana and to the Canadian border. My parents routed us through the spectacular Going To The Sun Highway in Glacier National Park, which curved through the blue mountains and carried us closer to the clouds than to the green earth below.

As we drove north, the diverse landscape we traveled through enthralled me. Still, the hours in the car often dragged by. To pass the time, my mom conducted rounds of I-Spy and various forms of counting games. During one leg of the trip, Mom offered my sister and me a penny for every Minnesota license plate we saw. I appointed myself the disc jockey of our trip and played popular forty-fives on my portable record player most of the way through Canada.

Once we reached Prince Rupert, British Columbia, we boarded a ferry to travel through the Inside Passage—the fjords and coastal area of southeastern Alaska. Rocky mountains towered on either side of the sea, and huge glaciers burst from the water. Orcas swam alongside our boat; dolphins leapt from the waves, and I spotted sea lions resting on shore. Eagles, as commonplace as pigeons, soared through the skies.

When we stopped at the ports in Ketchikan, Juneau, Petersburg, and Haines, Alaska, we learned about the Native people of southeastern Alaska who lived in these areas. The Native monumental art impressed me. For the first time, I saw magnificent totem poles. I learned that totem poles identify ancestral lineage of Native people, analogous to family trees done by many European cultures. The Tlingit, the largest tribe there, was divided between two clan-types—the gentle clans and the fierce clans. In totem poles, the images of frogs, geese, and other herbivorous animals represent the gentle clans, while killer whales, sharks, eagles, or bears represent the fierce clans. Marriage in the Tlingit tribe could only take place between the gentle and the fierce clans. A totem pole would then be constructed to represent the gentle and fierce clans in their lineage.

Our journey to Alaska, through the reservations in the Dakotas and the ports of Alaska, marked a new beginning for me, as I began to draw closer to my Indigenous identity.

3

Though my father's work was affiliated with the Air Force, we did not live on the base but rather in the city, at a home near the mouth of Ship Creek. Anchorage was then a small town nestled between the rugged wilderness of the Chugach mountains and the wildly-fluctuating tidal basin, Cook Inlet. When we moved, I was in junior high school—a period of time when my Indigenous identity began to shape and matter more. I attended school with a mostly Native peer group—my first prolonged connection to Native people. The diversity among us was tribal diversity. My classmates were from various tribal communities—Inupiaq from Barrow, Yupik from Bethel, Tsimpshian from Metlakatla, Haida from Queen Charlotte Island, Tlingit from Hoonah, Koyukon from Huslia, and Gwichin from Beaver—plus a dozen other Native groups from all the far reaches of Alaska.

Many of my junior high Alaskan peers and teachers possessed a unique pioneering and adventuresome spirit. Though the faculty was not as diverse as the student body, the faculty members exhibited more sensitivity and compassion to their students than my former teachers did. The curriculum, however, possessed very little information to honor tribal histories. Even Alaskan history was taught from a colonized perspective. Still, some of the teachers made their classes come to life. Mrs. Hilte, my Spanish teacher, stirred in me a nascent love for languages. I was fascinated by the new sounds and structures and the challenge of bending, twisting, and convoluting my tongue to create meaning. My science teacher, Mr Simpson, had a glass eye, and using secret code, he relied on me to let him know when his eye went askew. When I winked at him, he snuck a glance in the mirror and readjusted his glass eye. One of my favorite teachers, he conducted research on edible mushrooms, took our class out to collect them, and facilitated lively discussions afterward.

My parents encouraged me to join the team, as I loved swimming. I practiced every day with my friends on the team. After two months of preparation, we competed in our first meet, and I finished second place out of twenty. I watched as my peers celebrated their wins and denounced their losses. Parents berated the children for losing. I found myself repulsed by these attitudes and realized that competitive athletic sports were not for me. Though the competition fostered excellence, the stigmas attached to winning and losing created ugly standards by which to judge people. I did not want these stigmas attached to my performance, so I quit the swim team.

The net result of this decision? I became even more intensely competitive with myself. My mission was to always outdo myself and push on to the next horizon, irrespective of what my peers were doing. Sometimes, I studied my peers and concluded that avoiding some of their behaviors was the best course. By independently investigating the truth, I had ventured away from the status quo and discovered my own views and interests, many of which I still embrace.

After that, I didn't mind playing various sports with my friends, as long as it didn't involve a winner or loser. Even if chosen for a team, I played with total detachment from the outcome. My peers sometimes called me the "class klutz" because of this attitude. I played for the sheer enjoyment of the process, which never again qualified me for the coveted status of *athlete*.

Alaska was an outdoorsman's paradise. Though the temperatures could swing as low as thirty below—still more moderate than the extremes of interior Alaska—snow and cold never stopped me from spending time outside. I ice skated, usually for an hour every day, at a rink near school. I loved the pure exhilaration of picking up speed and flying across the ice. I went sledding and tobogganing in the steep hills near our home. I picked up a paper route to earn enough money to buy my own skis to go cross-country skiing. I also spent time trout fishing in the lakes around the outskirts of Anchorage with my dad and his buddies. During spring break, when the ice covering the rivers began to break up, I hiked to Ship Creek and jumped from iceberg to iceberg. We called this *iceberg rodeo*. The goal was to see how far we could ride the iceberg without slipping off into the frigid waters below. As spring neared, I waited impatiently for temperatures to reach the sixties. When the weather was just warm enough, my friends from school and I ventured three miles through melting snow to Goose Lake for a cold swim.

Once during winter, I went sledding after school several miles from home in minus 30-degree temperatures. With no wind, I was able to trek around for hours without a sense of the intensity of the cold. But by the time I reached home, my hands and feet had purpled with frostbite. I placed my hands in lukewarm water to let them thaw. The process was excruciating. Ever since, because of subsequent damage to the tiny capillaries, I have had poor circulation and a hard time keeping my hands warm in cold weather. But this has never dampened my love for the seasons. After all, there is no such thing as bad weather—only bad clothes and a bad attitude!

During the 1960s, an awakening emerged throughout the country and the world. Systemic changes were enacted that reflected a shift in the general consciousness. The Civil Rights Movement ignited historic changes. Protests to end the Vietnam War reflected the growing desire to find peaceful, just means to resolve conflict. A growing number of people questioned and objected to institutionalized and personal discrimination. Marches for racial equality occurred throughout the country. African-Americans sought to achieve equality within the American system.

During this time, members of Indigenous communities were mostly concerned with tribal sovereignty. Most of the Indigenous population lived in rural areas, and tribal sovereignty was a more pressing concern for them during the Civil Rights movement than equality. Such sovereignty would empower tribal communities to create their own educational policies, rather than have the state or federal government provide irrelevant curriculum. A culturally relevant curriculum could instill healthy pride and determination, so critical in creating prosperity. Sovereignty would also enable tribes to administer their own housing needs, to depend less on an urban electrical grid, and to retain hunting and fishing rights.

My mother began to skillfully surf the tempests of change. A pioneer in helping to empower Indigenous communities, starting first with our community in Alaska, she moved to the forefront of creating positive change for Indigenous folks who had been shoved to the margins of the dominant society. At that time, multitudes of Indigenous people were relocating from rural villages to urban areas such as Anchorage. Alaskan Indigenous villages operated on a subsistence economy, and tribal members lived simply but abundantly off the land.

Still, many sought to escape alcoholism and poverty. Many villages were geographically isolated fly-in villages, and leaving them was a challenge. Individuals who found their way out, however, embraced dreams typical of most immigrants. They sought better lives, and they wanted to acquire the skills or use the gifts and talents they possessed to make a living. They wanted to provide for their families. In reality, however, they traded one set of challenges for a new set of obstacles, as they could no longer rely on the natural world to meet their basic needs. Obtaining employment, finding health care, and recovering from addictions were all pressing concerns. In addition, language barriers made communication difficult; learning English became a necessity. Most Indigenous villagers did not know the first thing about renting a home or signing a contract, and prejudice was a day-to-day reality that manifested itself in the areas of housing, healthcare, education, and employment.

My mother's initial dislike of Anchorage changed as she became more involved with the Alaskan Native community. My mother, a very practical person, recognized a need and arose to meet it by organizing a center in Anchorage for Indigenous families who had newly arrived to the city. The Native Welcome Center offered classes, recreation, and meeting places for Native people in the city. It provided newly relocated Natives with basic health care, child care, budgeting courses, and job services. My mother ensured that the Center also had ESL courses; Mom had a natural empathy for those encountering, for the first time, a non-North American language: English. The Center was located on Fourth Avenue in Anchorage, near a strip of bars frequented by many Native people. The location of the Welcome Center proved fortuitous and transformed the desperation many felt into hope. The Center provided new possibilities and tangible ways to improve the lives of urban Natives.

To obtain funding and support for the Center, my mom forged alliances with like-minded local leaders. She possessed the powerful skill of creating a unified vision with others and then mobilizing them to translate that vision into action. She interacted with myriad people of influence, including tribal leaders, local priests, experienced medical professionals, and government officials. In particular, Ernest Gruening, the state senator, became an advocate and ally. He always ensured that funds were allocated so the Center could continue to provide free services for Natives. Though she served Native people, Mom skillfully built connections with the non-Indian world, and she encouraged and inspired them to contribute to the well-being of Native people.

My mother initiated an arts and crafts cooperative at the Welcome Center. In this space, people could share their artistic heritage and folk arts. At the time, new awareness was dawning about the importance of preserving Indigenous heritage; these efforts at the Welcome Center were crucial in this preservation. Traditional arts—including basket-making, mask-making, weaving, beading, feather-work and so on—expressed the aspirations, prayers, and visions of the Native peoples. The artisans imbued their crafts with powerful universal feelings, which transcend differences and connect us all to one another, to the past, and to the future. The cooperatives gave opportunities for artists to teach and mentor others in various arts and crafts. Tapping into the great need to find marketing outlets for the creative talent of so many individuals, the cooperative helped artists sell their creations at hotels, airports, and other venues for the tourist trade. This helped to set standards of authenticity for the crafts sold at these venues.

Through my mom's efforts at the Welcome Center, I began to connect with other Native people and was profoundly influenced by many of the craftsmen, artists, and elders who worked there. I spent a lot of time with Frank Mercer, a master carver from the Tlingit tribe, the largest Indigenous population in Southeastern Alaska, renowned for their artistic gifts. Frank specialized in the tourist trade and carved miniature totem poles and animal figurines, purchased as decorative souvenirs by travelers to Anchorage. He possessed a warm and genuine spirit. We often sat together at the Center, and he shared stories about growing up in Southeast Alaska, his family, and his art. His stories uplifted me; our time together was comfort food for my soul.

Frank talked about the village he grew up in and about his family, especially his grandparents. He spoke about the fish they caught and the berries they gathered. The way his community lived off the land was similar to living in the garden of Eden, he said. That way of life was part of the sacred covenant his people had with their Creator—to maintain balance with the world. This was the goal of life. His art celebrated this harmony and balance with the land. Frank coped with urban life in Anchorage; though the city was his physical reality, his spirit transcended this and remained connected to the natural world through his art.

I learned from Frank much about the Tlingit, including the importance of honoring the simple things of life. The tribe punctuated life with ceremonies. Similar to the Maori in New Zealand, they formalized occasions and brought order to what might seem mundane. For instance, when a guest came from out of town to visit the Tlingit, the guest would be welcomed at the airport with greeters and special songs. At an airport, most travelers remain totally anonymous according to social protocol of the dominant society, but not to the Tlingit. They instead made human interactions sacred and mastered the art of finding beauty in the ordinary.

In many respects, Indigenous cultures inspire mindfulness and presence through art and ceremony. I have heard people remark that the Lakota have a song for everything. In many respects, Indigenous cultures, such as the Tlingit and Lakota, can assist us to practice "the power of NOW." Despite facing colonization and oppression, every second is a miracle, and every sunrise and sunset, every sign of life, every gift, is worthy of singing and celebration. Even the most mundane aspects of life are cause for regard.

Through my mother, I also came to know of Paul Tiulana, a truly kind and encouraging man from a village called King Island—a small island in the Bering Sea. The King Islanders had regarded their home as the center of the universe, the axis around which all the quarry of the sea and air (marine and migratory food sources) centered. They shared cultural heritage rooted in their island homeland, but the government deemed the island to be too isolated for education, health, and human services. Government officials and missionaries had forcefully evacuated the island's inhabitants from their paradise and relegated them to the lower margins of existence—as refugees in Nome and later Anchorage. Because of his innate leadership qualities through consensus building, relinquishing the ego, and serving others, Paul had become a social, spiritual, and cultural leader in Anchorage. He frequently helped out at the Welcome Center, collaborated with my mother, and served on the Board of Directors. A cultural warrior, Paul spearheaded the revival of Eskimo music and dance.

As a young man, on a walrus-hunting expedition, Paul had been injured and had had his leg amputated. The accident ended his days as a master hunter. Instead, he became a repository of the traditional ways. Specializing in carving ivory, whale vertebrae, and walrus tusks, he was a great carver and crafted skin-boats of driftwood. Paul was also well-versed in traditional music and dance. He understood folk arts as a reflection of the human spirit's desire to create order, harmony, and beauty. These arts, part of our ancestral heritage, were passed down through generations and influenced by the spirit of our ancestors from the spiritual worlds. When these folk arts were threatened, people like Paul arose to champion them.

Paul and my mother organized a dance group with the other King Islanders. True folk artists, they upheld their music and dance as a medium through which the spirits of all things connect. The King Island dancers used drums made from a walrus stomach membrane stretched over round wooden frames. They created rhythms by tapping wooden sticks on the underside of the drum. Their songs started with a slow, steady pace. The dancers followed the music. As the rhythm and the cadence of the song accelerated, the dancing would grow more animated.

The songs and dances pantomimed stories of everyday life and were performed in perfect synchronicity. One dance imitated the journey of the King Islander boats to the hunting grounds. Another dance imitated berry-picking. Masks depicted the creatures encountered in each story; for instance, the walrus dance involved wearing the mask of the walrus. In their music and dance, the hunters, the gatherers, and the hunted and gathered were assembled and portrayed in a space of balance and peace.

I learned so much about the Arctic Natives by watching their dances. These dances, which fostered unity, love, and spirit, reflected how Indigenous cultures depended on group dynamics and harmony. In order to survive, Arctic tribal members had to have unity of thought and great love for one another. The severity of the climate and conditions left no room for mistakes and required a high level of cooperation among the people. If a group of whale hunters, for instance, was preparing to set out on the Arctic Ocean to capture an eighty-foot long whale, one mistake could mean death. Thus, the hunters needed be organized amongst themselves and responsive to the needs of the collective. They needed to value unity above all.

Years later, while touring an exhibit about Micronesian culture in the Marshall Islands, I viewed a replica of the traditional boats used to navigate the seas. Every part of the vessel was perfect and ready to endure rough waters; however, a saying held that no matter how perfectly the boat was made, it would never sink from external forces. Instead, the truest danger the crew faced was from the internal conditions that caused discord. Arguments and a lack of cooperation could lead to death. Knowing this, the captains of the expeditions held feasts in order to bring the crew together to sing, dance, and pray. This process of building unity among the crew could last for a few days, a week, a month, or on occasion, a year or more. A crew would not dare go to sea until all the participants of the journey were in complete unity. No matter how perfectly a boat had been built, if the crew were not unified, the journey would not be successful.

* * *

As I spent more time with the elders, artists, craftspeople, dancers, performers, and new friends from school, I discovered a new reality, one that was not reflected in the dominant media and culture that had influenced me in my earlier years. My formal education had never exposed me to traditional Indigenous systems of knowledge and information. I was now learning a worldview outside of the prevailing Eurocentric model, thanks to the guidance of elders and friends. Everything in the world, I realized, was interconnected, inherently one, and a reflection of God's handiwork. I began to recognize and revere the spiritual reality that ran, like a current, through everything and everyone. I learned of true spiritual strength from the example of tribal members who went to great lengths through ceremonial practices and the arts to connect us to spiritual realities, to create harmony and beauty, and to restore balance after a history of oppression and trauma passed through generations. Moreover, I now knew that without unity, no progress could be achieved.

The exposure to these new perspectives piqued my sense of wonderment and awe of Native cultures. Perhaps because of this, I applied for the Institute of American Indian Arts, a notable boarding school run by the Bureau of Indian Affairs in Santa Fe, New Mexico. I had first read about IAIA in a feature article in *Life Magazine*. Several prominent Indian artists and educators, notably designer Lloyd Kiva New, who became the founder and director, had dreamed of opening such a school. From the moment I read about the school, I had the desire to attend. Even as a child, I felt called to express myself through art and to be a part of something greater than myself. When I read about IAIA, I sensed that I had found my chance to connect with a higher purpose. I completed the application process, obtained letters of recommendation, and wrote an essay stating why I hoped to attend the school. Fortunately, I was accepted in 1969 to attend tenth grade, my sophomore year, there.

4

The green carpet of early summer blanketed the earth below me, as I flew over the Black Hills on my way from Alaska to Rapid City, South Dakota. The pine forests engulfed rocky pinnacles. Our plane took a curve, and we flew over the badlands, highly eroded and complex geologic formations. Though the land was infertile, variegated shades of red and brown colored the undulating topography. Right then and there, I fell in love with the Dakotas.

I was headed to visit Arthur Zimiga, a family friend in Rapid City. I would be his sidekick for the summer before I started school at Institute of American Indian Arts. Art, his family, and I would venture into the Black Hills and other back-country places around the state to fish, swim, and explore.

Rapid City is nestled in a trough between the Black Hills and the expanse of the prairies. Legend has it that the oval shape of the Black Hills once served as a "racetrack" for all of creation. Centuries ago, the creatures of the earth vied with one another in a race around the Black Hills in order to establish dominance of the land. The larger, four-legged animals crushed the small animals underfoot, giving the whole area a markedly red hue. Just as Buffalo was about to win the race, Magpie shot out from behind and crossed the finish line first. Magpie claimed victory on behalf of all *wahúnuŋpa*—two leggeds creatures (birds, humans, and, on occasion, bears). He turned over preeminence of the land to human beings, whose victory secured for them a special stewardship over the rest of creation.

That summer, I pitched a tent right outside Art's trailer near Rapid Creek, which flowed straight out of the Black Hills. Art lived with his wife, sons, mother, and aunt. Having grown up in the area, Art knew all the good swimming holes and fishing spots. An avid fisherman, he dedicated his summers to fishing, and since I didn't like to fish, I ventured through wide-open, undeveloped canyons near the creek. Some days, in the blistering heat, Art's family and I would cruise up to the Pactola Reservoir. While the family fished, I dove off cliffs and swam in the crystalline waters. When we returned from exploring, I gutted and filleted the fish Art had caught.

Both Art's mother and aunt spoke Lakota as their first language. Hearing them speak back and forth to each other, I began to pick up words and phrases. I learned the basics: *Toníktuka he?* How are you doing? *Tókhiya la he?* Where are you going? *Loyáčhiŋ he?* Are you hungry? I memorized various words by associating them with similar words in English. *Akíčhita*, the word for soldier, sounded like a familiar English word—cheetah. I also learned names of places. The Black Hills are *ȟé sápa*. *Makȟóšiča* is the Badlands. *Mnišóše* is the name of the Missouri River. Through language immersion with Art's family, I began my path of Lakota language acquisition.

I was one of the first people to learn Lakota as a second language in recent times. As I spent more time in Art's home, immersed in Lakota, I realized that learning the language would unlock new forms of knowledge outside the dominant culture and that I would limit my understanding if I spoke only English. Art's mother and aunt encouraged me to continue my studies of Lakota. Most of the people of their generation were overwhelmed by the all-consuming forces of acculturation. When they found receptive souls like me, they did their utmost to support us to learn and preserve our Native linguistic heritage.

* * *

Most weekends, Art's family and I traveled around the state to attend powwows. During these social gatherings, people from across the reservation came together for a weekend of music, dance, and prayer. These were not my first powwows—I had also attended powwows in Montana with my parents—but I was a little older and could appreciate these gatherings in a new light.

The powwow emerged during pre-reservation life in the mid-19th century. The well-being of tribal societies was maintained by the *okȟólakičhiye*, organizations that performed self-abnegating acts of service for the community. They organized hunts. They served as the first line of defense of the tribe. They coordinated logistics for moving camp. They offered care for the elderly and orphaned. Throughout the year, these organizations held feasts for the people to share their own unique traditional music and dances.

In the latter-1800s, a service organization from the Iháŋktȟuŋwaŋ (Yankton) people took the hides and meat from a buffalo hunt downriver in hopes of trading for corn and beans. When they arrived at the Omáha village down the Missouri River, the Omáha were beginning a celebration of the Helushka ceremony. In the 1860s, the Omáha elders had a vision of a spiritual revolution happening in the world. They were inspired to create a movement that would galvanize the people so that they could align themselves with the Holy Power moving through the universe. This inspiration took the form of a unique musical genre with potent lyrics. The lyrics motivated the people to arise and to perform acts of magnanimous brave service and to praise people that had already arisen. Upon witnessing their first Helushka, the Iháŋktȟuŋwaŋ determined that they needed to obtain this spiritual food for their community. In lieu of corn and beans, they brought back the rights to perform the dance and learned the songs to take back to their people. From that meeting of the Omáha and the Iháŋktȟuŋwaŋ, the Helushka was renamed by the Iháŋktȟuŋwaŋ for its benefactors: Omáha-Wačhípi, Omaha Dance. The Omáha-Wačhípi spread and became a powerful movement. It unified earlier forms of expression among the diverse tribes. Every modern powwow grew out of this history.

When American Indians were confined to reservations, all traditional gatherings for devotional and social purposes were outlawed, including the Omáha-Wačhípi. The only time Indians could obtain permission from government officials to hold an Omáha-Wačhípi was on the 4th of July, as a celebration to honor military veterans. The new focus on military service aligned powwows with "American" culture, while realigning connections to tradition. Thankfully, the essence of the powwow lived in the hearts of the people and was kept alive through the language and through underground practice. Today, the Omáha-Wačhípi bolsters the health and well-being of the entire community.

One of the many powwows we attended that summer was held at the fairgrounds in Rapid City. Rows of tents covered the expansive grounds. For the event, people from throughout the surrounding region attended. A powwow was not hosted as a tourist event but was by and for the community itself. People camped out with their extended families. Children ran and skirted between the tents. Women cooked fry bread and stew. When Art, his family, and I arrived, we too pitched a tent.

The powwow was comprised of five sessions, beginning Friday evening and continuing through Sunday. For the commencement of the powwow, the community flocked toward the arbor, the large circular enclosure at the center of the powwow site, for the Grand Entry. Each of the five sessions was initiated by a prayer and then the Grand Entry song. Hundreds of spectators were already seated under the shade surrounding the arena. We gathered around the shaded periphery and waited. When the singing began, a line of dancers entered the arena to the Grand Entry song. In recognition of their military service, veterans led the procession, followed by all the dancers of each category clad in their unique regalia, with the elders in the lead. Male traditional dancers wore headdresses made of porcupine hair and deer tail. Grass dancers donned brightly-colored fringed outfits. Children of all ages, also wearing traditional outfits, followed these groups. Though I didn't understand much about the history of the powwow, as I watched the Grand Entry, I felt a strong sense of how important this expression of unity was for the community.

After all the dancers were sung into the arena, the flag song was offered along with a song for the veterans. The lyrics for the flag song were:

"*Tȟuŋkášilayapi tȟa-wápaha kiŋ haŋ, oíhaŋkešni he nážiŋ kte. Iyóȟlateya oyáte kiŋ héhaŋ wičȟáǧiŋkta čha léčhamuŋ.*"

Tȟuŋkášilayapi translates to *He whom they have for a Grandfather.* This term used for Grandfather is the same term used for *the One to Whom all prayers are sent; Grandfather* can also refer to our ancestors, or to the President. *Wápaha* was the original term for the eagle staff, the original Lakota flag. Depending on who you asked, this opening phrase— *Tȟuŋkášilayapi tȟa-wápaha kiŋ haŋ*—could be interpreted as *the president's flag,* or perhaps as a reference to the original Lakota flag, the eagle staff of our ancestors. I would come to personally interpret it as the flag of the Divine Standard, belonging to all creeds and peoples, God's Emblem. The next phrase—*othaŋkešni he nážiŋ kte*—translates as "it will stand forever." The final phrase—*Iyóȟlateya oyáte kiŋ héhaŋ wičhíčağiŋkta čha léčhamuŋ*—could be translated as *beneath the Divine Standard, the nations shall flourish, thus I arise to be of service.* This song, I realized, ingeniously confirmed every Lakota's belief, regardless of whether they were patriotic, traditional, or simply spiritual.

After the Flag song, the announcer introduced the veterans, followed by the powwow princesses. Visiting intertribal singing groups, sitting along the periphery of the arena, were then invited to share a round of intertribal songs, in which each group offered four beginnings of one song. As about a dozen tribes were present, this process took quite a while. The singers present from the various Lakota reservations shared generously their own traditional musical expressions. I found myself drawn to their unique vocals, so unlike Western music. The singers, intending to project their music in an outdoors environment, threw their voices into the air in almost a falsetto, with a high volume and vibrato. I learned that while standard traditional songs were shared, many of the melodies were new compositions.

The basis of each session was song and dance. The sessions always began with an opening prayer song and could include dance and singing contests, traditional naming ceremonies, and other special events. Many times, the special events were sponsored by an individual family, in honor of a new birth or deceased loved one. The sponsoring family often held children's games—three-legged races, egg tosses, and tug-of-wars—giving away school supplies as prizes at the end. Every evening, the host community provided a feast for the participants, and we ate together in the arbor, with bowls and utensils we had brought from home, as community members circled around to serve everyone their meal. I enjoyed the children's games, the meals, and especially the songs. As the sessions continued, I tried to sing along to as many songs as I could. I even used my cassette recorder to record and learn new songs. Understanding the music, I realized, was key to understanding the culture—my own culture, which was still new to me in many ways.

In each session, the music and dance inspired unity among those who had gathered. The music provided deeper meaning to every event and ceremony. Though most powwow attendees were just spectators and only a few sang or danced, the virtuosic dancers inspired the audience's love of beauty, harmony, balance, and color—all the elements that uplift the human spirit. Each motion was sublime, ineffable. These dances could have looked spectacular with their rhythmic movements and stirring music—a kaleidoscope of color and rhythm.

Dance, though often considered superfluous in the dominant culture, is essential to life. The power of motion aligns with basic emotional and spiritual expressions. Even in Lakota language, one of the names of God— *Takú Škaŋškáŋ*—means *the animating force of creation*. As human beings, it is our nature to align ourselves with this pervasive force of movement in the world around us. In Indian cultures, every occasion is marked by music and dance; it is obligatory. For Indigenous people, even prayer—which can be spoken or sung—is most efficacious through dance. Music and dance establish connections between everything in this world—between the past and the future, between the earthly and the sacred.

That summer, I also attended my first Sundance. On the first day, Friday, I arrived with Art and his family at Pine Ridge Reservation, nearly one hundred miles south of Rapid City. A Sundance site had been constructed east of the village. The Lakota believe that everything in this world is a physical manifestation of a spiritual reality. One Creator has created everything in the seen and unseen realms, and the same spiritual laws apply to both. Thus, each component of the Sundance site had a spiritual symbol. An opening in the Sundance lodge faced east, toward the rising sun. A sacred tree stood at the center of the lodge, representing the tree of life, a symbol of the connection between heaven and earth. An arbor of willow branches atop ash rails formed an arbor encircling the center tree. Everyone would gather beneath this arbor for the Sundance.

That summer's Sundance was significant: the first time the Sundance had come out into the open at Pine Ridge. Many prominent traditionalists attended; I met many of them for the first time. Among the elders instrumental in reviving the Sundance was the esteemed Frank Fools Crow. He conducted the Sundance ceremony. Prior to the Sundance, he mentored the dancers and taught the singers the traditional songs, which were powerful, potent prayers for the dance.

Every dancer had a special reason for dancing; they would consecrate their dance as prayers for a sick loved one, for overcoming family crisis, or for personal growth. Along with their individual motives, the dancers, as a collective, symbolized the prayers of the entire community. The entire community would come to participate in and support the Sundance—seeing in each of the dancers the fulfillment of individual prayers as well as the whole. The dance would require total commitment and dedication of the dancers to achieve the prayer goals. Over the days of the dance, they would accept neither food nor water. This was the spiritual law of the people of the prairies, who endured great peril and hardship in their lives.

Even though no words were spoken, the Sundance was the most powerful prayer for the Lakota. It was said that one could think one's prayer, one could say one's prayer, one could sing one's prayer—but the prayer that involved the total being was the most potent prayer. As such, the Sundance required the whole being of the dancers and exerted great power over the entire community.

Early the next day, the singers sat and began to sing under the arbor. The dancers emerged from the compound on the west side and circled around the dance arena to enter at the eastern gate. They created a north-south line to witness the morning star rise in the night sky. This first point of light on the horizon appeared at the darkest, coldest hour before dawn. The morning star symbolized the promise of a new day, the summoning of the red dawn on the eastern horizon. The star offered hope that the darkness would be transmuted into a world of color, fragrance, movement, and light.

While the dancers began to greet the star in dance and the singers began to sing, the birds too, awoke, and their melodies intertwined with the singers. I stood watching at the periphery with other community participants. The collective song moved me. For those of us watching, we longed for this dance. We wanted our own goals to be fulfilled, our own prayers to be answered. We wanted to be led out of the darkness.

The dance itself was neither fancy nor acrobatic. The dancers stood in place with great dignity. They bounded up and down to the rhythm of the song. Even as a spectator from the community, I participated in the dance, bending my knees and moving up and down to the music. I was drawn to the Sundance music. The songs used in the Sundance are said to have originated in a vision and thus had a heavenly origin. Melodically, these songs are very beautiful. To this day, the Sundance music is a solace to my soul and the soundtrack of my life.

For each round of dancing, the singers offered a set of seven songs. Each round lasted about forty minutes to an hour. Four rounds occurred between sunrise and noon. After a break, another four rounds took place before sundown. As his vision unfolded throughout the rounds, Frank Fools Crow, the intercessor of the dance, and his helpers positioned the dancers in various configurations. The directions the dancers faced, the circle they made around the center tree, and the different movements were done as a great collective prayer.

Each of the dancers blew an eagle bone whistle in sync with the song. The shrill call of the whistle represented the communication of the eagle with the heavens. It was said that when an eagle spiraled upward on a convection current and disappeared from sight, the eagle communed with God and conveyed the voice of Creation in ineffable accents. The dancers aligned themselves with this devotional force when blowing on the eagle bone whistles. With their whole beings and with the whistle, the dancers appealed to the Source of Life.

That weekend, I didn't understand all of what I witnessed. Still, I felt the sheer power and magnitude of the Sundance. As I attended powwows, met with Lakota elders, and participated in this first Sundance, my attraction to the history and knowledge of the Lakota expanded. I launched myself into studying more about my own traditional culture. I was intrigued to learn about the history of the Sundance, one of the foundational laws of the White Buffalo Calf Maiden. The dance, I learned, reenacted the sacred time, according to Lakota belief, when the Maiden joined the people on earth for four days. During these days, she revealed spiritual and social laws and prophecies. The Maiden foretold of the day when The Grandfather— the One addressed in all prayers and songs—would appear and lead the people to the Source. A symbol of her visit and revelation, the Sundance was the highest form of prayer for the Lakota people.

I also learned that my mother's aunt, Margaret One Bull, participated in a Sundance in the 1930s. Margaret was Sitting Bull's granddaughter—a lively, intellectually-gifted individual. One of twenty others, she made a vow a year in advance to dance that particular Sundance. The dancers took the full year to physically, emotionally, mentally, and spiritually prepare. Every day, Margaret consecrated herself to the dance. As the principal dancer, she represented the White Buffalo Calf Maiden. She was the dancer who would hold the pipe and dance at the center of the lodge, closest to the Tree of Life. Praying with words alone was insufficient. Her whole body became her tongue. Every fiber of her being was directed to spiritually disciplining herself to the goal of the dance. Her preparation resembled climbing a mountain to reach a sacred place. Margaret's father, One Bull (Sitting Bull's nephew, who was more like a son to him after his own son died in childbirth), sponsored the Sundance around 1933 as a petition / prayer to end the devastating drought, during a period of time known as the "Dust Bowl Years." For three years, there was zero precipitation. The leaves did not appear on the plants. The grass did not sprout. The rivers were bone dry. Indigenous people of the prairies historically believed that the Dust Bowl was divine retribution for prior atrocities. In the late 1800s, the federal government had ordered the slaughter of the bison, bear, elk, and wolves to remove the food supply of the plains people. The ecosystem was devastated, and the prairies were opened to European homesteaders. The Europeans further damaged the environment through deep plowing of the topsoil that had built up over the years. The deep plowing opened the way for the Dust Bowl. Local traditionalists believed that the revival of one of the pillars of the ancient Covenant, the Sundance, would restore cosmic balance. Shortly after completion of the Sundance, it began to rain steadily for two weeks, followed by solid and regular precipitation.

Even though the dance harmed no one and benefited entire communities of Indigenous people, the United States government outlawed the Sundance in the late 1800s; people caught practicing this sacred rite faced arrest and incarceration. Despite the ban, the dance was practiced in secret throughout remote communities in South Dakota. Because of this, elders retained pivotal knowledge about the ceremony. During the sixties, when the dance was revived, these elders shared with younger generations the wisdom they had salvaged. I was one of the fortunate recipients of their knowledge.

That summer after my first Sundance, having attended several powwows and having learned more about sacred traditions, I realized why I had never connected with the dominant culture of the United States. The educa-

tional system, the political institutions, and the popular media had indoctrinated me with the allure of materialism, the popular notions of *success*,
and ideologies of class, race, and gender. I felt deeply and intuitively that
the messages of this culture were alien, skewed, and out-of-sync with the
natural order of life. I now felt a resounding pull to the traditional culture
that surrounded me.

5

The year before my trip to the Black Hills, my parents divorced after about seventeen years of marriage. They were seldom happy in their relationship. When they were together, I felt caught between the two, afraid of being pitted by one parent against the other. Their split came as a relief. No custody battles or horrendous, emotional processes affected my family during the divorce. My mom joked that their only "alimony" agreement was that she would pay my father exactly one dollar every year.

Soon after their divorce, my mom accepted a job in Utah working for a nonprofit agency called Project Necessity. My father stayed in Anchorage. I went to Santa Fe to start boarding school at the Institute of American Indian Arts.

As a teenager, I felt the need to be among my people—and I was happy to be with other Natives. I was exposed to myriad diverse tribes within the student body. I had friends from the Seminole Reservation in Florida, from the Meskwaki Settlement in Iowa, and from Little Diomede, Alaska, which was just a few miles from Russia. Several of the students at IAIA could barely speak English; they had gone to schools and lived in communities where only Indigenous languages were spoken. I learned about my peers' cultures and about the history of their tribes for the first time—not in our classes but rather through my general nosiness and many questions. I found new commonalities between us. For instance, my peers from the Seminole reservation practiced an annual ceremony of renewal, the green corn dance, which was similar to ceremonies done by my Choctaw friends. Even in the Northern Plains, corn had great symbolic significance as the harvested result of the seed of faith.

Though we came from different cultural backgrounds, my classmates and I shared a common purpose; all of us had applied to IAIA in order to develop our talents in the arts. I took classes with many gifted young people in sculpture, painting, and creative writing, along with regular academic classes. I wrote and created illustrations for the school paper. Though regimented, the environment suited me. I also appreciated the fantastic instruction for which IAIA was renowned. The late Edward Wapp taught the choir. A genius composer and musician, he arranged traditional melodies in a cappella choral arrangements. Allan Houser was another notable instructor, a master artist in any medium. An Apache man, born in captivity after the US military defeat of his Chiricahua Apache band led by Geronimo, he had received international acclaim for his sculptures, paintings, and mixed-media art. Professor Houser was a patient, low-key teacher who led by example. In his sculpture class, when I showed him the block of wood I was working with, he examined the grains, then guided me to sculpt a human figure. I witnessed firsthand his ability to look at a piece of wood and release the sculpture he saw latent within.

As many students came from the powwow culture of the northern tribes, a weekly powwow club formed. Our club was comprised of several powerhouse singers who continually created new compositions. We met in a large classroom and held powwows there, singing and dancing together. In the late sixties and early seventies, powwows had not fully emerged in the Southwest, and we hoped that our small efforts could contribute to the emergence.

* * *

I made the decision to leave IAIA at the end of tenth grade, first to stay with my mother in Southern California and then to start eleventh grade in Arlington, Virginia, where my father had accepted a job. In Arlington, I had a lot of autonomy. Every day after school, I took a bus to Washington D.C. for only forty cents. I knew the bus schedule by heart and explored most of the city that way. I took my first yoga class there, and I visited the Smithsonian museums and attended their lecture series. I went on organized tours to waterfowl sanctuaries and to the foothills of the Appalachian mountains.

Silent Spring by Rachel Carson had come out around that time, and it catalyzed an environmental preservation movement. Carson's examination of the uncontrolled use of pesticides and mankind's thoughtless interactions with the natural world penetrated my own thinking. I began to read more about this subject—first by reading *Silent Spring*, then *Mother Earth* news and other under-the-radar ecological publications. Through literature, I learned about recycling, avoiding waste, and the importance of conservation. I attended a huge rally on the National Mall to commemorate the first Earth Day. Different political leaders and activists spoke about the environmental devastation caused by large corporations, war, industrialization, and the American consumerist lifestyle.

My connection to this movement was an extension of my love for the natural world. The significant experiences of my life and my greatest memories—from my first Sundance to physical activity as a child—had occurred outdoors. I had felt a deepening stewardship and sense of ethics toward the earth long before my move to Arlington, and I had learned from many Native people who once lived a subsistence lifestyle that cooperation and peaceful coexistence with the natural world were possible. In middle school, I had developed an awareness of the damage humanity could inflict upon the earth. I had learned about the negative impact of the Alaska Pipeline, read books on endangered species, and participated in a thirty-mile walk to raise money and awareness for food shortages in Africa. Much to my parents' chagrin, I had also started to refrain from eating meat. For many years while living in Alaska, I had gone out fishing with my dad and his friends. As I filleted the carcasses, I realized that these animals' lives were sacrificed so that we could eat. I saw that every time I consumed meat, something had to die first, so I avoided eating meat whenever possible. I was deeply sensitive, believing that my own choices could have great effect.

In Arlington, I immersed myself in this alternative lifestyle. I volunteered at an eco-center near Georgetown a few times a week, where I sorted the glass and paper products that people brought to the facility and took them to a nearby recycling center. The more involved I became with the environmental preservation movement, the more I became something of a militant non-consumer. I never drove and always rode my bike, took the bus, or walked to get from place to place. I made sandwiches for myself in mass quantities—peanut butter and jelly, or cheese, raisin and mayonnaise—and stacked them in a bread bag in the freezer. Each day, I took two sandwiches in a plastic bag for lunch, and at the end of the day, I washed out my plastic bag to reuse for the next day.

Now as an adult, I have grown to be somewhat fanatical about conservation and recycling, to the point of driving close friends and family insane. Almost fifty years later, I still reuse my plastic bags. I have never used a clothes dryer because I do not want to use the additional electricity it takes to dry my clothes. Instead, I enjoy being outside, hearing the birds, and hanging my clothes on a line. I will not go shopping unless I have reusable bags with me because I do not want to contribute to the need for disposable bags. I take a thermos with me to cafes and convenience stores, as well as my own eating utensils. Of course, I have lapses in my efforts, but I strive to ask myself: *How can I be a minimalist here? How can I reduce the amount of harm done to the environment?*

My father changed jobs at the end of my junior year, so I moved to Boulder, Colorado, where my mother was living. At my new high school, I felt isolated by the lack of diversity. My peers had nice cars and had all taken fancy vacations during the summer break. Though I desperately longed for a place to fit in at my school in Boulder, I had none. So I decided to return to IAIA. I loved it there and wanted to feel again that sense of belonging. By this time, I had attended quite a few high schools and was grateful that I would complete my studies at IAIA.

Indeed, graduating from IAIA was a significant milestone. My graduating class did not wear the traditional caps and gowns; instead, we each made our own graduation garments—ribbon shirts and belts in vibrant colors and bold prints. During the ceremony, as we made our way, one by one, to receive our diplomas, a singing group from Taos performed a traditional honor song. Two heads of school spoke words of encouragement afterward. Then a closing prayer was shared.

Though many of my peers had career goals and plans for the future, I did not have any particular educational goals or professional aspirations. Of all the places I had lived and visited, I felt the strongest connection to South Dakota and wanted to return there. Over my adolescent years, my mother had helped to strengthen this connection; she arranged for me to work over a few summers at a tribal youth camp in Sisseton and had introduced me to Art Zimiga. At the time, she had so much going on in her life—most significantly, her activism to improve educational opportunities for Indigenous people; to support their cultural, spiritual, and linguistic heritage; and to eliminate discriminatory practices toward them. However, she wanted to strengthen this connection to South Dakota, for herself as well as for me.

Mom had a cousin at Black Hills State College, who had learned of and encouraged me to apply to a scholarship program there. I applied and was accepted. Though I did not know it yet, this marked a turning point in my life. From that time onward, no matter where I traveled, I would remain oriented to South Dakota.

6

In 1972, having just started my studies at Black Hills State College in Spearfish, South Dakota, I took a long drive to Vermillion to attend an Indian awareness seminar at the University of South Dakota. Upon my arrival, I was thrilled to learn that Richard Fool Bull, the oldest and most well-known Indigenous North American flute player, was offering a seminar on the flute. I had heard him play once before at a powwow in Pine Ridge. He was one of a select few who had devoted himself to keeping alive the traditional art of the flute.

When I slipped into Richard Fool Bull's presentation at the University Student Union, I chose a seat in the far back since I was a bit late. I listened as he shared the history of how he obtained the flute from his father and his grandfather. His songs, he told us, were all derived from vocal compositions, as was all traditional flute music. He played several songs, then sang them. I recognized some of these songs from recordings my mother used to play.

Then he displayed an array of his own flutes. He shared how he made his flutes, the meaning of the designs on the flutes, and the reason for the different colors. Every Indigenous flute-maker created unique flutes based on their own personal visions, or perhaps designs passed down to them by elders. These carvings could include horses, elk, deer, buffalo, cranes, or eagles. On Richard Fool Bull's flutes, green and blue duck heads had been carved into the bottom tip of the instruments.

When he finished his presentation, the audience began to trickle out of the room. I made my way forward, eager to see his fine workmanship and artistry. Richard Fool Bull smiled, shook my hand, and asked me my name. Standing closer to him, I could see the great age and wisdom in his face. He must have been in his late nineties. I introduced myself and asked about his tradition and whether anybody was carrying it on.

"Nobody's interested," he said, reaching for the flutes to pack them away.

"No grandchildren or great-grandchildren?"

"No," he responded. "There's no one."

I could tell he was deeply troubled by this. "That's too bad," I said. "Someone should carry this on."

Richard Fool Bull looked at me and with swift, intentional movements, put the flutes that he had been putting away back on the table. His face glowed with vigor and alertness, and his gaze on me was strong. "You're right," he said. "You should do this. You should carry this on."

I looked at the flutes on the table. I had never considered this possibility—and though I didn't discount it, I was not ready to commit to learning the flute and carrying on this legacy. I shook his hand, thanked him, and left without saying anything more.

That was the last time I saw Richard Fool Bull. A year or so after that, while I was visiting my mother in Boulder, I heard that he had passed away. Because he was prominent for his work with flutes and for the wisdom he bore from the pre-reservation days, news of his death spread quickly among the Indigenous population.

"Wait," my mother said to me, when we learned of the news. She disappeared into her room and returned with one of Richard Fool Bull's flutes. She handed it to me. My mother liked to collect things of this sort and must have bought this flute directly from Richard Fool Bull at a powwow or seminar years ago.

I attempted to play a few notes, then tried to give it back to her.

She shook her head. "It's just collecting dust," she said. "You keep it."

Initially, I didn't know what to do with the flute. One day, however, I borrowed some of my mother's vinyl records of traditional songs, both sung and played on the flute. Throughout my childhood, my mother would often play these records for my sister and me. Several recordings were of eminent twentieth century flute player John Colhoff; they were taken by a researcher from the Library of Congress who had visited South

Dakota in the 1930s to document traditional music. The son of a Russian immigrant and Lakota woman, Colhoff was something of a renaissance man—a scholar, singer, and gifted flute musician. He spoke English, Russian, and Lakota with great eloquence. As the official translator at Pine Ridge Agency, Colhoff was assigned to accompany the researcher from the Library of Congress. So humble was Colhoff that he never mentioned his own musical talent to the researcher. Only at the end of his trip to Pine Ridge did the researcher learn of Colhoff's talent and ask him to make a recording of his playing and singing.

To learn the flute, I listened to Colhoff's songs over and over until I could sing along with them. The recordings of Collhoff truly captured his mastery of the flute—the precision of his fingering and breathing, the resonance in his intonation—as well as his excellent vocals. Once his melody had been imprinted in my mind, I picked up the flute and began to imitate the same tune using the instrument. I learned a few flute melodies, which were instrumentalized vocal compositions, and I played them often.

Although I never knew Colhoff or Richard Fool Bull during my flute-playing years, I am indebted to them; their influences have shaped my musical vocation. Decades after learning the flute, I met John Colhoff's elderly son and had the opportunity to express my full gratitude for the introduction his father gave me to flute music. In turn, Colhoff's son expressed his pleasure that I had learned to play and sing his father's songs, thus keeping alive a waning musical tradition. I have also visited the gravesite of Richard Fool Bull, just north of St. Francis on the Rosebud Reservation. I have prayed there and thanked him for the gift of selecting me, of encouraging me to carry on his legacy. As I prayed, I knew he was still guiding me from the next realms.

As I taught myself to play the flute, I learned about its history and the features that distinguish it from other world flute traditions. The Indigenous North American flute originates from the bird-bone whistle, perhaps the oldest-known wind instrument; in fact, the Lakota word for both flute and whistle is the same—šiyóthaŋka—which highlights their connection. Carved from soft wood, the flute has a rich, vibrant sound. The scale of the flute—standardized across North America—is a step off of a diatonic scale. With cross-fingering and some technical prowess, one can play a chromatic and diatonic scale, as well as two minor pentatonic scales. This gives the flute special versatility. Perhaps most unique, the flute creates a natural vibrato, a kind of melodic warble, when steady air pressure is applied to it. Unlike other wind instruments where vibrato is produced by the musician, this is a feature of the flute itself.

Flute-playing was once a widespread practice amongst the tribes of North America. Sixteenth-century Spanish explorer Francisco Vazquez de Coronado described in his travel journals how his crew could always tell when they were approaching civilization by the sound of flutes. However, in the centuries that followed, twelve to twenty-four million Indigenous people perished in the face of constant warfare and disease. With this instability of life, traditions—including the flute—could no longer flourish.

* * *

Years passed, and word spread that I could play the flute. As very few people in Native communities were playing the flute at that time, I began receiving requests to perform. The first performances I did were during powwows; I played during the supper breaks. I had amassed a wonderful repertoire of songs from elders who were knowledgeable singers and whose generation was better acquainted with the flute than mine. After the powwows, I was invariably approached by additional older community members, who recognized the songs I played and wanted to share with me the songs that they knew. They had learned these songs from the generations before them, while riding during hundred-mile cattle drives, or when gathered around the fire in wintertime. I met a man in his nineties, Eli Taylor, the great tribal historian of the Bdewákhaŋtuŋwaŋ Dakota, at a powwow in Minnesota. Eli could still recall songs from his early twenties, and his grandson had a reel-to-reel recording of him singing fourteen songs over the course of fifteen minutes. I was amazed by his vast storehouse of traditional songs and acquired many new songs from him.

I primarily learned songs of the traditional genre, songs of love and courtship. During pre-reservation times, the flute was used to play a specialized genre of music pertaining to romance. In that pre-reservation social structure, adolescents, upon reaching puberty, were separated by gender in order to acquire the subsistence skills required to thrive in an unforgiving environment. Boys learned hunting, tracking, and martial arts skills, while girls learned the domestic arts. Only after years of rigorous formal training and after achieving proficiency in these skills were these youth then eligible for marriage. However, having been separated over the years of their training, the young men and women suffered from a communication barrier. Music became a means of expressing themselves and creating relationships. A new genre of music that related to love thus emerged.

Though these tribes were separated by thousands of miles over most of North America's prairies, woodlands, and Great Lakes regions, uniform rules of composition for this musical form emerged. The opening line, repeated three times in the first half of the song, consisted of cryptic or mysterious lyrics, while the second half of the song revealed the true meaning of the initial lyrics. Whether sung in Omaha, Ponca, Kiowa, Cheyenne, Arapaho, Lakota, Meskwaki, Kickapoo, Menominee, or Ho Chunk, any song was instantly recognizable as a love song because these songs followed a poetic style analogous to the haiku and always had the same structure.

Similar to Western musical traditions, these love songs portray a full gamut of human emotion. Some songs are romantic and sweet; others are tragic and remorseful. Songs may explore unrequited love; others may reveal bitter disappointment. As they derive from pre-reservation times, the songs preserve the unique vocabulary, idioms, and sentence structures of those eras. These ballads each tell a story. They provide a poignant snapshot into the heart of the people who lived centuries ago, revealing experiences of joy, pain, loss, and love that are truly universal.

While older generations primarily played romantic songs, I also learned to play many different types of songs on the flute, including many powwow songs and prayer songs.

One of the first places I traveled for a performance that included the flute was Florida. At the time, my mother was assisting Buffalo Tiger, the chairman of the Miccosukee Tribe of Florida, with grant proposals for their tribal education department. This was in the era before casinos, and most of the tribes were desperately poor. Tourism provided an obvious avenue for economic development; one of the Miccosukee Tribe's many initiatives was to start a festival to showcase tribal arts. When Buffalo Tiger asked my mother if she knew of anyone who could perform during the festival, she recommended me. When I went down to the festival that first year, I experienced "climate shock" because I departed from Bismarck, with its thirty-below temperatures, and arrived in Miami, where I was welcomed by a symphony of songbirds, explosions of flowers, and a sweltering eight-five degrees.

For nearly twenty years afterward, from the '70s to the '90s, I traveled to the festival to perform and lead educational workshops. This began my career in storytelling, music, and dance.

Graduating college, I started my teaching career and found it useful to incorporate the flute in classroom settings. Richard Fool Bull had inspired this method; in his seminars, he would share a song and then tell the stories associated with this song. I followed this same style—first in classes, then in all of my presentations. I shared the original stories from the lyrics of the songs, including romantic episodes and anecdotes.

In 1981, when I was nearly twenty-eight, I went on to make my first full-length recording at a studio in Australia. I had been invited to attend the World Council of Indigenous People, a conference held in Canberra, Australia. I met a man who was working in Aboriginal Education in Sydney, who invited me to do presentations around the schools there. He was quite interested in the music, so he arranged for professional studio time for me to record. I sold the few impromptu recordings we made during the tour. My next full-length recording was with Indian House records out of Taos, New Mexico; after that, I made between thirty to forty recordings under several different labels, only a few of which are still available.

* * *

I am often asked to play the *Native American flute,* but I do not have this type of flute and do not know how to play it. The Indigenous North American flute, the flute traditionally used across North America by Indigenous tribes, differs greatly from the popularized Native American flute.

In the 1980s, an individual from Arizona who had been crafting flutes according to the traditional tuning system—a step off of a diatonic scale—determined that flutes in this scale were not accessible for wider, commercial use. He created a flute according to a simpler melodic scale that was less versatile than the traditional flute but easier to use and well-designed for improvisation and individual expression. Later, a Navajo man from Arizona and classically-trained musician recorded several gold and platinum albums on this new flute. This spurred thousands of people to buy and make flutes of this sort, on the melodic scale. With the popularization of the new "Native American flute," many began to confuse these flutes with the traditional flute of Indigenous North America, though this new flute had little connection to the traditional musical aesthetic.

Nowadays, it is nearly impossible to find flutes on the original scale or musicians who can play them. People have lost sight of the rich heritage of the flute, which has never seemed right to me.

In learning the flute, I became interested in collecting and preserving traditional songs. I interviewed elders and expanded my repertoire of pre-reservation songs. In recent years, I have collaborated with noted music educator Richard Dube to create an affordable flute from synthetic material using the traditional scale. We host workshops in schools to accompany students in making their own flutes and learning basic flute-playing skills; students have now made thousands of flutes on the traditional scale. We have also worked to produce an accompanying flute curriculum book with information on the history, cultural context, fingering and breathing techniques, and most importantly, a notated songbook for beginners. I hope to bring awareness of the flute heritage and the traditional genre to the current generation of young singers who remain unaware of its existence. Perhaps, in time, this type of composition will be revitalized.

7

"O Son of Man! I loved thy creation,
hence I created thee.
Wherefore, do thou love Me, that I may name
thy name and fill thy soul
with the spirit of life."

Bahá'u'lláh, The Hidden Words,
Arabic no. 4

When a person dies, according to Lakota tradition, his soul begins the journey heavenward on *Wanáǧi Čhaŋkú* the Spirit Path, the expanse of light that is the Milky Way. On a dark night, if you look straight up, you can see where the Spirit Path forks. The main road continues straight, brilliant and strong. The smaller fork of light trails off into nothing. At this junction, there is a bright star called the Owl Maker, Hiŋháŋ Káǧa. As a newly-departed soul traversing the Spirit Path approaches the Owl Maker, the Owl Maker shouts out, "*Nitúwe he?* (Who are you?) *Táku enčiyapi he?* (What is your name?)"

At that moment, the wayfaring soul must announce his name. When the soul says his name, the reality of his life becomes apparent to the Owl Maker. The extent to which he honored and upheld his name in his lifetime—whether he was just, compassionate, or gentle—is manifest.

The Owl Maker looks upon this soul's doings; he then makes a judgment. If the soul has lived up to his name, the Owl Maker steps aside and allows that soul to continue straight on his journey throughout the ascending worlds of God. If the soul has failed to live up to his name, the Owl Maker remains motionless, blocking access to the straight path, in which case the newly departed soul has no option but to go on the trail that fades off to nothing.

* * *

In 1973, when I was nineteen years old, I received my Indian name: Tȟokáheya Ináẑiŋ, meaning First to Arise. The practice of giving a name comes from the Lakota belief that every human soul is the repository of the names and attributes of God. All creatures on earth may reflect a quality of God. A human being, the apex of creation, has potential to reflect the full spectrum of the attributes of God. Each soul manifests a unique combination of all the attributes of God but also may have certain dominant spiritual qualities that distinguish it, such as a thirst for justice, a compassionate heart, or a deliberate mind.

When a child is born to a traditional family, she is typically given a kinship name, which may reflect their birth-order or lineage. Later, she can receive a formalized name, an honor from leaders or elders in their community. Her name would be selected after extensive prayer and deliberation and would be announced in a presentation at a powwow or other formal occasion. Long ago, everyone was given a formal Indian name, though the practice has faded. As part of the process of acculturation and the subsequent loss of Indigenous languages, less emphasis has been placed on the Indian name.

Alice Iron Necklace gave me my name. Alice was born in Canada in the 1880s and came to the United States as a child, becoming a citizen of the Dakota territory around 1889. She cared for, comforted, and solaced my grandmother, Eva, after Eva's family perished in 1918 in an outbreak of Spanish Influenza. I first met Alice in 1966 during my family's visit to Standing Rock on our route to Alaska. Because Alice so dearly loved Eva, she requested to name me as a sign of love and honor for my late grandmother. Prior to formally giving me the name, she had the responsibility to pray for me daily, using the new name she had chosen. She also had to perform good deeds, especially focusing on hospitality, in my honor. These duties she took very seriously.

Both my sister Winona and I received our names at a powwow at Standing Rock in August of '73. After working for the summer at a youth camp in Sisseton, I drove over two hundred miles up to Fort Yates, North Dakota—the administrative center of the Standing Rock Sioux Tribe and host community for the largest annual celebration on the reservation. The summer powwows were among the largest of the year. People gathered from all around the country and surrounding reservations. As very few people had cars, everyone camped out on the grounds. This deepened the sense of togetherness and the ability to socialize. My mother had come to this powwow from Boulder. She loved occasions to gather with the community and was expert at setting up camp out on the open plains.

That weekend's powwow had an especially upbeat atmosphere because of Ted Bison, the powwow announcer. Originally from Pine Ridge, Ted was an active traditionalist, a medicine man and healer, one of few who knew and could articulate Lakota ways. He was known to be a *heyókȟa*, or *thunder-dreamer,* someone with a jovial spirit who clowns around and can make anyone laugh with his antics.

The powwow committee identified him as someone with the qualities of a strong powwow announcer. This role would require him to act as an intermediary between the committee who had organized the event and the people attending. He would have to know the schedule and ensure the correct timing of events. In order to uphold the positive spirit among the attendees, he would need to navigate the diverse personalities within the crowd, including bad tempers and strong egos. Throughout the weekend, Ted was on the mic, announcing the sessions of dance and music through-out the days, calling for dancers to prepare and stand at-the-ready. His announcements were infused with humor and storytelling, and his friendli-ness and organization set the tone for the entire weekend.

On the Saturday afternoon of the powwow, I did not know what to expect when Ted Bison called me, Winona, and our name-givers to the bowery for the formal name-giving. Anticipation and excitement swelled inside of me as I walked with Alice towards the crow's nest, the slightly ele-vated place where the announcer stood. When we reached the crow's nest, we were met by Joe Flying By, the officiant of the ceremony. He had talked with Alice and Mrs. Zahn, my sister's name-giver, beforehand, preparing extensive mental notes on their process and reasoning for giving us these new names. My sister and I took our place behind Joe.

Joe began the ceremony in Lakota, as this was the main language spoken at Standing Rock. At the time, I was not yet fluent in Lakota and did not understand much of what Joe was saying. I was later told that Joe spoke to everyone about our genealogy and history. He talked about why Alice had initiated the naming and shared details about the beloved station of my grandmother, Eva. Then Joe revealed our new names—Tȟokáheya Inážiŋ and Tȟa-Niyaŋ Awíčhableze Wiŋ—and why they were chosen. He faced west and began to pray in song. His resonant tune propelled the prayer out to that direction. In one hand, he held an eagle plume and feather, which he swept through the air. The plume and feather symbolized the virtues inherent within Winona and me, virtues that would enable us to soar to our fullest potential. To continue, Joe turned and prayed to the north, east and then south. He then held the plume and feather up to the heavens and prayed, then held them down toward the earth while still praying.

Finally, Joe announced to all of creation the appearance of two new individuals using our Indian names. He asked the powers of creation to recognize and bless us, the honorees. Then he handed the feather to Alice and the plume to Mrs. Zahn. Alice tied the feather to a small braid made right down the middle of my head, near the soft spot, a very sacred spot. Mrs. Zahn did the same with Winona. Both feathers represented our names.

In my new name, Tȟokáheya Inážiŋ, "Tȟokáheya" means to move from a place not in front into the first position. "Inážiŋ" signifies the transition from a non-standing position into a standing position. Both words reflect movement. They are difficult to convey in English, but the closest translation would be: *the first to arise.* The first time I heard Joe Flying By share my name, I did not know why "First to Arise" would have any significance. I was not aware of the meaning and depth to my name when I first received it, nor why Alice would have chosen it for me.

To conclude our naming, Joe joined the Lone Man Singers for a traditional song. When someone receives an Indian name, they also receive a song that extols their name. In our case, our song was a standard song that had been rewritten to include our new names. Joe and the Lone Man Singers sang, "The people see how much Tȟokáheya Inážiŋ and Tȟa-Niyaŋ Awíčhableze Wiŋ cherish their traditional heritage. So now, look towards the center and behold Tȟokáheya Inážiŋ and Tȟa-Niyaŋ Awíčhableze Wiŋ there." Alice took me by my arm; Mrs. Zahn took my sister. We began to dance around the periphery of the arena, and everyone lined up to shake our hands. They greeted Winona and me as their own relatives, welcoming us on our journey. *Hi Grandson. Hello Cousin.* This was how the community at the powwow honored the significance of this occasion—that we, two people of the younger generation, had been newly named.

Following the name-giving ceremony was a gift-giveaway. For months, Alice, my mother, and Alice's daughter Florence had accumulated various items, including star quilts made by the extended family, to give out to the community after Winona and I received our formal names. These quilts represented the morning star, the summoner of dawn. Ted Bison called the names of various community members to come receive these quilts. Several people in mourning accepted quilts, as did others who had travelled long distances to participate in the powwow. Elders and visitors, too, were gifted quilts.

Later that evening, Alice, her children, and others in our extended family oversaw a great feast. They provided a meal for the people who had witnessed our formal naming, over five hundred guests. The main dish was a soup made with beef from a newly-butchered cow. Alice's sons had skinned the cow, quartered and cubed its meat for the soup. The organ meats, delicacies, were specially-prepared. Fry bread was another staple of the meal. Everyone sat on the ground around the arbor, holding their own bowls and utensils. Members of my family and I went around the circle with pots of the soup, serving the meal to those gathered there. This feast was a spiritual feast. We partook of the food on behalf of those who had passed on, those in the spiritual realms. Even with hundreds of people, it felt like an intimate gathering between us, cementing the closeness of our community. This concluded what was a true celebration of our collective heritage.

* * *

I received my name around the same time my mother gave me the family pipe. The pipe's bowl and stem were made of catlinite, which was very rare. The stem had broken. She asked me to hold onto the bowl of the pipe for her and to retrieve the stem from an elder in White River, South

Dakota, after he repaired it. When I acquired the stem, my mother gave both bowl and stem to me. As with my name, when I received the pipe, I did not understand its significance. Both receiving the pipe and my Indian name set me on a path, a spiritual quest for understanding better my own purpose.

Only in more recent years have I considered what the naming ceremony must have meant to Alice. Alice was filled with excitement during my naming. The thoroughness of her preparation and her participation were tokens of the love she had for my mother, my grandmother, and me. There is a Lakota word, *hokší̌chaŋlkiyapi,* for a favored child, which literally translates to *a child whom they use as a heart.* This child from birth is unique and destined for a significant standing in the community. She is lavished with every possible honor and benediction. My grandmother Eva, as the sole survivor of her family line, was this hokší̌chaŋlkiyapi to her community. Alice and the entire Wakpala community poured their heart and soul into her. Eva's Indian name—Išná Máni Wíŋ, or "She Who Walks Alone"— was a reflection of her cherished station as the remaining descendant of her family line.

My mom had received an Indian name a few years before we did, in part out of gratitude for her activism and also out of respect for her mother. Now my sister and I were the beneficiaries of Eva's highly-regarded station; the love that Alice, Mrs. Zahn, and the community held for her had transferred to us. I am grateful to have been given this honor.

Ms. Iron Necklace passed away two years after my naming. At the time, my first child had just been born. I have a photograph of Alice holding her, beaming. Alice was nearly one hundred years old at that time, and it was the last time I saw her alive. I regret that I never had the chance to ask her why she gave me the name Tȟokáheya Ináži̇ŋ. In retrospect, I see that she gave it to me as a benediction, as a prayer to help me in my life. Even now, I find it difficult to live up to my given name. My name refers to someone who leads, who champions a cause, whereas my nature has always been more introverted and reserved. I strive to understand what my Indian name means and the ways in which I can grow to live up to it.

8

In 1973, I attended Haskell Junior College in Lawrence, Kansas, partly because my grandparents had gone there. At the time, the school served as a two-year junior college, though it was first established nearly a century earlier as an industrial school for members of federally-recognized tribes. I did not know what field I wanted to go into, so I took general courses. I felt without purpose, without direction, like a rolling stone. At the time, I was heavily involved in the party scene at Haskell. I frequented parties and other alcohol-related activities during most weekends. On the weekdays, I tried to maintain my studies and keep balance. Then, when the weekend arrived, I'd let myself go again. It was something that most of my peers were doing—the natural pattern of life at the college.

Starting in my senior year in high school, I had begun experimenting with alcohol and marijuana. Most of my peers drank, and growing up, both my parents drank alcohol, especially my father, and my relationship with him suffered because so much of what he did revolved around drinking. As I was immersed in this drinking culture, it was a wonder that I did not start drinking until the end of my high school career. Once I started, however, I became more dependent on alcohol during my first two years at college.

Alcohol use was never a part of Indigenous North American culture; it was brought over by Europeans. Since its introduction, it has been the cause of incalculable suffering and grief. In Indigenous cultures, people have little ability to resist the cruel effects of alcohol; there is a deep-rooted, biological intolerance to this toxin. This intolerance runs to such an extent that the Founding Fathers saw the introduction of alcohol to tribes as a means to exterminate Indigenous people, or at the very least, remove them from their land. Benjamin Franklin once said that "if it be the design of providence to extirpate these savages in order to make room for cultivators of the earth, it seems not improbable that rum may be the appointed means."*

I began to realize what a destructive force alcohol was in my life—the moral laxity and degradation it caused. I saw the stark contrast between the alcohol abuse at Haskell and the traditional ways of living I learned through my exposure to powwows and Sundances, receiving my Indian name, and inheriting the family pipe from my mother. I knew that in order to commit to a traditional lifestyle, I would have to renounce substance abuse. It would be some time, however, before I would be able to do this.

* * *

During my two years at Haskell, I enjoyed attending a series of seminars on art, crafts, and history taught by tribal elders primarily from Oklahoma. A friendly Ponca elder, Joe Rush, from White Eagle, Oklahoma, taught fanmaking classes. In other classes, I learned hand games and even participated in hand game tournaments with some of my classmates. I also attended a workshop and discovered that hand games were formerly a major cultural expression at Standing Rock. As a culminating event for one class, we traveled to Carnegie, Oklahoma and unimaginably beat the famous Kiowa hand game team, the Carnegie Road Runners!

Hand games were a traditional Indigenous system of conflict resolution with an offensive and defensive team. The offensive side hid sticks or bones. They sang and scored points as long as they were able to fool the defensive—or guessing—side. The guessing side's object was to retrieve those sticks to receive points. A line was drawn between the two sides, and each side put up a wager. One side, for example, would put up a pair of

* "The Electric Ben Franklin, In His Own Words," page 57, http://www.ushistory.org.

moccasins, and then the other side would put up a pair. The team that won received all the goods that were wagered back and forth. Since the games were done in the context of prayer, the team that lost did not really lose, since everything that was lost would be waiting for them in the next world.

This kind of game resulted in a win-win situation. The team that won was responsible for providing a feast and redistributing gifts for the whole people. The victorious team thus had the opportunity to show generosity and magnanimity.

Hand games were a classic mechanism for conflict resolution and totally antithetical to gambling in the Western sense, where a person has an addiction and a lust for self-aggrandizement. But Christian churches did not see this aspect of hand games. They only saw the gambling aspect and not the spiritual aspect. Because of the church prohibition on gambling, hand games were banned in their entirety, and the church enforced the bans on singing, dancing, the language, and games through coercion and force. The ban, initiated by the clergy, was enforced by the government edict, and the prohibition extended from the church to the entire community.

The most memorable seminar at Haskell, for me, was given by Mr. Ernest Mihecoby from the Comanche Nation in Oklahoma. Ernest was well into his eighties. He was raised with the stories and oral traditions of chiefs and intellectuals from the nineteenth century—leaders who championed the Comanche nation's efforts to preserve their way of life. Ernest was educated by a most prominent Comanche leader, Quanah Parker, who was the son of Chief Peta Nocona and famous captive, Cynthia Ann Parker. Quanah, in his youth, arose to a leadership role in repelling Euro-American intrusion and was instrumental in the establishment of the Native American Church and the formulation of its devotional practices. Ernest was his strongest living disciple.

The Native American Church of North America, the most widespread Native American religion, was characterized by mixing Christianity with traditional beliefs. It spread rapidly around the time of the military conquest of the Plains Indians and soon became a legally-chartered religion in the United States. The Native American Church was noted for its sacramental use of the spineless cactus peyote. Peyote had been used for thousands, if not tens of thousands, of years in the Western Hemisphere. Because of its hallucinogenic properties, in recent years, peyote was classified as an illegal, controlled substance. Only an American Indian member of a federally-recognized tribe and card-carrying member of the Native American Church was legally entitled to ingest peyote.

Even though Ernest's seminar was not about the Native American Church—it was about storytelling—the staff and students of Haskell petitioned him to conduct a half-moon prayer meeting the weekend after his seminar. I had attended Ernest's classes that week and had taken a liking to him. Like many of my peers, I had grown up knowing other Indians who were involved in resisting displacement and acculturation, and I was fascinated by Ernest's related accounts from his upbringing. When I heard about his prayer service, I was eager to attend. Besides, as I was still wrestling with my alcohol habit, I did not want to lose myself to yet another weekend of drinking.

On a Saturday in early spring, Ernest and his helpers erected a thirty-foot thípi for the half-moon prayer meeting. The Native American Church utilizes a thípi as a place of worship, similar to a portable cathedral. They went to great lengths to construct the thípi with perfection—to arrange the poles just so, to roll out the cover without a wrinkle, and then to stretch the cover around the poles until it is as tight as a drum. The thípi was a part of the prayer, a sacred architecture. Once erected, the Fire Chief built a fire at the center of the thípi. One of the four basic elements of life, fire was a universal and common element shared by all the disparate peoples of the world. No matter who you are, it is believed, your ancestors gathered together around the fire. Every one of the traditional practices—from the Sundance to the fasting ceremonies—uses the fireplace as an integral element of the devotional practice.

Over seventy of us, students and Haskell faculty, had gathered outside of the thípi. Then Ernest stepped forward. In this ceremony, he served as the Road Man, the one leading the people on the path of worship throughout the ceremony. The title Road Man drew from the abundant North American symbolism of the spiritual way of life as a road, often called the Red Road.

At sundown, Ernest started to pray. He led us in a procession around the outside of the thípi. Then he entered the structure, followed by the men who would serve as Drum Chief and Cedar Chief. The Drum Chief had prepared the drum—a cast-iron kettle partially filled with water, with a hide stretched over the top—ensuring that the sound created had a penetrating, healing effect. As Ernest and the other chiefs took their place at the back, we filed in behind them and sat around the perimeter, forming a circle around the fire. I could see the faces of each of my peers, glowing from the light of the flames.

Ernest sat behind the half-moon altar, a crescent-shaped sand construction that followed the bend of the thípi. A thick line drawn in the sand followed the curve of the crescent. This represented the road of life, from birth to old age; the line was only half a circle as a gesture to the life after this one in the unseen, heavenly realms.

As Ernest sang an opening song, the doorman passed around corn husks, and we each took one. Tobacco was passed around, and everyone took a pinch. We then rolled the tobacco into our husks. The fire chief took a stick from the fire, and one by one, we lit our rolls and passed the glowing stick around. Everyone began to pray at the same time. Different words of devotion in languages unknown to me resonated through the thípi. Even though Ernest was officiating, everyone participated fully in the songs and prayer, which struck me as egalitarian. Not used to expressing myself aloud in prayer, I wondered what I should pray about. I remained silent. The words that came to my heart were, "God, help me make it through this weekend. I don't want things to continue as they are. I want to make a change."

On the altar, Ernest had reverently placed a single, large, perfectly formed heirloom peyote button. Peyote is prepared in one of several ways. Once the peyote buttons have been cut up and dried, some people grind them into a powder. Others serve the peyote fresh, like a vegetable. On this occasion, it had been ground into a powder, then mixed up with water so that the consistency resembled oatmeal. Four spoonfuls—one for each time the peyote was passed around the circle—would be served throughout the night.

This was not the first time I had used peyote; I had attended a half-moon prayer ceremony in Alberta a few years before where peyote was given. It was considered a medicine, holy and pure, in contrast with us error-prone human beings. When taking this medicine, we understood that the process of our purification could be painful. Along with intense nausea came mental anguish. The worse it tasted, the more desperately we needed to be purified.

At sundown, during the opening songs, we passed the peyote around the circle. When I put the peyote to my tongue, I instantly felt sickened by its bitter taste. The taste could gag a maggot, but I ate my spoonful. Although a part of me did not want to experience the effects, I knew from a place deep within that it was time to get out of the rut of depending on alcohol and marijuana. I had to overcome such dependencies in order to progress down my path. Eventually, I would encounter new tests and challenges; I needed to be ready for them.

Pain coursed through my entire being, and I excused myself from the circle. I stepped outside the thípi, walked several yards away, and threw up. I breathed in the cold night air, and after a few minutes, I returned to the circle. I sank to the ground and bowed my head, still sick and miserable. I felt the weight of someone's stare on me, and when I looked up, I met Ernest's gaze. He motioned for me to come to him.

As I reached his side, Ernest took the bag of cedar from the Cedar Chief, one of the four officiants who had earlier gathered the cedar in a ceremonial way and placed it in a bag embellished with beads specifically made for this occasion. He began to pray in the Comanche language. His words rang with sincerity. He removed the cedar from the bag and sprinkled it on the embers, which lay to the side of the central fire. The cedar represented purity. Taking his fan, Ernest wafted the fragrant smoke in the four directions. Though I did not speak his language, I felt, deep within me, that I knew the meaning of his prayer: that my eyes and ears would open so I could see a better way. Ernest fanned the cedar smoke over my head, spreading purity over my entire body.

I returned to my place, released from the sickness that had overtaken me. A newfound euphoria settled in, along with a firm resolve. I had been wrestling with the demon of alcohol for quite some time. As I listened to Ernest's prayers, I arrived at the clear conclusion that I had to eliminate alcohol from my life. Though I never saw Ernest again, I remember this night with him as a great transformational experience, one that saved my life.

9

I graduated in 1974 with an Associate Degree in General Studies from Haskell and came to Standing Rock. At Haskell, I had met the woman who would become the mother of my three oldest children. She was now pregnant with our first child, a daughter, and I knew I needed to provide for them both. My cousin and I found steady work for a farmer a few miles southwest of McLaughlin, South Dakota. We worked fifteen-hour days, seven days a week as farm hands. We stacked hay and bucked bales that rainy summer. For this, we earned sixteen dollars a day, plus meals.

By August, I was thinking there had to be a better way to earn a livelihood. One day, while at the Standing Rock Agency, I heard a friend call out my name. Terry, who was working for the tribe at the time, shared with me that he was applying for a two-year Teacher Corps program at the University of North Dakota. An initiative of the Kennedy administration, the innovative program provided the opportunity for teachers-in-training to earn a Bachelor of Education while working full-time in their respective school districts. The program provided stipends for participants, as well as their dependents, so I would have additional provisions for my growing family. I immediately filled out and mailed the application. I was not particularly interested in teaching, though I enjoyed working with kids. As I was without an alternative plan, the ability to earn a living while obtaining a degree seemed to me a good option.

Part of the requirements for acceptance into the Teacher Corps was approval by the tribal school board. The Teacher Corps was quite competitive. A limited number of slots for the program existed because of the scarcity of available teaching positions on the reservation, and tribal politics often factored into who was accepted into these positions. Mr. Peter Taken Alive, a tribal leader on the board, advocated for me. Mr. Taken Alive's endorsement was significant, and I appreciated his vote of confidence. His recommendation played a big part in my eventual acceptance.

* * *

I taught in school district number four at Standing Rock Community Elementary School for two years. I taught fifth grade during the first year and sixth grade during the second. I was responsible for developing lesson plans and executing them in the classroom under the supervision of a head teacher. I did university coursework through distance-learning modules, and I traveled once or twice a semester to the UND campus in Grand Forks, North Dakota for weeklong sessions. I also spent two full summers taking classes on campus through the Teacher Corps, which was the best and most well-developed academic training that I have ever had in my educational career.

In the Teacher's Corps, I received a modest stipend—close to five hundred dollars a month, which barely covered our basic necessities. I counted every penny and budgeted with precision. I drove to Bismarck once a month to buy our groceries in bulk. To this day, I cannot believe how we survived on so little; this experience contributed further to my lack of a consumeristic lifestyle.

I had an aptitude for teaching, though I lacked classroom management and disciplinary skills. To compensate for my shortcomings, I created other activities using cultural music, dance, and storytelling to pique the interest of the students. I invited elders to teach traditional games. Several teachers and I even held powwows for the children.

I learned much from working alongside the teachers and administrators at our school; they were exemplary in their pedagogy and expertise in the field. In addition, they had a great love for and commitment to the children. Most of the teachers were tribal members. Those who were not, such as Bea Umber, my mentor, had lived on the reservation most of their lives. Bea's mother had come out to the reservation as a homesteader in the late

1800s. When I met Bea, she was in her seventies and past retirement age; she had continued in her teaching position because she loved the work. For most of her career, she had taught in the one-room schoolhouses on rural areas of the reservation. Bea had great compassion for her students, yet she also could sense what the kids needed—which most often was tough love. The children we worked with responded well to her methods and attitudes.

Within the schools, we saw the full range of capacities in the children. Some of the children in our classes came from families whose parents were educated off the reservation but had returned because of their desire to be near their homeland. Their parents occupied a wide-range of professions and had extraordinary skills in parenting their children. Some of the other children in our classes came from broken homes. They lived in the chaos of alcoholism, domestic violence, and abuse; and they did not receive proper attention and care in the home. This lack of attention manifested in their behavior at school. They came to us hungry, distracted, withdrawn, or lashing out.

These children were most often the products of intergenerational trauma stemming from a parochial educational system implemented on the reservations in the 1880s through the 1970s. In the late 1800s, various Christian sects put pressure on Congress to allocate various denominations to random tribes. Through this "crap shoot" process, Standing Rock was given the Catholic, Episcopal, and, to a lesser degree, Congregational churches and their attendant education systems. Representatives of these churches systematically and forcibly removed Indian children from their families and communities and placed them in boarding schools. These schools operated under the premise of "kill the Indian; save the man." In the regimented environments of these schools, Indian children were taught that all they knew from their culture and traditional ways was savage and sinful. They were indoctrinated in this oppressive mindset, which effectively dismantled Indigenous cultures and languages.

Years ago, an elder explained the effect of this system of education to me. "Look around," he said. "See all the problems on the reservations? Look at the alcoholism, the suicides, the neglect, the domestic violence, the depression, the health crises. Do you want to know who started all of this?"

He waited a moment before he said, "Me. I'm the one who started it."

This elder went on to share that as a young child, he was raised out in the prairies by his parents and grandparents. He spent time outdoors, hunting, and with the community in his village. He had long hair and had never worn store-bought clothing. He felt confident in his identity. But then his people were forced to settle on reservations. He was removed from his home and taken to a school far away, where he learned that everything he had come to know and all that he inherited from his community was erroneous. The clothes he wore and the way he kept his hair was not civilized. How he prayed and worshiped God was Satanic, and if he did not renounce these ways, he would be consigned to eternal damnation.

Over the course of his adolescent years, as the elder was forced to live this way, he gradually began to accept what he learned in school. When he grew older, and it was time for him to marry and raise children, he found a wife who was raised within the same educational system. Their children inherited their self-hatred and identity crises. And so this self-hatred and identity crises were passed through the generations from the first generation to be extracted from traditional culture and indoctrinated into the dominant culture, up until the present. In my work, I saw its continued effects in the social disintegration present in our classrooms. How many of my students were the victims of this intergenerational tragedy?

"You see all the problems that exist on the reservations?" the elder had asked me when he finished his story. "It all started with me."

This elder used satire to emphasize his point. Though he obviously was not responsible for what happened, his insight enabled him to see that he was part of a process that resulted in the effort to destroy a culture. He was forced to believe that what he learned from his parents was wrong, the way he looked was wrong, his language was wrong, and his practices were wrong. Though he initially resisted what he was taught, day after day of being pushed down caused him to question his identity and view himself as inferior. Though it never completely eradicated his core beliefs, this systematic oppression deeply affected him, along with every other Native child from his generation who was subjected to this form of brainwashing.

This particular elder was a classmate of my grandmother, Eva. As he shared his story with me, I realized that she had endured the exact same injustice and had, to some degree, internalized this trauma. Perhaps it became manifest in her physically, in her fragile health: she died young, in her fifties. What else of this devastating legacy had been passed down through the generations of my family? In what ways had I, like the children in my classroom, inherited the oppression of the past?

* * *

Our daughter, Kimímila, was born during my second semester with the Teacher's Corps on February 24, 1975. She was one of the last babies born at the old Standing Rock Agency Hospital. Since no obstetricians were on duty, a midwife—Sister Clarice—singlehandedly delivered her.

In the delivery room, as her mother was in labor, I remember hearing a strange, eerie sound resonating from outside the hospital. I went out into the cold to determine its origin. The Missouri River, running alongside the hospital, was frozen solid. Above me, the Northern Lights shone in a brilliant display. The sound reverberated off the frozen river, emanating between the heavens and earth. The ice on the river, in such frigid temperatures, expanded and contracted, sending crackling sounds up and down the river. It was mystical, amazing—the song of the Northern Lights.

A significant Chippewa dance for women, the Jingle Dress dance, originated from the Northern Lights. Legend tells of a man who, while praying for his sick daughter, was transported from this earth into the heavens. There, he was shown the power of the Northern Lights, symbolic of a God-born force from the realm above. He saw how the lights shimmered and danced in a curtainlike wave. And he heard a sound, much like the one I heard the night Kim was born. When the man came back to this world, he aspired to recreate the majesty of the Northern Lights in dance regalia. He formed the Jingle Dress—a dress embellished with hundreds of small metal cones. When dancers wore this dress, the cones created the same movement and sounds as the Northern Lights. Now practiced among Midwestern tribes, the Jingle Dress dance represents both the heavenly power from above and the exalted station of womanhood.

We named our daughter Kimímila, which means *butterfly*. The butterfly, a symbol of regeneration and transformation, is a physical form with a spiritual essence, and it represents the connection between the heavens and the earth. Kimímila was a plump baby, with long, straight black hair. Her dark eyes were bright and absorbed her surroundings. From the start, she was radiant and outgoing, and she remains so today.

* * *

After completing my undergraduate degree in 1976, with two years of teaching experience under my belt, I was recruited for a graduate program in educational administration at the University of South Dakota in Vermillion. The non-thesis degree required two semesters of intensive summer study on campus in Vermillion. I received a stipend and also began an internship at Little Eagle Day School. There, I had the privilege of working with the principal, Adele Little Dog. Years ago, she had been selected by Sitting Bull's adopted son to perform a pivotal role in the revival of the Sundance. Her dedication to preserving Native culture revealed itself every morning at the school; she conducted all-school assemblies entirely in Lakota, the children's first language, though many of the teachers did not speak Lakota and had no idea what she was saying.

My son was born the autumn that I started the Educational Administration program at the University of South Dakota. The summer before his birth, I danced in my first Sundance at Green Grass. I pledged my dance as a prayerful and joyful support of his arrival, to honor this new life coming into the world. My mother came from Boulder to support me and attend. With her close friend and mentor, Eunice Larrabee from the Cheyenne River reservation, she helped prepare a feast in honor of my participation, which would be held at the end of the four-day dance.

Frank Fools Crow, whom I had met at my first Sundance, was the mentor for the dancers that year. Frank had conducted many Sundances and had direct knowledge about the dance. In the months before the Sundance, he taught us the formations and directions for each dance during the different prayers. He did not speak English, so a translator always accompanied him to these meetings.

The dance was one of the most physically-grueling ordeals I have ever experienced. The air was dry, and the heat soared to over one hundred degrees. As required for the dancers, I did not partake of food or water during the course of the four days. Because of the unusual heat, we dancers were given the option to return to our camps at night to sleep and eat.

Many chose this option. A few of us decided that we would continue our dance in the traditional way. We would remain through the night near the sacred tree, without food or water, as a means to propel our prayers.

At the end of the four days, I was exhausted. After the Sundance concluded, I lay on the ground, breathing hard. A close friend walked over to where I had collapsed. Without saying a word, he poured a big jug of water over me. The jolt of water revived me, and I sat up, spluttering and laughing. I joked with him to go get another jug of water, which, without hesitation, he did.

On September 18, 1976, my son Ohíyes'a was born. I had chosen the name, which means *the one who wins or succeeds*, after the famous Charles Alexander Eastman, whose original name was Ohíyes'a. I greatly admired Eastman, who was born in the 1850s in Minnesota. Though as a child he spoke only Dakota, he learned English as a teenager in South Dakota. Intellectually gifted, he went on to graduate from Dartmouth and earn his medical degree. As a physician, Eastman treated victims of the Wounded Knee massacre. His Lakota patients loved him, as he could speak to and understand them in their own language. Eastman was also a founder of the Boy Scouts and wrote several incredible books documenting Indigenous history and culture. In many ways, his story reminded me of my great-grandfather. My great-grandfather, also born in Minnesota, was bilingual and a truly brilliant man. I hoped my son could aspire to these qualities.

When Ohíyes'a was born, I commissioned a friend whom I had met at the previous summer's Sundance to make a cradleboard for my son. Centuries ago, these baby-carriers were commonplace throughout North America. The infant would be laced up in the cradleboard and kept secure and comfortable as his parents carried him on their backs. My friend, Mitchell Zephier, crafted the cradleboard from richly-stained wood, tanned buckskin, and ornate beadwork designs. From his infancy, Ohíyes'a was tucked in this cradleboard, so that his mother and I could carry him around. He would have been the first baby to use a cradleboard in decades, and he made quite a sight!

Ohíyes'a was a quiet, healthy boy, and he instantly became Kim's playmate. She took him for wagon rides around our home in Little Eagle, where we had moved for my Master's practicum. Ohíyes'a's sister loved him so much that even before he learned to speak, she became his spokesperson.

My mother lavished a lot of attention on her grandkids. She loved to spend quality time with them and cook for them. Though she was living in Boulder and was at the height of her activist career, she tried to visit as often as possible. Because we always drove to the Bismarck airport to pick my mother up, Kim became convinced that her grandmother lived in the airport; she called her grandmother her "airport uŋčí."

By the time Ohíyes'a was born, I excelled as a student. I loved the intellectual stimulation. I knew how to write papers, cram for tests, and perform all of the survival skills of a professional student. Giving up the party scene put me at a great distance from my peer group; I gravitated, instead, toward an older generation whose mindset and interests matched my own. At the University of South Dakota, I met plenty of interesting and wise elders, many of whom became my mentors. I loved to sit in on the language class of James Emery, an elder who taught the Lakota language. Emery could never remember a time when he could not speak both English and Lakota. An intellectually gifted individual, he was a storehouse of information and stories. Whenever I could, I snuck out of my regular academic classes to join his. I also met Charles Kills Enemy at the home of one of the history professors. He became my mentor for the Lakota fast.

I also grew close to another elder, Joseph Rock Boy, from the Yankton reservation. I had met Joe years ago while attending an Indian Awareness seminar in Vermillion. He remembered me and became like a grandfather and mentor to me. Friendly, outgoing, and an encyclopedia of traditional knowledge, Joe often shared stories and wisdom with me over coffee. He encouraged me to continue to seek answers to my questions about my purpose in life. Joe was an active member of the Native American Church, and together, we went to many peyote meetings. I often invited Joe to my home, where he visited with my children and told them traditional stories about the exploits of Iktómi, a trickster character. Joe had learned these stories from his grandparents, and he passed them along to Kim and Ohíyes'a.

* * *

Just after Ohíyes'a was born in 1976, I arranged for my children to be given Indian names. I asked Joseph Rock Boy to name Ohíyes'a, and I asked Margaret One Bull, my mother's aunt, to choose a name for Kimímila. Then I immersed myself in the preparations for the feast and the gift-giving. Elders with knowledge of traditional crafts helped to make gifts for the giveaway. Jim One Feather made buffalo horn spoons and beautiful quillwork. Margaret Brave Bull crafted star quilts. I felt that drawing on the skills of these artisans and providing handcrafted gifts would add to the significance of the event.

The formal name-giving—one of the first after a long hiatus—took place at a Sundance at Standing Rock. After the completion of the dance, my children received their names. My wife held Kimímila's hand, and I carried Ohíyes'a to the center of the bowery. Joe Flying By officiated the ceremony, as he did for me, and shared with the community my children's new names: *Kiŋyáŋ Tȟa-Óyate Nawíčhakičhižiŋ Wíŋ*, *She Flies to Defend Her Nation*, and *Makȟá Okíŋyaŋ*, *Flying Over the Earth*.

I had asked Joe Rock Boy to give Ohíyes'a the name *Makȟá Okíŋyaŋ*, which means *Flying Over the Earth*, because it was my great-grandfather's name. The name is indicative of the eagle and represents the sky's vastness and the physical manifestation of spiritual qualities. The name points to the eagle's ability to rise above obstacles. My grandfather was remembered for always speaking in his own dialect, the minority Minnesota Dakota dialect, though he lived among Lakota speakers. Joe spoke this same dialect and used this dialect to share with the community why this new name had been chosen for Ohíyes'a.

My aunt Margaret and I had consulted upon Kimímila's name as well prior to the ceremony. Her name, *Kiŋyáŋ Tȟa-Óyate Nawíčhakičhižiŋ Wíŋ*, means *She Flies to Defend Her Nation*. Margaret gave Kimímila this name in honor of my mother's work championing Indian rights. Margaret saw my mother, with her activism and marshaling the forces of justice, as a true defender of our people. She wanted Kim to receive this name in honor of her grandmother.

This occasion was very significant to me. My name—*First to Arise*—held great meaning in my life, and I hoped my children would find the same blessing.

* * *

The responsibilities of fatherhood weighed heavily on me, especially in regards to finances. When I completed my degree at the University of South Dakota, I was looking for a job and learned that Standing Rock College was looking for teachers for freshman-level English and math classes. I started teaching there in the fall of 1977. I did not enjoy working in adult education, but I remained at the college for two semesters until I learned of a new job opportunity with the Youth Conservation Corps Camp in Wakpala.

I enjoyed this position. I organized recreational activities for the teenagers who participated in the camps. I had the freedom to incorporate my own interests, and I took the youth to local powwows and arranged to have elders come in to share traditional stories and legends.

Because of my work schedule, I did not get to spend as much time with my children as I would have liked. When I was home with them, I read all types of children's books to them, before bed and in the mornings. I took them to powwows from the time they were born. When they were old enough to walk, they began to dance at the powwows. We made all of their little dance outfits—tiny cloth dresses with beadwork and beaded belts—by hand.

Though I enjoyed loving and attending to our children, I was dismayed by the growing tension between their mother and me. My way of handling the tension was avoidance, which can be dangerous but seemed safer than confrontation. How could I resolve the dilemma of wanting to be with my kids but not their mother? I prayed for opportunities to leave the home.

As the years went on, my prayers were answered as I transitioned away from a routine teaching career to giving presentations and seminars around the country and the world. This took me away from our home for days at a time. I arranged to travel with my children so that we could spend as much time together as possible outside of the home. While this did not necessarily solve my marital tension, the travels reduced the chances of our children having to experience it.

Witnessing my children's births and these early years of their lives reinforced my determination to find something of substance in the world. I often felt as if I were sinking into quicksand. Feelings of rootlessness and hopelessness intensified in me. *What am I doing? Is there hope for my little children? What is the purpose of life? What is the Red Path for me?* I wrestled with these questions—questions that would intensify and lead me into the Lakota fast of 1979, the fast where I beseeched the Creator for understanding.

PART III

HUPÁGLUZA
(TO LIFT THE PIPE IN PRAYER)

1

One day in the fall of 1975, when I was teaching at Standing Rock Community Elementary School, I walked over to the Bureau of Indian Affairs office in Fort Yates on an errand for my mother and her sister. They had inherited large landholdings on the reservation from their mother. Since I was the only member of our immediate family living on the reservation, my mother had asked me to research and visit these lands.

When I walked into the Bureau, located in an old brick building, I met Gerald, a new employee. I gave him my requests for information. Gerald printed off photocopies of maps of the landholdings. He took out colored pencils and outlined the lands that my mom and aunt had inherited. Though soft spoken, he had a deep kindness about him, and I was grateful for the extensive services he offered.

I visited Jerry at the realty office several times to get more information about our landholdings. We quickly developed a friendship. Although Jerry was mild-mannered, I sensed that he was an advocate for justice in the Bureau's land dealings. Jerry defended the rights of the Indian lessees, who historically had been taken advantage of by the bureaucratic system. Because of this, his colleagues had gave him the nickname "the mouse that roared." I admired this about Jerry—how he served others with the utmost integrity.

After we had seen each other several times, Jerry invited me over for dinner. He and his wife Dianne lived in a government housing unit two blocks away from my home in Fort Yates. When I arrived, they welcomed and invited me inside. Adorning the walls of their home were posters emblazoned with sayings such as "The earth is but one country, and mankind its citizens,"* and mementos from their global travels. The proclamation of a global sensibility, rare in rural North Dakota, greatly appealed to me.

Over dinner, the Henriksons shared with me that they were members of the Bahá'í Faith, a world religion whose aim is the unification of humankind. They had just returned from Haifa, Israel, where they partook in a nine-day pilgrimage to the Bahá'í holy sites.

"We visited the region where Bahá'u'lláh, the Prophet and Founder of the Bahá'í Faith, resided, and where His remains and the remains of His predecessor are interred," Jerry explained. "The holy site of their entombment is the point of adoration for all Bahá'ís, the sacred place we turn toward in prayer."

"It was a blessing to be able to go," Dianne added.

The Henriksons shared photo slides depicting the highlights of their pilgrimage, the Shrines, and surrounding gardens. I marveled over the photographs of the majestic golden-domed Shrine built on a mountain and surrounded by, interestingly, cedar trees. I was reminded of a Lakota prophecy, which held that a mountain covered in cedar was the birthplace of the Thunder Beings, the forces that heralded and sustained life in the springtime. Prophecy foretold that, when the time came, the force of light and goodness would emanate from this mountain. I began to ponder this prophecy, as I looked at the photos of Mount Carmel and listened to Jerry and Dianne describe the Báb and Bahá'u'lláh as Divine Messengers from God for this day. The Báb came as a Herald to the Prophet, Bahá'u'lláh, Who brought a message of peace and justice to transform the whole of society. Bahá'u'lláh's teachings included the Oneness of God and of all religions and the oneness of humanity.

I was also struck by the aerial photographs of the gardens around the golden-domed Shrine of the Báb. The flowers and shrubs were laid out in perfect eight-pointed star designs. "What is the significance of the star design?" I asked.

"I'm not sure," Jerry replied. "What about them interests you?"

I began to tell them about the significance of the morning star—how this star appeared at the darkest hour before the dawn, the harbinger of

---

* Bahá'u'lláh, *Gleanings from the Writings of Bahá'u'lláh*, no. 117.1.

a new day, a sign of hope after the confusion and bewilderment of night. The morning star sacrificed its life to escort a crimson path to the horizon, preparing the way for the day star, the sun, to launch its own hero's journey. Throughout North America, the gallant morning star appeared in a plethora of traditional tales, always with the principle duty to usher in a new day.

"Your description parallels the story of the personage of the Báb, Who is interred in this Shrine," Jerry said. He proceeded to tell me how the Báb prepared the way for the Prophet Bahá'u'lláh and how He came at a time when many people were searching for the Promised One, Who would bring truth and salvation. Jerry told me how, in Persia in the nineteenth century, a scholar named Mullá Husayn had prayed and fasted to purify himself so that he could find this Promised One. When he met the Báb, one fateful night in Shiraz, he did not know that he had met the one for whom he was searching. But that night, Mullá Husayn had a question in his heart—to understand the significance of the Surih of Joseph. Though Mullá Husayn did not articulate this to the Báb, the Báb spontaneously revealed a commentary on the story of Joseph, one of the most enduring stories in world religious scriptures. This prompted Mullá Husayn to believe that he had, indeed, found the Promised One.

Because the Báb brought a revolutionary message of spiritual and moral transformation, He and His followers faced cruel persecution within the corrupt Islamic regime. The Báb Himself was martyred at a young age. Thirteen years later, a new revelation would be ushered in by Bahá'u'lláh. The brief life of the Báb mirrored the brief life of the morning star. Both appeared for a fleeting time in order to herald the dawn.

I left Jerry and Dianne's home that night intrigued by the stories they had told me. I felt something within me shift, as if I had come across a new path, one I was eager to venture down, though I was unsure of where it would take me.

* * *

That night at the Henriksons was not the first time I had heard of the Bahá'í Faith. As a teenager in Washington D.C., I had met a young man and woman who were teaching the Bahá'í Faith. Introduced to me by a mutual friend, this young man and woman had shared with me stories of Bahá'u'lláh and the Báb—stories of Their persecution and suffering. I was struck by the young man and woman's conviction and earnest energy; they spoke as though offering me a gift and treated me with the highest respect, much as Gerald and Dianne did.

Their sharing differed from the unsettling interactions with evangelists, both in my teenage years and as an adult on the reservation. Many missionaries on Standing Rock went door-to-door to try to convert new followers to their faith. When they came to my door, I was open to learning about Christ's teachings. Both my parents had been raised in Christianity but had grown disillusioned with it in their adulthood. They disliked "Churchianity," as they called it—the semblance of worship, the illusion of steadfastness, the manmade pretenses, the worship of an empty shell—all of which they felt was disconnected from the true spirit of Christ. As a result, I never knew much about the religion and next to nothing about any of the Divine Messengers.

Though I was willing to talk with the missionaries who came to my door, whenever I shared with them that I practiced Lakota spiritual traditions, they always informed me that I was a heathen. They considered anything outside of their own religion as satanic; to them, my practices were devil worship. They were unwilling to continue our conversation once they realized I would not convert to their narrow ideals. "Nice to meet you," they would say as they left my home, and unbelievably add, "You're going to hell."

As I heard these varied messages—each of which conflicted and condemned the one before—I wondered what could bring these conflicting creeds to a single truth. Where is the compass that guides to a true North?

The Lakota traditional beliefs, taught to me by my different mentors, were the only compass I had. Yet, though the practices had a broad appeal, the Lakota spiritual tradition was revealed only to the people of a certain time and place. And with fewer speakers of Lakota in each generation, fewer people fully understood the provisions of the covenant. Thus the essence of the teachings of the White Buffalo Calf Maiden—embedded in the language and preserved in traditional songs—had begun to erode. I longed to find a new belief system, congruent to my Lakota beliefs, one that could wrap the entire world in its embrace.

I noticed how greatly Gerald and Dianne's approach differed from the missionaries who inhabited Standing Rock. They had no hidden agendas, just true interest in getting to know me. So often on the reservation, missionaries would come and go; however, Gerald and Dianne knew that in a rural community where everyone knows everyone, relationships are built slowly and to last. That was how our friendship formed. They learned about and accepted my Lakota spiritual beliefs, and they were the first white people I had ever met to do so.

Jerry and Dianne endeavored to learn more about the joys and challenges of my life and my spiritual journey. I opened up to them with my questions on child-rearing, my marital struggles, and my desire for unity and to see reconciliation amongst the divided racial and ethnic groups in this country. With humility and consideration, they shared with me concepts from the Bahá'í Faith that related to my journey. As wise teachers who were deepened in the Bahá'í Faith and its writings, they drew from the ocean of its guidance to offer remedies that applied to the problems I shared and spiritual food that satisfied my appetite.

As my last year as a teacher drew to a close, I continued visiting Gerald and Dianne. Our friendship grew. I accompanied them to Bahá'í Holy Day celebrations. Their daughter, Shahin, was close to Kim's age; whenever I visited Jerry and Dianne, our girls played together. Jerry and Diane shared prayers for my children and family with me whenever I went to their home, and I was impressed that they had memorized so many of these prayers verbatim—not realizing that the practice of memorization was common across faith traditions.

That March, Jerry and Dianne participated in the Bahá'í fast—a nineteen-day fast during which they abstained from food and drink from sunrise to sunset each day. Though I was not yet a Bahá'í, I decided to participate in this sacred time of renewal and purification. Like the Lakota fast, the Bahá'í fast was a potent expression of devotion and provided the meditational opportunity to develop one's relationship with God. I knew I would not have a problem fasting during daylight hours, since I had observed the Lakota fast of completely refraining from food and water for four days straight.

During that first Bahá'í fast, I noticed some minor physical differences. The sensation of hunger had switched off after the first twenty-four hours in the Lakota fast, and the feeling of thirst had intensified. This did not occur during the Bahá'í fast. I experienced some hunger pangs daily. I figured this was because I was breaking the fast at sunset each day. All in all, the two fasts are like comparing apples and oranges. The purpose is one and the same—to take time to draw closer to God.

As I grew more interested in learning more about the Bahá'í teachings, the Henriksons told me stories of the Central Figures of the Bahá'í Faith—the Báb, Bahá'u'lláh, and 'Abdu'l-Bahá. Learning about the persecution of the Prophets of the Bahá'í Faith captured my attention. I discovered that all of the Prophets of the world religions had suffered intensely through torture and persecution. I wondered how they endured those trials and tribulations.

One story that moved me was the story of the death of Bahá'u'lláh's youngest son, Mírzá Mihdí when Bahá'u'lláh and His family were wrongfully imprisoned in Acre. None of Bahá'u'lláh's followers could visit Him. Mírzá Mihdí had been praying on the rooftop of their home and chanting as he circled a skylight. During his prayer, he missed a step and fell through the skylight to the ground below. Bahá'u'lláh rushed to His beloved son and offered to restore him to full health. But Mírzá Mihdí refused, asking instead that his life be offered up as a ransom in order for the Bahá'ís to draw closer to Bahá'u'lláh. Though it grieved Bahá'u'lláh, He accepted His son's offer. Mírzá Mihdí died. Soon after, the restriction on visitors was lifted, and Bahá'u'lláh could receive His followers as visitors.

At the time I heard this story, my son had just been born—and I better understood the great sacrifice this would have taken, to lose a child. The sacrifice took on greater heights knowing that Bahá'u'lláh had the ability to resuscitate him. This story and many others revealed to me the role of sacrifice in this Faith, and to me, that made it all the more sacred. Another personal point of resonance with Mírzá Mihdí is that we share June 23 as the date of his passing and my birth.

* * *

One night as I left their house, Gerald and Dianne gave me a slim volume of the writings of Bahá'u'lláh called *The Hidden Words*. The book contained a collection of spiritual truths written in simple yet profound form.

While walking the few blocks back to my home, I pulled the book out of my pocket, opened it to a random page, and began to read. Suddenly, the small letters on the page became illuminated, and each word seemed to leap off the page, right toward me. I shut the book. After a moment, I reopened it, and the same phenomena occurred. I forced myself to read on: "Noble have I created thee, yet thou hast abased thyself. Rise then unto that for which thou wast created."*

The truth of these words anchored into my heart. Was I preventing myself from reaching my own inherent nobility? What patterns and habits were holding me back? The words challenged me, yet I still felt torn, resistant to change. As I reread the text—shocking, powerful as it was—I realized, deep in my being, how I had taken myself away from this nobility. Remorse enveloped me. I needed a course correction, a spiritual jolt of sorts. Perhaps these profound words had found me at the time I needed them most.

* * *

Born and raised in North Dakota, Gerald and Dianne were both of Norwegian descent; Norwegians had emigrated en masse from their homeland in the mid-1800s, many to the homesteading territory of North Dakota. Both Gerald and Dianne became first generation members of the Bahá'í Faith. Dianne and Jerry met while attending firesides at the home of a longtime Bahá'í couple, Marian and Orviell Kadrie. Marian was raised by devout Muslim-Syrian parents in Driscoll, North Dakota, and she learned both Arabic and English as a child. Her father often told her stories with moral, spiritual lessons, and he had learned these stories from his time in Acre, Palestine. When Marian's father went to the markets in Acre, he had encountered a man named Shaykh Effendi, whom he considered a mentor. During the 1970s, after becoming a Bahá'í, Marian went on pilgrimage to Israel. There, she met a member of the Universal House of Justice, the Bahá'í international administrative body. In conversation with him, she discovered that her father's mentor was none other than 'Abdu'l-Bahá, the

---

* Bahá'u'lláh, The Hidden Words, Arabic no. 22.

son of the Prophet Bahá'u'lláh. When Marian met and married Orviell Kadrie, a Bahá'í of Middle Eastern and Ojibwe descent, the two first moved to Long Beach, California. Then, upon hearing of goals to form Bahá'í communities in North Dakota, they moved to Fargo.

After becoming Bahá'ís, the Henriksons came to Standing Rock from Bowman, North Dakota as pioneers, and joined the Bahá'í community there. The move was not a drastic change, though the cultural divide and living among many non-native English speakers proved challenging. In a true spirit of pioneering, they met these challenges cheerfully. Their genuine natures and pure spirits were attractive and distinguishing qualities to the Lakota community.

* * *

After I moved to Vermillion, South Dakota, to start my Master's program in Educational Administration, I kept in touch with the Henriksons, and I made sure to visit them whenever I traveled back up to Standing Rock. When my program finished in 1977, I moved back to begin work at Standing Rock College. Jerry and Dianne continued to share the Bahá'í Faith with me—telling me about the conferences they attended and the communities they visited. I enjoyed our conversations, and details of the Faith stuck with me, though I never considered a deeper commitment.

In 1973, when I received my Indian name, my mother had passed onto me the family pipe. Since that time, I had determined to find my path in life. Lakota tradition holds that, in both the material and spiritual worlds, each of us seeks to traverse the spirit road connecting the earth and heavens. In my pursuit of traditional ways, I sought to understand this relationship between the spiritual realms and the world in which I lived and moved. I wanted to discover where I belonged and to truly know my purpose. And now as a father of two, I hoped to offer my children a spiritual foundation. Like so many, I wanted to find meaning in my life.

The elders had advised me that the only way I could attain true understanding was to fast. Every year for the past four years, I had fasted, starting in Pine Ridge under the guidance of the revered Pete Catches. As we approached the summer of 1979, under the mentorship of Charles Kills Enemy, I prepared to embark upon another fast.

2

After the 1979 fast, I had felt a strong sense of failure. Though I had survived the physical ordeal of the fast, I had not felt that I had accomplished the goal of finding my path in life. My prayers had seemed to go unanswered.

I spent the days following the fast in quiet meditation, as is advised for one who follows devotional practices such as the fast to aid the transition from the material realm to the spiritual and then back again. Moments of contemplation often turned to frustration. I had no idea what direction my life would take. I returned to my small rental home and my full-time work at the Young Adult Conservation Corps.

One afternoon, later that summer, the Henriksons dropped by my house in Wakpala. I invited them outside, and we sat on a bench in the yard. They were leaving the country, they told me, and were going to the Falkland Islands to serve as pioneers. Before they left, they wanted to ask me something. I waited, curious.

Jerry spoke: "You've come to our firesides, learned about the Bahá'í Faith and its teachings. You've shown such interest, but we realized we've never asked you if you'd like to become a Bahá'í. So we thought we'd ask." He paused. "Would you like to join?"

I did not have a response to his question—other than *yes*. I had learned much about the Bahá'í Faith and had come to believe in Bahá'u'lláh and His teachings. "How do I join?" I asked him.

"You'll sign a declaration card."

"If I sign the card, what does that mean?" I asked.

"It's an administrative procedure that identifies you with the Bahá'í community," Gerald explained. "There are Bahá'ís all over the world, and you would become a member of our worldwide community." I had already met Bahá'ís in Standing Rock at the Holy Day celebrations and gatherings at the Henriksons' home. I had a conceptual understanding of a greater Bahá'í community around the world, though I would not come into contact with this global community until later in my life.

"You've learned a lot about the Central Figures of the Bahá'í Faith, Their sufferings and persecutions, Their message, and Their laws," Gerald continued. "Should you become a Bahá'í, you would strive to follow the laws and to promote unity."

I was familiar with many of the Bahá'í laws relating to marriage, divorce, death, and burial. Holy wars, slavery, the burning of books, gambling, and the use of intoxicating substances were prohibited. Though I was a child of the anti-establishment era of the sixties, I had a sense of what it meant to be obedient to spiritual laws. Lakota traditional ways require the strict adherence to laws of sanctity, chastity, prayer, and fasting. I found myself attracted to the Bahá'í laws of prayer and fasting, which I saw as the renewal of traditional laws.

Without hesitation, I agreed to sign the card. If the Henriksons were not good friends, if I had not spent time with them, I would have felt reluctant about signing my name to anything. Historically, signing official documents had led to many tragedies for Native peoples. When the United States government made treaties with Indian Nations, many of the Indigenous people were not literate in English. Officials encouraged Natives to merely touch a pen with their index finger, then allow a scribe to write down their names. As the Natives could not read or write in English, they trusted the officials and with a mere motion of their index fingers lost all their possessions, land, and culture. Unknowingly, they forfeited all they held dear; the act of touching a pen caused them to lose their continent. In the Lakota language, the word for someone who loses their identity, *wičazo ayúthaŋpi*, translates literally to "one who touches the pen."

A joke shared tribally illustrated the legacy further. The joke is told as follows:

After the Lunar landing in 1969, officials from NASA visited the people of rural Indian tribes who did not have access to television or news. They showed the people footage of the lunar landing. Unbeknownst to them, according to Indian tales of Iktómi, the trickster, the people who fell under Iktómi's trap and committed immoral acts were punished by being banished to the moon.

One elder remarked to these officials that his people had already been on the moon for many generations. "Send a message to our relatives on the moon," he told the officials. "Tell them first that we forgive them for their crimes and they are welcome to come back for a grand reunion powwow and feast. And second, most important of all, tell them this—"

He waited a moment before he said emphatically: "Don't sign anything."

"Don't sign anything" became a humorous, ironic refrain—but it reflected the historically rooted fear among Indigenous Americans of signing any type of documentation. Even the Bahá'í declaration card would have been repugnant to many.

Later, I would come to appreciate that literacy is a divine gift. Writing, at its truest form, allows the Word of God and His Prophets to be documented for future generations. This enables the enlightenment of the people, aiding them to recognize their own nobility. Yet the great gift of literacy has been perverted for selfish ends. The written word can be used to persecute, enslave, and disenfranchise people—a tool for usurping human dignity.

The act of touching a pen and signing the declaration card would later enable me to see that those of us who have faced oppression can recover what has been lost. This act of writing can be renewed as an act of volition and empowerment, for us to arise to our truest nobility.

As I signed the card, I did not think of this moment as a turning point. It did not register within me what this declaration would mean in my life. I did not feel a great sense of commitment or transformation. Only in the months and years that followed did I begin a process of understanding the significance of Bahá'u'lláh's Revelation and of becoming affiliated with the Bahá'í community.

After signing the declaration card, I asked the Henriksons about Bahá'í prayers. They gave me a small prayer book with a deep green cover. I had heard some of these prayers shared at Bahá'í gatherings and also when I visited Jerry and Dianne in their home. Holding the small book in my hand, I was surprised by the sheer number of prayers that had been revealed by the Báb and Bahá'u'lláh.

I randomly opened to a page that had the prayer for the Central States—a prayer that believers residing in that region are encouraged to say daily. The prayer, revealed by 'Abdu'l-Bahá, read:

O Lord, my God! Praise and thanksgiving be unto Thee for Thou hast guided me to the highway of the kingdom, suffered me to walk in this straight and far-stretching path, illumined my eye by beholding the splendors of Thy light, inclined my ear to the melodies of the birds of holiness from the kingdom of mysteries and attracted my heart with Thy love among the righteous.

O Lord! Confirm me with the Holy Spirit, so that I may call in Thy Name amongst the nations and give the glad tidings of the manifestation of Thy kingdom amongst mankind.

O Lord! I am weak, strengthen me with Thy power and potency. My tongue falters, suffer me to utter Thy commemoration and praise. I am lowly, honor me through admitting me into Thy kingdom. I am remote, cause me to approach the threshold of Thy mercifulness. O Lord! Make me a brilliant lamp, a shining star and a blessed tree, adorned with fruit, its branches overshadowing all these regions. Verily, Thou art the Mighty, the Powerful and Unconstrained.*

The opening words of the prayer struck me deeply: "For Thou hast guided me to the highway of the kingdom." I had prayed and fasted to find my path. During the fast, I had suffered four days of over one-hundred-degree temperatures; I didn't know if I would survive. I was worn down. I recognized my utter nothingness. During those brutal days out in the hills, no vision or revelation came to me. I questioned whether God had even

* 'Abdu'l-Bahá, in *Bahá'í Prayers*, pp. 211–12.

heard my prayers. "Praise and thanksgiving be unto Thee for Thou hast guided me to the highway of the kingdom . . ." I reread the words of the prayer. "Suffered me to walk in this straight and far-stretching path . . ." Was this highway of the kingdom, this straight and far-stretching path, the red path? My path in life?

In that moment, my whole being resounded with recognition. *Yes.* This was my red path.

On that sacred day many years ago, I made the commitment to say this prayer every day. The words expressed the sentiments of my heart: how precious and blessed life is. I would utter this prayer daily, praising and offering thanksgiving to God for having guided me to His Kingdom, the holy red road. He would continually enable me to walk along this far-stretching path. Every day, I would ask that the light of God, the light of Divine Revelation, illumine my inner eyes and allow me to see His creation anew.

Over the years, I reflected on the words "so that I may call in Thy name amongst the nations and give the glad tidings." I came to understand that after a long, dark winter of spiritual deprivation, the most beautiful sound, the most joyful noise, was the first songbird of spring announcing the coming of a new revelation. Those whose hearts were attracted were drawn into the circle of love. There, in that circle, confirmed by the Holy Spirit, we were prepared to call out God's name and to share the glad-tidings of God's new Manifestation to humankind.

Since my declaration, I have reread the prayer and meditated on its words. I have testified to my weakness and God's power, to my impotence and God's might. I have asked God to enable my tongue to commemorate and praise Him and to honor me through admitting me into His Kingdom. I continually prayed to draw closer to the threshold of His mercy and requested to be made into a blessed tree, adorned with fruit, with its branches overshadowing all regions.

The analogy of the tree intrigued me. I visualized the power of God as light descending from heaven, and I realized that we were all like trees, reaching for the light. Like trees, our branches grew and roots extended. We eventually produced fruit, a product of the seed of faith planted when we first start to believe. I pondered how each and every one of us could grow and produce something unique from our faith.

Years later, I visited the Bahá'í holy places in Haifa. Outside of the Shrine of Bahá'u'lláh, I stood on a red stone path leading from the Shrine, a path that pointed to the north and west, in the direction of the central United States. A huge tree grew from the center of this path. The branches overshadowed the surrounding paths, providing shade from the direct sunlight. Since my visit to the Holy Land and noticing this particular tree, I began to visualize this tree whenever I said the prayer for the Central States. I prayed to become more like the tree, offering shade and protection to those around me.

The prayer for the Central States, in all of its different images and elements, provided answers to the prayers I had uttered out on the butte during the four-day fast that I had barely survived. Out in the hills, I was broken down; this prayer revealed to me that, though I may have felt abandoned then, I was not, nor would I ever be alone. In saying this prayer, I testified to what I experienced in a deeply profound and powerful way during the fast. The words of this prayer allowed me to express my lowliness, blindness, deafness, and frailty. My weaknesses, however, could be transmuted and transformed into strengths through the power of God. I needed to continue to open myself to His Divine Hand, trust in Him, and allow Him to change me.

After the first day that I read and pondered the prayer after signing my declaration card, I devoted myself to the process of transformation. I strove to overcome the challenges that occurred daily, by asking for God's assistance. I made an ongoing effort to be worthy of His divine bestowals and to live in a state of prayer. This commitment to prayer and transformation assisted me in the years ahead. Though I did not realize it then, I would visit many diverse lands of the world, meet many diverse people, and through these blessings, receive a small glimpse into the immense power of the Holy Spirit.

3

At the end of that summer of 1979, the Henriksons left for the Falkland Islands, and my family packed up our home and moved to Vermillion. I had applied to law school, with my mother's encouragement, and was accepted to the University of South Dakota. Located in the southeast corner of South Dakota, Vermillion, a small and beautiful town of barely twelve thousand people, extended along the northern stretch of the Missouri River valley. There, the glacial hill formations gave the topography of the land an exquisite contour. I would once again spend my days on the small nucleus of the University of South Dakota campus, whose courtyards were peppered with stately older buildings.

After my first few days of law school, I began to question whether law school was a good fit for me. The intensity sunk in during orientation, which was similar to boot camp. I decided to withdraw from the program, but I did not leave law school without a safety net. I had learned about another graduate program—a Master's in Community Education—which offered a living stipend. Even after I switched to this program, my investment was halfhearted; I was not all that interested in getting another degree. I knew that I was forestalling growing up and was biding my time through my continuing studies.

During the fast of the previous summer, my uncle Charlie had advised me to focus my energy and prayers on a single goal—to avoid feeling scattered. Now, I was juggling various priorities. I continued to hone my flute practice and took opportunities to perform when I could. My study of the Lakota language intensified as well. Having returned to Vermillion, I often visited good friends and mentors—Joe Rock Boy and his wife, Nancy; they patiently taught me new vocabulary words and aided me to construct more complex sentences.

On weekends, we would occasionally travel the forty miles from Vermillion to the neighboring Omaha and Winnebago reservations just south of Sioux City, Iowa. There, we attended powwows, hand games, round dances, and all other kinds of community gatherings. Ohiyes'a and Kim often came with me and played with the other children there. I always encouraged them to dance with me. I tried my hand at crafting regalia for us to wear and channeled my childhood love of art into learning complex feather and beadwork.

Round dances, hand games, and other social dances commemorated community members' birthdays, anniversaries, and graduations. On these occasions, everyone danced to the round dance songs; between songs, there were talks and prayers. Elders shared stories in the Omaha and Ho Chunk languages. Back then, everyone who was a part of the older generation spoke either Omaha or Ho Chunk, while today only a handful of people have retained this knowledge. Feasts were served for everyone who attended.

Music was the binding agent at these events. The drum served as a unifying force, representing the voice of the ancestors that spoke to us from ancient times and roused the people out of hibernation into wakefulness. It symbolized the first thunder, the animating force of all of creation. Comprised of a wooden frame and animal hide, the drum signified the plant and animal kingdoms on which all people depend, a representation of harmony amongst all of creation.

At the University of South Dakota, I was reunited with Harley Good Bear, a friend and fellow student in the Community Education graduate program. Harley and I had met in 1972 when he came to a conference at Black Hills State College. After many years of not seeing each other, we found ourselves in the exact same classes at USD. Like me, Harley kept up with many traditional practices, including the sweat lodge. We decided to start a weekly sweat lodge in Vermillion and chose my backyard as the location to construct one. After a while, a few friends began to join us— both Indian and non-Indian—and we had to move the sweat lodge to a home with a bigger yard. The interest of non-Native people in Indigenous traditions had been growing since the early '70s. In university towns such as Vermillion, residents were open to exploring alternative spiritual practices. We welcomed them because, we figured, the more prayer warriors and sweat hogs, the merrier.

Care in raising Kim and Ohiyes'a was an intense focus in my life at the time. My children were just starting school at the time we moved to Vermillion. I helped them get ready for school in the mornings. After school and during summer, I taught them how to swim in the Missouri River. With the strong rush of the current, I kept them close to me. They showed a liking for the water, just as I did as a child. Today, we all laugh over my daughter Kim's exaggerated recollection that I would toss them in the river then drive down to Sioux City and pick them up an hour later.

* * *

I soon became acquainted with the small Bahá'í community of Vermillion, comprised of students and working adults from diverse backgrounds. I learned much from attending the community gatherings. I attended the Nineteen Day Feast, a gathering held every nineteen days that served as the bedrock of the Bahá'í community. Three components—devotions, consulting over community issues, and socializing—united and refreshed those of us in attendance. At these gatherings, I met Bahá'ís of Iranian descent for the first time. They offered rich perspectives on the history and culture from which the Bahá'í Faith originated.

The Bahá'í community in Vermillion was able to form a Local Spiritual Assembly because we had just over nine members in our community. After prayer, reflection, and without campaigning, in a democratic process, we elected nine qualified and devoted individuals to serve on this institution. As the Bahá'í Faith does not have any clergy, this local administrative body shouldered the responsibility of meeting the spiritual, material, and social needs of the community. The Assembly arranged devotionals, children's classes, and study programs for adults, as well as the Nineteen Day Feast. The institution was not just concerned about the Bahá'í community but the affairs of the larger community as well. 'Abdu'l-Bahá, the son of the Prophet Founder of the Bahá'í Faith, stated about the functioning of the Local Spiritual Assembly that its deliberations must be focused on "spiritual matters that pertain to the training of souls, the instruction of children, the relief of the poor, the help of the feeble throughout all classes in the world, kindness to all peoples, the diffusion of the fragrances of God and the exaltation of His Holy Word."*

With my increased involvement in the Bahá'í community, I began to immerse myself more fully in the reservoir of the Bahá'í sacred writings. Back in Standing Rock, I had realized the Bahá'í writings challenged me because of the lofty language. One of the first Bahá'í books I had read before becoming a Bahá'í was *Epistle to the Son of the Wolf.* I had no reference point with which to understand the contents of the book. From the moment I opened to the first page, I could barely comprehend the meaning, yet I felt compelled to continue reading. The act of reading these eloquent, meaningful words without understanding their significance was mystifying and solidified my attraction to the writings of the Faith. Later, I would learn that this particular book was the last major written work of Bahá'u'lláh, in which he admonishes Shaykh Muhammad-Taqiy-i-Najafi, a Muslim cleric and the son of a prominent family, and calls upon him to repent for his involvement for the persecution of the Bahá'ís in Iran and the horrific torture and death of two brothers.

I began to study the writings of Bahá'u'lláh in depth, and I was determined to let their contents penetrate my mind. I read The Hidden Words, *the Seven Valleys and the Four Valleys,* and *Gleanings from the Writings of Bahá'u'lláh.* To engage fully with the Sacred Word and to allow the information to penetrate, I read each text multiple times and meditated on each word and sentence. Each time, the passages took on a new meaning, and I wrote summaries and notes in the margins in bold print. To this day, I can find the quotes and passages I need in any Holy Book by searching for the bold handwriting in the margins. This was the best way I knew how to interact with and learn about the significance of the Faith.

As a new Bahá'í, I not only studied the Bahá'í writings, I also prayed every day. Just as we sustain our bodies with food and exercise, our spirits need the nourishment of conversation with their Creator. The spirit is impelled to pray, similar to the bird's urge to sing and the flower's to bloom. When I first became a Bahá'í, Jerry explained to me the importance

---

* 'Abdu'l-Bahá, quoted in Shoghi Effendi, *Bahá'í Administration,* p. 22.

of obligatory prayer, which Bahá'u'lláh enjoins His followers to recite at least once daily. He pointed out the three Obligatory Prayers from which I could choose, and he drew my attention especially to the first and shortest.

I found the Short Obligatory Prayer very convenient, but occasionally, I took a look at the longer Obligatory Prayers. I sometimes tried to recite the longest one, which requires genuflections: during the prayer, the supplicant raises her hands toward the heavens, then bows, then kneels with her forehead to the floor, and then sits. As I tried to perform the motions with a prayer book in hand, I often ended up contorting myself into odd positions; needless to say, I did not often turn to the Long Obligatory Prayer.

My attitude toward the Long Obligatory Prayer changed profoundly in 1987 when my father died. My father was a lifelong smoker and, a few years prior to his death, was diagnosed with lung cancer. In December of 1987, his wife, Roberta, called Winona and I, asking us to drive to Denver to be with our father in his last days. We left Standing Rock right away and drove the 650 miles to be with him.

I prayed fervently during that ten-hour car ride. I was not ready to let go of my dad. He and I had never had the best relationship; his drinking habit had impaired our closeness during my adolescence and early adulthood. To lose him, to lose the hope of regaining what had been lost in my formative years, was too hard to bear.

When we arrived, we were devastated to see his declining condition. The cancer had so consumed his body that he had lost the ability to move and speak. He lay on the floor in the living room, as he did not want to be confined to a bed. I knew he was nearly gone.

During his final hour, I witnessed a miracle. Moments before he died, when it was only the two of us in the living room, my father—who had been resting on the floor, immobile—suddenly rose to his feet, like a marionette pulled by invisible strings. He turned his gaze upward and reached several times toward the ceiling, in supplication to the realms above. He then bowed to unseen royalty, placing his hands on his knees. Finally, he knelt to the ground and rested his head on the floor in prostration. He then sat up on his knees, eyes wide open, face intense.

I was speechless, shocked. How could someone with no strength, in the throes of cancer, move with such conviction?

We sat in silence until, overwhelmed by emotion, I left the room to say my own prayers. When I returned, I found my father, collapsed on his side, his face frozen in the same intense expression. I brushed my hand over his face to close his eyes.

After his passing, it dawned on me that my father's motions matched the same genuflections as the Long Obligatory Prayer. He would have had no way of knowing this prayer—he had never shown interest in the Bahá'í Faith—yet he carried out the same exact movements: the raised hands, the bowing, and the kneeling.

I had never known my father to pray, nor had I ever heard him mention God. Yet at the end of his life, his entire being was compelled to offer itself to God through movements of intense devotion. His final act on this earth was compelled by a supernatural, omnipotent force to do the impossible. I realized then that, throughout the remainder of my life, I could, through my own free will, choose to recite this prayer and perform the required genuflections. I vowed, from then on, to say the Long Obligatory prayer daily. To this day, every time I say this prayer, I cherish the memory of my father supplicating his Creator. I am grateful that his final act on earth has allowed us to connect throughout all the heavenly, eternal realms.

Within my first year at USD, many of the Bahá'ís in our community left Vermillion and moved away for work or to continue their education. I became an isolated member of the Faith, as the nearest Bahá'í communities lay several hours' drive away in every direction. Without the support of a community, I resolved to continue learning as much as I could about the Faith on my own.

I have always been open to alternative ways of looking at and understanding the world around me. Since adolescence, I had felt that life was a chimera, fleeting and evanescent. Knowing the horrors in human history and especially in the history of the Lakota people—that all they had hoped for and loved had been taken from them—made the world seem especially impermanent. I had no way to make sense of it. Rearing my children had intensified this feeling, and I longed to provide them with a framework for understanding and a spiritual foundation.

When I read the following passage from *Gleanings from the Writings of Bahá'u'lláh,* I found words that clearly and most eloquently expressed what my own heart had felt for so long. I clung to every word: "The world is but a show, vain and empty, a mere nothing, bearing the semblance of reality. Set not your affections upon it . . . The world is like the vapor in a desert, which the thirsty dreameth to be water and striveth after it with all his might, until when he cometh unto it, he findeth it to be mere illusion."*

Indigenous spirituality had given me a foundation through which to come into the Faith. The traditional Lakota spiritual practices—the songs, the stories, the language—were still dear to me. The part that made little sense to me was that this spiritual way of life was only revealed to the people of a certain time, place, and culture. According to Lakota beliefs, the Grandfather had spoken directly to the Lakota, his grandchildren, through the White Buffalo Calf Maiden, and her prophetic teachings mentioned that she would return and that our people would be led to the great and heavenly road—the red road. *When would her return occur?* I had always wondered. *Would her new revelation connect us to the world and the world to us?*

"Unto the cities of all nations He hath sent His Messengers," Bahá'u'lláh wrote in *Gleanings*. He then described Messengers of the prophetic cycle, who attracted the peoples of a certain time and place to the "Haven of abiding security," offered them laws and teachings, and prophesied to them about the return of a Promised One.**

The Lakota, too, have awaited the return of *Ptehíŋčala Ska Wiŋ*, the White Buffalo Calf Maiden. Lakota sacred songs have told of Ptehíŋčala Ska Wiŋ, the White Buffalo Calf Maiden, and Tȟuŋkášila, the Grandfather. The White Buffalo Calf Maiden directed the people to pray to and invoke the Grandfather and shared that it was the Grandfather who authorized the Maiden to establish her Covenant.

I had come to understand that God had not forsaken us and had sent a great message through Bahá'u'lláh to connect the Lakota spiritual traditions with the other great world religions. The White Buffalo Calf Maiden is not directly mentioned in the Bahá'í writings, as Abraham, Zoroaster, Buddha, Moses, Jesus, and Muhammad are. The Bahá'í writings further

---

* Bahá'u'lláh, *Gleanings from the Writings of Bahá'u'lláh*, no. 153.8.
** Bahá'u'lláh, *Gleanings from the Writings of Bahá'u'lláh*, no. 76.1.

clarify that the names of some Prophets "seem to be lost in the mists of ancient history."*

My growing understanding of Bahá'í teachings did not undermine Lakota spiritual traditions. Rather, the Lakota ceremonial life and the practices I cherished so dearly were given new meaning, and I did not have to abandon my background but could appreciate the gems within it more fully.

For the first time, in the Bahá'í Faith, I had direct and lucid answers to many of my questions. I sensed that my search for meaning—for the red road—was not over, however; it was beginning afresh every day.

* Letter written on behalf of the Guardian, *Compilation of Compilations*, vol. I, p. 22.

4

In the summer of 1980, as I finished my Master's degree in Community Education and was preparing to start my doctoral studies, a Bahá'í friend, Ed Roberts, gave me a call. He was traveling to a gathering at the Bahá'í House of Worship for Native American Bahá'ís and pioneers to the reservations in North America. Over the course of three days, this gathering, the Continental Indigenous Council Fire, would include teaching workshops, prayer, and fellowship. The National Spiritual Assembly of the Bahá'ís of the United States, as the national administrative body for the Bahá'í community, was hosting this gathering. Representatives from this body would be present throughout the weekend and would be among those offering workshops.

"Would you like to come with me?" Ed asked. His enthusiasm was so contagious that, though unprepared, I readily agreed to join him. I packed my dance outfit, a couple of flutes, and a few other items in an overnight bag. This would be my first exposure to large numbers of Native Bahá'ís and my first time attending a large Bahá'í gathering. I was excited, though I did not know what to expect.

Ed picked me up in his beat-up Peugeot, and we drove for hours along Highway 20 through the open Midwestern countryside and chatted. Ed was one of the first Bahá'ís in South Dakota. He was originally from Sioux Falls and was now living in Pierre. I had met him years before at a gathering at the Henriksons' home, though we had never spent much time together until now. Truly an illumined soul, he radiated warmth and love and possessed an infectious zeal for the Bahá'í Faith. Though he was of European descent, he had been involved in teaching efforts to Native populations for years and was the driving force behind large teaching projects on Rosebud and Pine Ridge.

Along our way to Wilmette, two of the balding tires on Ed's Peugeot blew out. Thankfully, spare tires and roadside assistance from other drivers enabled us to continue on our way. We were not the only attendees who endured a difficult journey to the Council Fire. Members of tribes from as far away as Alaska and Mexico had crowded into rickety, poorly-functioning cars for a long drive to Illinois. Ironclad determination and enormous faith enabled over one thousand individuals to attend this gathering.

When we arrived in Wilmette, we checked into the dormitories at North-western University, which the National Spiritual Assembly had reserved for the Council Fire attendees. The morning after our arrival, I woke early in eager anticipation of my first visit to pray at the Bahá'í House of Worship, a short walk away from the Northwestern campus. The white, stone, domed temple graced the edge of a quiet suburban community along the shores of Lake Michigan. The gardens surrounding the nine-sided structure burst with color and fragrance. Fountains gushed on each side. As I climbed the steps of the House of Worship, I noticed the symbols from all the world religions etched in the intricate stone design. I felt alive with the spirit that pervaded this place.

A short man with a wide smile on his face stood at the door to the sanc-tuary. To everyone who entered, he offered a hug and a kiss on the cheek. Unaccustomed to the show of affection from a stranger, I descended the steps to wait for him to depart. When he showed no signs of moving, I decided to walk through the gardens, hoping that with time, he would leave and I would have successfully avoided him. After walking several times around the House of Worship, I realized the strange man was not going to leave. I waited behind a line of visitors to enter the House of Wor-ship, watching as he embraced person after person. When I approached him, the man greeted me with great kindness and humility. I was surprised by how uplifted I felt by his warm embrace.

Later, I learned this man was Zikrullah Khadem, an appointed Hand of the Cause, a member of a select group of people appointed to protect and propagate the Bahá'í Faith. At the Council Fire, I knew little about the

Administrative Order and the role of the Hands of the Cause, though I eventually realized that Mr. Khadem had a significant role.

After Mr. Khadem welcomed me, I stepped into the sanctuary of the House of Worship. I had never experienced anything similar to the spiritual ambiance I felt in that space. Under the high arched ceiling, many other visitors were seated in rows of chairs, offering silent prayers. Inscribed on the walls around the edifice were familiar quotations from The Hidden Words, including "Thou art My lamp and My Light is in thee" and "Thy paradise is My Love, thy heavenly home reunion with Me."* Prayer book in hand, I found a seat and began to offer my own prayers of thanksgiving for the opportunity to visit and worship in this sacred place.

* * *

Later that day, the Continental Indigenous Council Fire commenced. When all the attendees gathered together, our spirits were electrified. Many attendees were the only Bahá'ís in their families and in their tribes. These heroic souls had taken a leap of faith in identifying themselves with Bahá'u'lláh's Message for today. The non-Indian people who attended the Council Fire had pioneered and put down roots in remote Native communities in order to build relationships and teach the Faith.

The Council Fire, a festive reunion for isolated souls, was driven by the conviction that Native people had the capacity to contribute greatly to the advancement of society. We had long heard from elders in our tribes that our people were awaiting the day of fulfillment, and now we knew that day had arrived. We were receptive and eager to take in all that the weekend had to offer to learn how we could arise to new heights of service and how we could empower ourselves and our people.

This gathering was the second one of its kind held across North America and initiated by the Continental Board of Counselors. This body was established by the international administrative body of the Bahá'í community, the Universal House of Justice. Its members foster individual initiative

* Bahá'u'lláh, The Hidden Words, Arabic nos. 11, 6.

and action and promote learning among the Bahá'í community. Individuals from the Board of Counselors such as Lauretta King, Athos Costa, Raul Pavon, and Angus Cowan had spearheaded great teaching work with Indigenous American populations throughout the continent. They recognized the receptivity within Native people to the unifying message of Bahá'u'lláh and had seen large numbers enroll in the Faith.

The Counselors identified a common prophecy amongst Indigenous people: that, in the future, the Native peoples of the Western Hemisphere would reunite as the sign of the coming of a new era. This emerged from the belief that all Indigenous people came from the same parent stock. Over time, we had dispersed throughout the hemisphere into culturally and linguistically diverse groups. As the Indigenous Bahá'í population grew, the Counselors started the Council Fires as a means of gathering together Native people of diverse tribes for our spiritual upliftment. I understood that one of the purposes of the Bahá'í Faith was to raise up the marginalized people of the world, a fulfillment of one of the few Biblical quotations I knew—"So the last shall be first, and the first last."*

Throughout the weekend, I attended various seminars and discussion groups with prominent Native and non-Native Bahá'ís. We deepened on the Bahá'í writings and developed travel teaching plans that would take us to Indigenous communities around the Americas. In these sessions, many shared their personal experiences with finding the Faith and how the Faith confirmed their Indigenous identity. Franklin Khan, a Navajo member of the National Spiritual Assembly, offered a workshop, as did Dorothy Francis, an elder from Manitoba. They shared stories about their personal spiritual quests and the experiences that led them to the Bahá'í Faith.

One of the most powerful presentations that weekend was by an elder from the Tlingit tribe in Alaska, Eugene King. Eugene was a very tall man, over six feet, and had been blind all of his adult life. His erudite bearing made his presentation incredibly compelling. Eugene had descended from Tlingit Chiefs but had faced ostracization upon becoming a Bahá'í and had ultimately sacrificed his chiefdom. Hearing of his sacrifices for our beliefs

---

* Matthew 20:16.

moved me. Eugene talked about how the Bahá'í Faith fulfills both Christian and Indigenous prophetic traditions. He shared long passages from the Bahá'í writings and Christian scripture from memory. One of the common strands was how the light of the revelation enables one to see his or her own spiritual heritage and identify the universal aspects that will benefit all of humanity.

Mr. Khadem also spoke on several occasions. He spoke during plenary gatherings about Shoghi Effendi and his love for the Indigenous people of the world. He conveyed that the Guardian would have loved to attend this gathering but that he was standing in for the Guardian as a representative. Before this, I had not fully appreciated the station of Shoghi Effendi as the Guardian of the Faith and 'Abdu'l Bahá's successor. Mr. Khadem's presentations were incredibly insightful for me. A spiritual power radiated from Mr. Khadem when he spoke. Even in his presentations, it was evident how humble and magnanimous he was.

* * *

To close the Council Fire, a celebratory powwow, held on the shores of Lake Michigan, honored the spiritual upliftment of Indigenous peoples and the coming together of disparate tribes. The Chicago Indian community had been invited to attend the powwow. Chicago was one of the major destinations for the Relocation Act, a federal act that called for the relocation of Indigenous people from their rural reservation homes into urban settings. Laws such as this were strategies to acculturate Indian people to the dominant society. Spread out amongst the greater Chicago area, the Native community there represented many tribes. Mr. Ben Bearskin Senior, half Hochunk and half Dakota, was among those invited to the powwow. A pillar of the Chicago Native community, Ben was a brilliant man, fluent in Hochunk, Dakota, and English, and a leader in the Native American Church. As a representative of the ancestors of that land, the Hochunk, who are indigenous to the Chicago region, Ben offered a significant presence at the powwow.

The spirit was very high that evening. Ben sat at the drum and sang. A great traditional singer, Ben had recruited some of his best singers and dancers to join him. With a prayerful demeanor, they shared the music of the Hochunk people, which aimed to inspire the people to heroic deeds, to generosity and magnanimity. I wore my outfit and danced.

Mr. Khadem sat among the powwow singers, on the right-hand side of Ben Bearskin. He had his own drumstick and kept steady time on the drum as he sang along with the rest. It was a wonderful sight—this little Persian man amidst a group of Indian singers. As I watched him and Ben at the drum, I felt they represented the coming together of diverse people on a global scale. The powwow was remarkable, not because of the excellence of the dancers or the beauty of the singing, but rather because of the spirit of unity that prevailed throughout the night.

Later, Ben commented to me how moved he was by the spirit of that gathering. I, too, was stirred. The Council Fire provided me one of my first opportunities to see the spirit of unity within the Bahá'í Faith in action. While no physical fire had been lit that weekend, the spiritual blaze enkindled shone brightly on the 1,000-plus participants.

5

While completing my Master's degree in Vermillion, my friend Harley's younger brother, Arlo Good Bear, frequently came to visit his brother. Arlo and I struck up a friendship instantly because of our shared interests in music and dancing. Arlo was a hoop dancer, flute player, and brilliant storyteller. He had a magnetic personality and unforgettable charisma, with all the social graces and magnanimity one could hope for.

Arlo and Harley were members of the Mandan and Hidatsa tribes. These tribes historically lived side-by-side along the Missouri River but spoke different languages. As sedentary people, both tribes bore the brunt of smallpox and influenza epidemics, which reduced their tribes of tens of thousands to tens. Despite their small numbers, these tribes are renowned for beautiful expressions of dance and music, of which Harley and Arlo were worthy exponents.

Arlo was a student of John Rainer, a well-known musician and flute instructor at Brigham Young University in Utah. During our visits, Arlo taught me how to perform grace notes on the flute, an ornamentation that enhanced the melody line of songs. He coached me in different breathing techniques and vibrato as well.

During the summer of 1980, Arlo and I were both invited to perform as part of an American Indian Dance and Music presentation, which gathered performers from all over the country. The performance took place at an amphitheater in Liberty Park, New Jersey, adjacent to the Statue of Liberty. As a soloist, I performed Northern Plains traditional dance and flute music. Arlo hoop-danced and played the flute. The intricacies of

Arlo's hoop dance—poetry in motion—showcased his athleticism and coordination.

Arlo and I returned to the hotel after our presentation, just before an evening meeting to debrief and socialize with the performers from all over the country. Out of the blue, Arlo said, "I'm going to give you the hoop dance."

One must be given the "right" or "authority" before being able to present any aspect of traditional culture—be it song, dance, storytelling, or a craft or art form. In that moment, Arlo conveyed his authority to present the hoop dance to me.

Yeah, right. I thought to myself, certain he must joking. *And a cow can jump over the moon . . .*

"I'll give you four lessons," Arlo continued. "One lesson now and the rest later." I looked at him, trying not to show my incredulity. Arlo's ceremonial language and conveyance of tradition in giving me the dance was emphasized by the number four—a sacred number—pertaining to the stages of the bestowal of this gift.

Arlo looked at me, and his face softened. "Brother, I'll do my part by providing the lessons. You must do your part! Once you carry out what you've learned from these lessons, you will receive four gifts. One—you will meet many new people. Two—you will see many new places. Three—you will have profound experiences. And four—you will receive abundant blessings. But you have to do your part."

Arlo retrieved his hoops. He placed one hoop on the floor. "Now, there are two ways to pick up a hoop." He demonstrated both ways, then nodded at me, indicating that it was my turn to try.

I stood and set the hoop in front of me, just as Arlo had done, and stepped on the edge with the ball of my foot. With the slight pressure, the hoop flipped up, so I could grab it by hand. Even today, I prefer this method of picking up a hoop. I tried the other way as well. Years later, I would demonstrate these two methods to children around the world, just as Arlo did for me.

Arlo held one of the hoops. "When you use a single-hoop design, it expresses your relationship within the world of creation," he said. "We are all a part of the hoop of life. This hoop represents the interconnectivity we have with all created things." He spun the hoop with one hand, flipped it from hand to hand, then hopped over it several times like a jump rope.

"More and more designs will come to you," he assured me.

Arlo picked up a second hoop. "One hoops represents you and the physical world. The second hoop represents the interplay between the sun and the moon. The hoops can be woven into a dance narrative or a narrative without dance."

He spun the two hoops at the same time and manipulated them in a variety of ways. After he demonstrated, he had me attempt the same moves. Though I loved the movement, I felt incredibly challenged by the high level of coordination and physical skill required. Perhaps Arlo was expecting too much of me.

Arlo continued his instructions, as he picked up a third hoop. "With three hoops or more, you can create designs that represent transformation and the emergence of humankind into consciousness." Then, with five hoops, he demonstrated the design of the ladder, explaining that this design symbolized the ascent from the lower to the higher world. He then created the more complicated design of the butterfly. "The butterfly flies higher and farther from the world, becoming its true self," he said.

I was drawn to this final explanation of the designs of emergence. Oral traditions from all the different peoples of the world described the same narrative of transformation and enlightenment. The Bible told of Adam and Eve, Noah, and Abraham, who all moved humanity from lower states of consciousness to heightened knowledge and awareness. I was inspired by how the hoop dance showcased this same concept.

We concluded this first lesson. Even though I had privately questioned Arlo's passing me the dance, I was eager to learn more from him. The next day, I wished him safe travels back home, with the hope that we would soon continue our lessons.

Shortly after we returned home from the Liberty Park performance, I received a phone call from Arlo's mother. She informed me that Arlo had died in an accident. The news shook me. He and I had just performed together. He was only twenty-five years old. He had given me only the first lesson with the hoop of the four promised. Now, he was gone.

At the funeral, people from all over the country gathered to honor Arlo's life. Since he was a member of the three affiliated tribes of North Dakota— the Mandan, Hidatsa and Arikara Nations—people representing those groups came. As a youth, Arlo had become an elder in the Mormon church and served as a missionary on the Mescalero Apache Reservation in New

Mexico. There, he had had a great impact on the Apache people, as evidenced by the devoted friends who traveled all the way from Apache land to attend his funeral.

As an accomplished dancer, Arlo was well-known throughout Indian country despite his young age. He had traveled extensively with a Mormon performing group called the Lamanite Generation. In this capacity, he developed and honed his skill as a hoop dancer. His dynamic spirit enabled him to command respect and admiration wherever he went. He was known not only for his dance skills but as an accomplished flutist and orator.

The night before the funeral, a wake was held for Arlo in a thirty-four-foot thípi in the old ancestral community, Shell Creek, twelve miles south of Newtown, North Dakota. One hundred family members and friends sat around a fire kindled in the middle of the thípi. As many members of Arlo's family belonged to the Native American Church, they had asked an elder to serve as the Road Man, the officiant of the ceremony. At sundown, the ceremony began. The Road Man held a staff and passed it around the circle. Every one of us in the circle, when the staff came to us, took hold of it and sang. Our songs were offered with the intent of sending off Arlo's soul. The staff was passed around the circle four times during that evening, and we prayed and sang for our departed loved one till the sun rose.

The next morning, as one of the pall bearers, I helped to carry Arlo's coffin from the thípi to beside the open grave. Hundreds more people came to pay their respects. An elder knelt beside the coffin and let out a long, sorrowful wail, part of the traditional mourning practice. Before the coffin was lowered into the earth, one of Arlo's relatives offered a traditional oration—an instruction to the departed soul on how to get to the next world. The power of the words stirred me, even though I did not understand the Hidatsa language. Following this, four short songs were sung, each representing the four stages of life one must go through to enter the next world. As the songs were sung, Arlo's coffin was slowly lowered into the grave.

After Arlo was laid to rest, we gathered for a big feast at a church near the cemetery. Traditional dishes made with corn, squash, and beans were served, along with a soup made of tripe, a delicacy. A most interesting mixture of dried meat pounded into a fluffy texture, mixed with dried wild fruits and corn, was also offered. This is a spiritual food; when we ate it, we were symbolically partaking in Arlo's spiritual journey.

During the feast, Arlo's brother, Jacob approached me. Without saying much or offering an explanation, he presented me with Arlo's hoops. I was shocked. As far as I knew, Arlo had not told anyone that he had given me the dance or about our first lesson together. Wordlessly, I accepted the hoops. I had no way of knowing that these would be the hoops that I would dance with for over thirty-five years and that I would take to over ninety countries. They are the hoops that I still use today.

*　*　*

Back home in Vermillion, I had a dream that Arlo's family, friends, and I had gathered in the same cemetery where Arlo was buried. Arlo lay in his coffin. His hair, plaited into two braids, framed his cheeks. His forehead was painted with red ochre vermillion paint, a color belonging to and most pleasing to God. When a person wears this paint, it is said, God will recognize them. One line of the paint extended from his forehead through the part of his hair to the back of the neck—a symbol of the straight, red road of life. Arlo wore a shiny yellow ribbon shirt, most of it covered by a Pendleton blanket. His left arm was tucked inside the blanket, and his right hand grasped the edge. Intricately beaded moccasins with buffalo tracks as part of the beadwork peeked out from the bottom of the blanket. For the Lakota, buffalo tracks symbolized walking the path of the Maid of Heaven—the path that offered divine prosperity. When a person was following in her ways, this design was shown and represented bounty and blessings.

Arlo sat up in his coffin, the tired expression on his face giving way to sheer exuberance. Then, he stood up, and his body soared through the air to the tops of the trees. He was moving heavenward and was eager to do so. Just as I thought he was going to continue flying upward, Arlo halted in midair and gazed at all of us gathered below. A radiant smile broke through his face. In his eyes, I saw deep love for each of us. And then he was gone, rocketing upward until his body was indiscernible from the light of the sun.

In the years that followed, I would connect with other friends who attended Arlo's funeral and would hear that they had similar dreams following his death. In their dreams, they saw Arlo rise from his coffin and fly upward. They, too, recalled his luminous, joyous expression gazing back upon us. This was how we could let Arlo go: knowing that he was released from this world and merging with the eternal source of Light.

After that, I had several other dreams about Arlo. In the next dream, I heard a faint sound of a drum and a voice singing in the darkness. A dim light appeared. The song escalated in tempo. The light intensified, and I could see Arlo at the center, dancing. He lifted one hoop and began to make designs with it. The light spread. A crowd of people gathered around Arlo. I saw that the people were downtrodden, burdened, and in distress, and I realized that I was among them.

Arlo continued dancing with the one hoop—a representation of one-ness. The power of that single hoop enveloped all of us in the crowd. Arlo began adding several more hoops. He twirled and overlapped the hoops to form the design of a flower. This flower represented the potential we had to blossom and bring color and beauty to the world. Arlo proceeded to create designs representing the beauty and growth of springtime: flowers, trees, birds, butterflies, rainbows, and stars. With each design, the people gathered began to revive, to come together in joy and harmony. Just as the elements miraculously come together every spring—the blowing winds and rain, the sun's light and heat, the growth of the plant world, the regeneration of the earth—so the people in my dream were created anew.

Arlo performed design after design, and I saw how the power of the hoops encompassed the Indigenous North American people in the dream and extended to include people from every country, every ethnicity, and every background.

The vivid dreams continued for two more nights. Then they stopped.

Arlo had told me earlier that summer that he would give me four lessons—one lesson that first night and the rest later. These three dreams were my remaining lessons. Arlo had told me that he would fulfill his promise, that he would do his part, and that I would have to do my part. My part was to carry on the dance. By doing so, Arlo had promised that I would receive four gifts—to meet many people, travel to new places, have profound experiences, and receive abundant blessings.

In my little room in Vermillion, I pondered these dreams. The first dream of my benefactor rising up from his coffin and soaring joyfully heavenward portrayed the joy that Arlo experienced in reuniting with his

Creator. The next dreams showed the different colored hoops as symbols of the blessings of the Creator—unity, harmony, beauty, and balance.

Moreover, the dance in my dreams represented the coming of a new era. An old era had ended; people could go no further as distinct homogeneous peoples. Separation had led to despondency; the people of the world had lost their spirit and hope, as I had first seen in my dream. Even those with outward wealth, success, and power—were they truly happy? Or were they, too, suffering in the way my dreams revealed? As long as we remained separate by bounds of race, class, gender, and nationality, we were cut off from God's grace. The only way we could advance collectively was through unity. Together, as represented by the different colored hoops conjoined to create signs of life, the diverse peoples of the world could come together in a single dance.

In my dream, Arlo first danced with one hoop—a reiteration of his dance lesson with me in New Jersey. I understood this part of the dance was an exposition on the power of a single individual to serve as an agent of change. The dance revealed the responsibility of the individual to transform himself and, in so doing, to inspire transformation within the community.

When Arlo danced with two hoops, I saw the design of the sun and the moon. This dance portrayed how humankind must all turn to one divine source, the source that provides light, divine knowledge, and divine love. This source was the only effective means of uplifting humanity.

Arlo's dance with three hoops demonstrated the imperative for all people to overcome the obstacles of life. The dance portrayed how to make the transition from the dark world of restrictions to a world of spiritual enlightenment. The dance showed us how to emerge into that world, to scale the ladder of knowledge to greater heights and, like butterflies, activate our wings of knowledge and soar higher each and every day. As he made these designs in the dream, formerly downtrodden and despairing people were transformed and began to mirror the heavenly attributes symbolized in the hoop designs. The four different colors of hoops represented the paradigm of four—the directions, the seasons, the stages of life, the phases of the moon, the parts of the day, and the diverse peoples of the world. The hoop dance showed how each of us bring essential and innumerable gifts—gifts necessary for the upliftment of the human spirit and unity of humankind—from our respective backgrounds.

What I learned in these dreams was related to the significance of the dance. I did not, however, receive a formula on how to actually perform the dance. How then would I fulfill my promise to Arlo?

Interestingly, Arlo had been scheduled to go on an eight-week tour to nine countries of Africa with Arts America through the United States Information Agency (USIA). A part of the "Great Society" programs inaugurated by John F. Kennedy and backed by artistic greats such as Jazz trumpeter Dizzy Gillespie, Arts America was designed to promote international goodwill through the performing arts. When Arlo's mother informed the agency of his passing, they expressed their condolences and asked her if she could recommend somebody to go in his place. She recommended me.

When USIA contacted me, I knew that I could not replace Arlo; I did not truly know how to do the hoop dance. However, on faith, I accepted the invitation. I knew that I had a lot of work ahead of me to prepare for the tour.

In recent years, for the first time since Arlo passed away thirty-five years ago, I returned to his gravesite. I did not remember where his grave was located; however, I followed my intuition and made my way through the cemetery. I found his grave nestled between those of his mother and father. Around me, I heard the shrill call of crickets. As I knelt by his headstone, their melodies intensified. I looked up to see the deep green of the trees and the blue of the sky overhead. For a moment, I felt as if I had left the boundaries of time and space. I prayed for my friend and for the gift he gave me all those years ago—a gift that has taken me around the world, allowed me to meet many new people, have more meaningful experiences than I could have imagined, and has enabled me to plunge into an ocean of blessings. Arlo has fulfilled his original promise beyond my wildest expectations or dreams.

6

In the fall of 1980, before traveling to the capital of Senegal, Dakar—the first city of the African tour that Arlo had been planning to go on—I flew to Manhattan to procure the necessary visas for each African country in my itinerary. I was directed to go to "Pawt Athawty" for all my transportation needs. I wandered around downtown Manhattan for quite a while asking denizens directions to the "Pawt Athawty." Finally, in exasperation, one local pointed upward and said, "What hole did you crawl out from under? You idiot, you're standing right in front of it." I looked to see the huge lettering: "PORT AUTHORITY." I have since learned to distinguish and understand many local American English dialects.

Since I was a last-minute addition to the trip, I arrived in Dakar later than the rest of the tour group due to all the delays in obtaining the visas. Stepping off the plane, I was engulfed by intense heat and humidity. A mass of people, more people than I had ever seen in a single space, swarmed through the airport. A throng of locals approached the disembarking passengers. Offers in strange languages accosted us on every side, and beggars pulled at our arms. Local artisans approached us with their goods, and strangers indicated that they could drive us, carry our bags, or give us a tour of the city. I was taken aback by the chaos and finally relieved when a representative from the United States embassy arrived to take me to the University of Senegal, where I would join the rest of our tour group.

Dakar, during that time, resonated with French influence. French, the colonizer's language, was spoken by all and dominated the educational and political arenas; people also spoke myriad tribal dialects, Wolof being the dominant Indigenous language of Dakar. In fact, most of the Senegalese spoke at least three languages fluently. Restaurants served both Senegalese traditional foods and fine French cuisine. Much of the city had been developed during the era of French colonization. The layout of the streets mirrored that of Paris, and iron lattice work adorned the elaborate architecture, though some buildings had declined into slight dilapidation, and the tropical climate had caused rust to cover some of the iron work.

The other artists, representing the United States Information Agency, had arrived a few days earlier. Our group consisted of a tour manager, three performing artists from South Dakota, and a six-person dance company from New York. Together, we would represent the United States as goodwill ambassadors in cities and remote villages throughout Ghana, Senegal, and the Congo. With two weeks in each country, we would perform at universities, schools, festivals, community centers, and tribal ceremonies, sharing African-American, European-American, and Indigenous-American dance traditions, as well as modern dance styles.

Built and developed by the French government, the University of Senegal in Dakar hosted us. The French had added many modern provisions, including a spacious dance studio. Our tour group was given several days to recover from jet lag, which provided me time to teach myself some semblance of the hoop dance, in order to perform three to four presentations a day.

Shortly after I arrived at the university, thankfully on break, I slipped into the empty studio to practice. I began rehearsing—first with one hoop—the designs that Arlo had shown me during our first lesson. Hour after hour, I practiced spinning and reversing the hoop. I tossed it from hand to hand and whipped it around my body. Incrementally, I added hoops and practiced more complex designs.

Our tour group's first presentation in Dakar was at a school. When it came time for me to do the hoop dance, I was nervous. Jim Iron Shell, one of the performers from South Dakota, sang a traditional song. I moved a single hoop around my body. I added another hoop and yet another. During that first performance, I used five hoops. As I danced, I became immersed in each movement. Though I did not see the reactions of the audience, I sensed their positivity and appreciation, which further motivated me. Within a few days, I was dancing with eight, then twelve hoops.

By the end of that two-month trip, I would create designs using twenty hoops.

I engaged fully in the learning process, experimenting with different methods and design sequences. I practiced manipulating my fingers and the hoops in such a way as to create a varied performance. My new routine incorporated both standard hoop dance designs and my own unique configurations with the hoops. Having observed other hoop dancers performing designs with pauses in between each design, I considered creating a presentation that would flow from one design to the next without break.

Even as a part of a group of seasoned performers, I did not fear making mistakes in my hoop dance. In the United States, I may have felt inhibited from engaging in this learning process due to the cultural perfectionism that often manifests itself in a lack of tolerance toward adult beginners and can hold back this population of learners. Fortuitously, my dance career began with this African tour, where I did not feel pressure to perform at an impossible level of excellence.

I did my best to honor the responsibility I had been given when Arlo passed me the dance and appeared to me in dreams. At the time, I was not truly cognizant of the significance of the tour, especially as it had come together so quickly. Only later would I realize that this was a fulfilment of Arlo's promise to me. Even from the next world, Arlo was ensuring that this tour would launch me on my path.

*　*　*

One of our first performances in Dakar was at a national wrestling match—a great honor, as wrestling is a national sport of Senegal. Champion wrestlers from different regions of Senegal had come to compete in this traditional event. After our tour group presented several traditional dances, master drummer Doudou N'Daiye Rose performed. Upon his passing in 2014, Rose was hailed by *The New York Times* as "an emissary of his native culture's joyous and complex rhythms." A national hero, he was frequently invited to perform at and many times open major Senegalese festivals. Throughout our tour in Senegal, Rose performed with us at festivals and villages, often with his twenty-seven sons, who were all master percussionists.

At the wrestling festival, Rose and his sons performed a series of incredible percussion pieces. They layered rousing rhythms on top of each other, creating a complex weave of percussion. Rose played with great passion. His hands flurried over the drum so fast that it was impossible to distinguish his arms from the drumsticks. The people in the grandstands were ignited with the spirit. They poured from the stands and began to dance, fast and frenetic. Ladies dressed in vibrantly-printed cloth shook their entire bodies. Shoes flew off of people's feet. The energy and the dynamism of that performance is something I will never forget.

In our tour group's spare time, we visited the historical sites of Senegal. One of the most memorable experiences for me was a boat trip from the mainland to Gorée Island. At the foot of the island loomed a white stone fortress. As we docked and were escorted inside the fortress, tour guides offered explanations in French, which I did not understand. I followed the guide to a narrow opening in the stone, and when I stood in that portal, intense panic paralyzed me as I looked over the sea. I felt overpowered by the raw emotion of being there.

When I asked someone to translate the tour information, I learned that this doorway, known as *the door of no return,* was one of many ports of embarkment during the slave trade. Ships would pull up to that portal, and hundreds of human beings would be forced inside the ship, where they were transported as cargo across the ocean to be sold as property. A large percentage of people of African descent in America had their last contact with their continent of origin stepping over the threshold and through the doorway to generations of hardship, suffering, and bondage.

In the marketplaces of Senegal, I saw an array of specialty crafts made and sold by the people there. I bought wooden sculptures of traditional masks and animal figurines to give as gifts to my family back home. In one marketplace, an artist sold a canvas textured in reds, blues, and yellows. I looked closely and saw that the art had been made of butterfly wings.

At another market, a long line of people gathered around a food stand. I walked closer and peered around the ledge to see what food was being prepared. A vat of hot grease was bubbling, and next to it was a bowl filled with wriggling worms. I watched with surprise as the vendor tipped the worms into the grease, frying them to a golden crisp. He filled paper cones with the fried worms, offering them to the people standing in line. It was the most popular food item—a winning snack for many—but I decided against trying it.

Everywhere we went in Senegal, we received a warm welcome from the different tribal people there. I learned the basic greetings in each tribe. I was struck especially by the Wolof tribe—made up of lithe and sinuous people, highly distinguished, easily identifiable by the markings and scars on their cheeks. Even today, when I spot a member of their tribe, I am able to greet them in their own language.

From Senegal, our group transited through the Ivory Coast and went down to Ghana. We spent a day or two in Abidjan, a city similar to Dakar in its French influence. After our two weeks in Ghana, we drove through Togo. We also traveled through the Central African Republic, Gabon, and Nigeria. Our flights often did not stick to the listed schedule, and this resulted in layovers that lasted as long as a day or two in each of these countries. This gave us a chance to explore new cities and villages.

Flying, in Africa, was a big free-for-all. There were no safety rules—or if there were, the rules were not strictly enforced. Passengers stood in the aisles during the flight and smoked. Some people brought chickens in wire cages into the main cabin. As the airplane descended, everyone stood up in the aisles and began pulling their bags out. The whole experience was comical, to say the least.

Local drivers, in many of the cities we visited, pointed out monuments, educated us on local history, and shared stories as they drove us from place to place. In Ghana, a driver took us from Accra to Kumasi, a four-hour drive over rutted roads and rough terrain. Along the way, when we stopped for a lunch break, the driver asked us if we liked fruit. He went out into the abundant forest and emerged with a variety of fruit I never knew existed—fruit I have never had before or since.

As we toured through various communities, I observed how American companies pushed unhealthy practices and addictions onto the people of Africa. Billboards introduced tobacco products and advertised their false pleasure while concealing their detriments. Representatives of tobacco companies passed out free cigarettes on the streets and at major events. Other advertisements marketed baby formula, urging mothers of newborns to abandon breastfeeding for formula. Reps of these companies also distributed free samples of formula.

In Ghana, the University of Ghana in Lomé near Accra hosted us. The university was known for its incredible performing arts company. The company included artists from all the different major tribes of Ghana, each of whom retained unique music and dance traditions from their respective tribes. When we first arrived in Ghana, we met with the company and watched them perform. Their presentations integrated the diverse traditions in a dignified, powerful way. We later found out that the students taught each other their own tribal music and dance so that they could perform together.

This incredible display of unity deeply moved us, especially those of us from South Dakota. Though unique regional styles of music and dance among the tribes in North America exist, tribes do not typically share or integrate them with each other. Rules and regulations guide Indigenous North American tribal artistic expression, in part to uphold the excellence of each tradition. Restrictions exist as to who can share and participate in the music, dance, and language. A person cannot participate in sacred dance forms unless they have been given the dance from someone qualified to pass it on; my mother, for instance, could only hoop dance until she reached puberty, then had to put the hoops aside. Because I had been passed the dance from Arlo, I had received the authority to hoop dance. The same guidelines applied to music; a person first had to be qualified to sing any given repertoire of songs and then had to be able to sing the correct words and notes.

Fears of appropriation and suppression exist within these rules and are highly connected to the history of oppression: the prohibition of forms of spiritual expression, the indoctrination of the dominant culture, and the degradation of sacred music and dance forms by popular media. Many Indian cultures and languages have only survived because of a tribe's exclusion of outside influences. Safeguarding tradition has led to narrow, restricted ways of thinking and the imposition of regulations that restrict traditional practices from other tribal and cultural groups.

What I observed in Ghana was that the tribes were much less restrictive about their music and dance expressions. Though we had heard much about intertribal conflict in Africa, we witnessed instead intertribal sharing and connection, exceeding anything I had ever seen in North America. African tribes revered music and dance as essential elements for expressing social, cultural, and spiritual aspects of life, just as the tribes in North America did.

I continued to observe high levels of excellence and virtuosity in Ghana. The renowned xylophonist, Bernard Woma, was an instructor at the University of Ghana. During a sharing session between their performing arts company and our tour group, he performed for us. He played a traditional vibraphone comprised of wooden sticks of different thicknesses and length. When the wood was struck by a mallet, the sound amplified in gourds attached underneath. The reverberating tones, the speed with which Woma made music proved that he was truly a virtuoso. At the end of his performance, he contorted his body to play the vibraphone in all different kinds of ways. First he stood on his head and played it, then played it behind his back.

Woma explained to us that when he was born, his hands had a certain odd shape, considered by some to be a deformity: there was an unusual gap between the middle and ring fingers of his hands. An elder in his community told his parents that Woma was destined to perform the vibraphone, as the mallets of this instrument are held in each hand between the middle and ring fingers. Woma performed at venues around the world devoted to traditional folk arts and culture. From birth, it seems, he was ordained to carry on this essential aspect of his culture.

The talented people I met in Africa never had an inflated sense of self or notorious ego. Fame was not a part of their culture, unlike the popular culture in North America, which values the individual. The context from which these artists performed was entirely different. They believed that these traditional arts did not result from their own talent but rather originated from the divine. For them, the most powerful way of connecting with their art was to remove the self; art did not belong to the individual. I would later discover similar perspectives in artists of every ethnicity and nationality all over the world.

* * *

After we left Accra, we visited the Ashanti nation in Kumasi, Ghana, along with villages outside of Kumasi. There, we witnessed traditional ceremonies unique to the different tribes, including marriage rites and possession ceremonies. When we arrived in one village, we saw a large festival going on. The village chief paused to welcome us. He remarked that it was no accident that we had arrived on that very day, the day of his daughter's coming-of-age ceremony. "You are among many people who have traveled from across the region to attend," he stated. "God has sent you." He looked at us and gestured. "You have something unique to contribute to this special occasion. You know what to do. Now, we ask you to do that for us!"

The three of us from South Dakota looked at each other. Though we had not planned to do anything, we knew exactly what the chief was asking of us: to honor his daughter with our North American blessings for a woman's coming-of-age. Together, we performed the Buffalo Dance with the appropriate songs. In North American Indigenous tradition, the buffalo symbolizes the heritage of the White Buffalo Calf Maiden and the high station of women in this world.

To the delight of the tribe members, we invited the chief's daughter and several other young women of her age to join our dance. We taught them how to dance in the four directions then come back to the center. They learned how to motion as if they were pawing at the earth and to move their feet to a double-beat. In another movement, they bowed low towards the ground and rose again. At the end of the last song, they came forward. We offered a prayer for the girls, a prayer that they would always stay within that circle of love and unity and that this circle would remain unbroken for their children and the coming generations.

I often remember that particular presentation. I marvel at how the chief asked us to participate in honoring his daughter and that he somehow sensed that we knew what to do. When we had finished doing the North American coming-of-age ceremony for the people in the village, the other performers asked us how we knew what to do. We explained that the chief recognized that we were also village people from North America. He rightfully made the assumption that we observed similar practices and had comparable ways of welcoming our young people to adulthood. In our travels throughout Africa and in my later journeys, I found a deep, global connection among all tribal peoples and their traditions.

7

In the years that I have been performing the hoop dance, many elders have helped me to deepen on the history and practices of the dance. One of those elders, Asa Primeaux, approached me in the early 1980s just after a performance at the annual Bdé Iháŋke Wačhípi / End of the Lake Powwow on the Yankton Sioux Reservation. Over the course of many decades, Asa had seen the hoop dance move from a common devotional tradition to something rarely practiced among the people. He encouraged me to continue reviving the dance.

"When you do this dance," he said, "it is a prayer for the people. You're asking each sacred design to grow in the hearts of the people, to bless them and bring them together."

Historically, the purpose of the hoop dance was devotional. During the pre-reservation days, as the *okȟólakičhiye,* service organization, provided structure for tribal life, they hosted feasts as a way of expressing gratitude to the people for allowing them the honor of serving them. In the context of these feasts, they performed their own unique music and dances. The hoop dance was the signature dance of one such society, the Elk Dreamers Society. The Elk Dreamers Society would perform this dance as a choreographed prayer for the people. They utilized only a few hoops to create designs that represented the signs of spring. Each design was a prayer of renewal, peace, harmony, and love for the people. In Lakota language, the word for "hoop" connotes something sacred. To manipulate a hoop for this dance evoked mystical or holy symbols and invited viewers and dancers alike to participate in this prayer.

In the late 1800s, the government outlawed the practice of the hoop dance, along with other Indigenous spiritual traditions. The suppression of these practices resulted in the decline of the dance. At the same time, impresarios such as Buffalo Bill staged theatrical extravaganzas about the exploits of the "Wild West," and organized performance tours throughout continental United States and Europe. For these shows, impresarios commissioned singers and dancers from the Elk Dreamers Society to perform the hoop dance. As the Elk Society members often lacked translators and could not speak English, they could not explain the purpose and meaning of the dance to the impresarios. As a result, the hoop dance was grossly misconstrued as pure entertainment and was advertised as a side show. Because of this, it lost much of its exalted significance. Even today, the hoop dance is still practiced as entertainment and is not often connected to its spiritual heritage.

During the 1970s and 1980s, there were very few practitioners of the hoop dance. In the 1990s, the Heard Museum in Phoenix, Arizona began to sponsor a yearly International Hoop Dance Championship. This revived interest in the dance and encouraged a high level of athletic excellence and agility amongst the competitors.

Nowadays, competitions like this happen year-round throughout the country and have created an industry of top-notch competitive dancers who dance with the highest level of speed, strength, and dexterity. Some even perform with the famous Cirque du Soleil.

As I received the dance in a spiritual manner, I have no desire to perform the dance competitively or as entertainment. For me, the dance has always been a prayer.

My routine now has been the same for almost twenty-five years. In it, I use twenty-eight hoops to represent the 28-day lunar cycle. The lunar cycle is a period of transition from the cold and lifeless winter into spring. During these days, new signs of spring emerge—each day, a new insect chirps, a fresh fragrance exudes from a bloom, and color seeps back into the trees and grass. In a parallel way, my hoop dance sequence signifies the power of transformation in human history and the promise of a spiritual springtime that winter can never overtake. I have chosen designs that depict the effervescence of life during this time of year. The sequence of these designs showcases the progression from winter to spring, as I start with six hoops and move to twenty-eight.

In the mid-twentieth century, several of the remaining hoop dancers developed a distinctive dance style utilizing many hoops. This style, identified with the Northern Plains, is the style I perform today. Before I perform my dance, I often—facetiously—tell the audience that there are easy, intermediate, and difficult levels of hoop dance, and that I will be performing the easiest style, starting with six hoops. They often think I am joking, but by far, the most difficult style is dancing with one hoop. It may sound counterintuitive, but dancing with a single hoop is incredibly challenging. Every hoop added after one makes the dance incrementally easier to perform.

I often show them several basic designs with one hoop and explain what the patterns symbolize and that one hoop represents our place in creation. Then I put the first hoop down and pick up two hoops—a white and yellow hoop. "These hoops represent the sun and the moon," I share. I hold the white hoop up and talk about the powers of the moon to influence the tides and the growth cycle of plants. I then lift the yellow hoop and explain its purpose. "This hoop is as the sun, the source of heat and energy for all of creation." When I pick up another hoop to make three hoops, I speak of how the three hoops symbolize transformation. "In order to progress and transform, we have to transcend obstacles along our path."

I then pick up two hoops to add to the three hoops I have. With five hoops, I demonstrate several of the designs depicting the unfoldment of spring. One design shows a plant sprouting through the earth. "This parallels how human beings manifest our potentials." Another design shows a tree growing. "This represents the maturation of the individual, how as we grow, we draw strengths from our roots and heritage. The higher we reach, the more we gain new perspective on life. We live in a time where we can see the world through new eyes."

I scan the audience. "I don't see strangers here." I then make the design of a flower. "I see a room full of flowers, who can bring out beauty and divine fragrance, who can diffuse blessings to the world." I create the design of a constellation and share that they are all as North Stars of guidance. I speak of the meaning of the morning star, how it appears in the darkest, coldest hour before dawn. The morning star announces the coming of a new day and provides light for all of us to walk the sacred path of life and see each other, the colors, and beauty of all creation. I shift this design to an eagle and say, "I see a room full of eagles that can soar on the wings of knowledge and understanding."

I tell them that the four colors of the hoops—black, red, yellow, and white—symbolize the paradigm of four—the cardinal directions, the elements, the stages of life, the different kingdoms of existence. They also represent the diverse kindreds and peoples of the earth. "These hoops represent the people coming together to create something beautiful, something that will embrace all of us."

I offer these explanations, alongside the designs to inform the audience that the hoop dance is a spiritual activity, not merely entertainment. I prepare them for a sequence of designs that depict the effervescence of the human spirit and highlight a different manifestation of spring. "I will make flowers, mountains, trees, insects, and birds—everything we associate with the coming of a new day," I announce, informing them that I will begin my routine with six hoops and work up to twenty-eight.

"When you see the designs unfold, applaud," I guided them. "But don't applaud me. Applaud and encourage yourselves. Your role is to work together in ways that our ancestors could only dream of. In this way, we will create a new world together."

Then I begin my dance. It is a six-minute routine, most often done to a recording of the Black Lodge Singers, though I love working with live music as well.

When I dance today, I still use Arlo's hoops, as given to me by his brother, Jake. Unlike most hoops used in North America that are made of willow, Arlo's hoops are made of rattan, a reed material from Southeast Asia used to make wicker furniture. Willow only temporarily maintains its tensility; in the course of a year, the material can become brittle. Rattan matches willow in both its rigid and flexible properties but is far more durable.

In 1981, I was invited to perform in Australia. When I arrived after the long flight, I found ten of my hoops shattered, because, still an inexperienced traveler, I did not pack them with enough protection. I did not know what to do, as I had performances scheduled for the following day. Fortunately, the friends who had picked me up at the airport in Brisbane had some errands to do, and we stopped at a hardware store. I wandered with them into the store; in the section that had plumbing materials for boats, I noticed a lightweight, synthetic tubing material that looked to be the same size as the hoops. I purchased quite a bit of it, along with some wooden dowels. That evening, I set about creating new hoops. I cut and measured strips of tubing, connected the ends with two inches of wooden dowel, then wrapped them with electrical tape. The new hoops were light, flexible, and would not bind or crimp. They were exactly what I needed.

Traditionally, a hoop dancer will have to prepare his hoops based on what types of designs he plans to make. For designs that require flexible hoops, hoops must be soaked in water for an hour before the performance. Stiff hoop designs allow the hoops to be left dry. Arlo had instructed me in these particulars of preparation, and throughout my travels in Africa, I arrived early at every venue to prepare my hoops accordingly.

Currently, in my performances I use the sixteen original wooden hoops that I have had from the beginning and twelve synthetic hoops made with the material I found in Australia. I have been using these hoops now for almost forty years, through thousands and thousands of performances in over ninety countries.

I continue to work on perfecting new hoop designs. This is why I never describe myself as an athlete, a dancer, or a singer. I am simply someone who is persistent and committed to a learning process that involves much trial and error.

One design that took me a long time to create was the design using all twenty-eight of the hoops to create the image of the eagle transforming into an image (with fewer hoops) of the world. Originally, Arlo had showed me this design during our first lesson and had fashioned all of his hoops to make a globe.

Soon after I received the dance, I attended a meeting in Standing Rock with elders who were visiting different communities to share the vision of Crazy Horse. There, the elders shared the story of how Crazy Horse traveled to Bear Butte, shortly before he was murdered, to fast and pray for four days and four nights. On the morning of the fourth day, just as the morning star appeared above the hilltop, he had a vision. In the vision, Crazy Horse was transformed into an eagle and flew out over the world. As he flew over different parts of the world, he saw all of the *oyáte tȟa-čhánygleška*—the *hoops of the nation* or *hoops of humanity*. This phrase—*hoops of humanity*—refers to the socio-political structures, music, arts, and languages that serve the various people of the earth. These are referred to as *hoops* of the people because they are unifying forces that bind communities together.

Transformed into an eagle, Crazy Horse saw all these hoops—the diverse societies of the world and their beauty and strength. He realized how the same sun of reality shone on the people, uniting the people in spite of their differences—very similar to how the physical sun shone on the different flora and fauna in the different parts of the world, with one sun illuminating diverse beings, with each being unique and resplendent in its light.

Then to his horror, Crazy Horse realized that dark clouds were sweeping over the world and were blotting out the light and heat from the sun of reality. He saw humanity plunged into darkness. Greedy egotistical rulers began to seize control of the hearts of the people everywhere. These rulers threw the people into a swirling tempest of hatred, envy, and avarice. He saw brothers pitted against brothers, nations against nation. Every heart was broken; every mother was destitute; every child was forlorn. He witnessed carnage and gloom—the people dying, their bodies dead in mud, darkness and gore ruining the land.

Crazy Horse began to weep. He cried as he realized there was no hope, no future for the world. He pondered all the diverse peoples, their former glory and beauty; he began to pray that the people could see this beauty in themselves and each other. The energy of this prayer was as the wind beneath his eagle wings and propelled Crazy Horse upward. He flew above the darkness and looked into the future.

He saw the light of a new day dawn over the world, touching the people. The ruins of the earth began to stir and shake; the collapsed people rose, brushing away the dust and gore. Revived strangers reached out and embraced one another. They began to create new designs, new hoops of beauty and life. A new design began to form and to take shape in the world, starting first in the heart of North America where Crazy Horse himself was from.

This was the story that these elders shared. They emphasized that Crazy Horse foretold that this vision would begin its fulfillment in seven generations. The time was now, they said. We would witness this vision of the hoops of humanity become reality.

Right then, I determined to express Crazy Horse's vision in the hoop dance. And so I began. I tried to create or recreate the design of the world that Arlo showed me, but it was so difficult. I realized that the way Arlo had made the design was by soaking the hoops a precise length of time so they would have the exact tensile property to hold together in a global formation. I found it impractical to soak my hoops for the exact length of time before every performance. Through practice and experience, I learned to wind several layers of electrical tape on each of the wooden hoops to create the right amount of flexibility in the hoops. I perfected the process, which culminated in my goal of creating Crazy Horse's vision.

In this routine, I created a design with all twenty-eight hoops that represented an eagle. I began to spin. As I spun, the eagle design morphed into the world.

After this, I included one more design. Several hoops circled my legs—these were the tail of the eagle—and I took them to make one long chain with all the hoops. This represented all the people of the earth, intertwined, impossible to segregate. I spun and spun, and as I did, I moved this long chain to rest upon my shoulders. With the final beat of the drum, I created another image of an eagle, with its wings outstretched in flight.

8

As I had only been a Bahá'í for one year, my first exposure to large Bahá'í communities was during the tour in Africa. In South Dakota, I had only been a part of the small Bahá'í community in Vermillion, and due to friends moving, I had spent much of the year as an isolated believer. Though I had attended gatherings such as the Continental Indigenous Council Fire, I had never seen what a pattern of community life could be like for a Bahá'í community made up of hundreds of believers. Africa was where I first saw this.

In Dakar, Accra, and Brazzaville, whenever I had an opening in the presentation schedule, I would visit with the Bahá'í communities there. I attended the nineteen-day Feast. I went to vibrant devotional gatherings and visited Bahá'ís in their homes, and I visited the Bahá'í Center in Accra. Everywhere the people were of modest means but abundantly wealthy and prosperous in family, friends, and spirit. We were hosted by a lady who had no furnishings in her home; she cooked on a fire outside and feasted us on chicken feet soup. This memory lingers in my mind as a banquet fit for royalty because of the hospitality, generosity, and joy that pervaded that evening and lifted us up into the stratosphere of ecstasy.

During my travels to meet the Bahá'ís, I was particularly impressed with the focus on children in each community. Children actively participated in children's classes, the Nineteen Day Feast, and devotionals. My experiences in North American Bahá'í gatherings had been otherwise—with children remaining separate until the dessert and socializing at the end. Here, children sang and played the drums during prayers and were included in community consultation. Children were part of the rhythm of community life from womb to tomb, and music was a special glue that held together the hearts of the people.

In each locality, I met both native African and pioneer Bahá'ís. Many of the pioneers sacrificed the comfort and lifestyle of their home countries and the proximity to family and friends, to move to African rural communities to teach the Bahá'í Faith and establish communities there. They possessed so much faith. I remember their joy and the strength with which they involved themselves in establishing relationships, in sharing the teachings of love and unity to everyone who crossed their path.

Among the African Bahá'ís, I observed that those from minority tribes and those from the lowest rungs of society had a special place in Bahá'í community life. In Brazzaville, I saw how the minority Pygmy population, who were consigned to menial jobs and were generally considered outcasts by society at large, were at the forefront of participation in the Bahá'í community.

Though material resources were limited, relationships and connections were strong. People spent time with one another, and they went out of their way for one another. While in the Congo, I met a young Persian pioneer, Fati, short for Fatimeh. Fati was one of few who owned a car in Brazzaville, a community with dusty, rock-filled roads. She often piled ten to fifteen Bahá'ís in her four-passenger vehicle and drove them to devotional gatherings or to visit and encourage local friends. Her car resembled a clown car, packed with laughing people and bouncing along those pot-holed roads. When it arrived at its destination, an unbelievable number of people would extricate themselves from their contorted positions in the car and pile out—me included!

* * *

Before I left the United States, I contacted the Bahá'í National Center and obtained a list of contacts for the various countries on my itinerary. My first contact was in Dakar, Dr. Ardekani. He was serving on the Continental Board of Counselors at the time. He introduced me to the large, active community there and invited me to a community devotional gathering held in a local cemetery. The location surprised me; I was not accustomed to attending large gatherings in cemeteries.

We went to the section of the cemetery where many Bahá'ís were buried. There, the friends prayed, sang, and danced. The memories of ancestors, both family and friends, were always celebrated and invoked. This practice was repeated in each African Bahá'í community that I visited, and it became one that I enjoyed. Each community made a point to gather near the gravesites of the first native believers of their communities, as well as the gravesites of the Knights of Bahá'u'lláh—an honor given to the first Bahá'ís to ever settle in a given country or territory. Commemorating these souls was a priority in each community. These individuals were seen as gateways through which every Bahá'í in the community came into the Faith. The practice of holding devotional gatherings at their gravesites signified how precious the Bahá'í Faith was to the members of the community and how much gratitude they felt for the believers who brought the Faith to them.

During these occasions, we had big picnics at the gravesites, and we feasted on delicious food, including a variety of fruits I had never seen before or since. We shared prayers, often singing. Many friends brought drums, and people would dance and move as they sang. These were festive, joyful, deeply spiritual occasions. I felt at home to share my own devotional expressions. I sang Lakota prayers and played prayer songs on the flute.

I noticed quickly that the whole devotional attitude in the African communities was so different than what I had experienced before. In the United States, communities said prayers with a solemn, serious, and reserved attitude. In Africa, music animated our communication with God. Drums and song infused the prayers with great joy. Dancing—even in the cemeteries—was never separated from the devotional expression, similar to the Indigenous North American practices. Dancing was experienced as a physical manifestation of spiritual upliftment.

In Africa and in all Indigenous traditions throughout the world, the arts are inseparable from life. This differs greatly from dominant Euro-American culture here in North America, where the arts are relegated to "hobbies" and seen as a means of escape from the stress and freneticism of everyday life. In traditional cultures throughout the world, the arts are used for the opposite purpose: to connect with one's reality, with that which is holy, sacred, and ancient; to connect with one's family and all the generations that came before, with the dreams and prayers and hopes of the ancestors; to connect with the future generations; and to connect with the realms of creation surrounding us, the earth and sky. The arts eliminate the illusion of separation. The arts lift us up into the reality of goodness and beauty and harmony.

Wherever I went in Africa, I noted the high level of multilingualism and multiculturalism. The diversity of cultures and languages did not prevent the tribes from sharing with and accommodating each other, especially in the Bahá'í community. Most Africans spoke three to four—and sometimes more—languages from their different tribal groups. In Senegal, I noted that most everyone spoke the intertribal language—Wolof. Even though only a portion of the population belonged to that ethnicity, their language had been adopted as the lingua franca of that country. The language of commerce and education there was French, and since the country of Guinea, in the middle of Senegal, was an English-speaking country, everybody who lived near Guinea also spoke English. And since a large portion of the population was Muslim, many were literate in Arabic—the language of the Koran—as well.

The Bahá'í Feasts and devotional gatherings, consequently, reflected this type of multilingualism. Everybody in attendance at a gathering would switch fluidly from one tribal expression to another, even to the colonial languages, whether French or English. Everyone's native language was welcome at the gatherings. Friends said and sang prayers in their native languages; there had been clear effort made to translate Bahá'í scripture into various local languages. Even when different items were discussed, the consultation was done openly in a multilingual way so that everyone was included. In this way, everybody was a participant.

A document, *The Prosperity of Humankind,* prepared by the Bahá'í International Community Office of Public Information for the United Nations World Summit on Social Development in 1995, proposes concepts and themes relevant to a global strategy to advance the development of humankind. This next stage of advancement involves a challenge to reshape all of the institutions of society in order to expedite the unification and prosperity of all of humanity. To craft and implement a global strategy, the document proposes the consideration of numerous principles, such as an unquestioned loyalty to the recognition that we are one human family, a commitment to justice as the organizing principle by which we operate, the uniting of the religious and scientific community to hold a systematic dialogue about the development of human capacity. Such an effort requires dialogue skills that encourage participants to rise above their own particular views in order to function as part of a group with particular goals. Numerous other principles challenge all leaders, officials, politicians to see themselves as responsible for the welfare of all of humanity. The document aims to inspire a global effort to increase the prosperity of all of humanity.

Because of my global travels and concern for the preservation of cultural diversity, I appreciated reading in the statement "cultural expressions need to be protected from suffocation by the materialistic influences currently holding sway."* In the former Soviet bloc and other countries, the arts have been contaminated by materialistic views that oppress people. Artistic productions portrayed marginalized people as happy and content. This discriminatory practice needs to end. Theatrical productions in Africa or any "exotic" culture end up being processed and packaged much like a ride in Disney World where the viewer remains in his or her plastic vicarious bubble digesting a sanitized, homogenized semblance of an expression divorced from the context that gives it meaning.

The Bahá'í International Community also adds that diverse "cultures must be enabled to interact with one another in ever-changing patterns of civilization, free of manipulation from partisan political ends."** If distinct cultures never interact with each other, then their true worth will go unrecognized by anyone other than themselves. Despite the economic and political turmoil enveloping the African countries, I observed how the Bahá'í community transcended this turmoil through the arts and created a beautiful spiritual environment, where diverse cultural expressions were shared in a unifying, integrated manner.

---

* Bahá'í International Community Office of Public Information, *The Prosperity of Humankind*, Haifa, Israel, 1995.

** Bahá'í International Community Office of Public Information, *The Prosperity of Humankind*, Haifa, Israel, 1995.

9

After my tour in Africa, I returned home to Vermillion, where I had just begun to study for a doctoral degree at the University of South Dakota. Though I was still technically a full-time student, I began to engage in artists' residencies in schools. Such residencies integrated the folk arts into an existing school curriculum and expanded student creativity. The residencies lasted up to a week and took me through the Dakotas, from Yankton to Sisseton, all the way up to Watford City; and across the United States, from Oregon to New York, down to Florida, and to other parts of the United States.

The South Dakota Arts Council was the primary benefactor for my residencies. I had started working with them back when I was working with the Teacher Corps in the seventies. The Arts Council was searching for artists who could present in schools that served 90 to 100 percent of tribal children. They wanted to offer targeted culturally relevant programs for this significant population in South Dakota. With the encouragement of the director, Charlotte Carver, I began visiting schools around the state. A pioneer in the field, I continually tried different approaches until I found ways to hold the children's short attention spans. When I started these residencies in the seventies, virtually no one else offered comparable folk art presentations. In the ensuing forty years, an explosion of talent developed. I now have intense competition in an area in which I had, at one time, nearly sole occupancy of this genre.

The residencies offered me a lot of creative latitude. I created lesson plans from traditional stories, an extension of what I had already done as a teacher in the Teacher Corps. I taught the children traditional songs, led art projects, and played hand games with them. I even found elders whom I recruited to help me teach and lead the hand games.

Though I led workshops at festivals for people of all ages, I soon realized that I especially loved working with kids. I tried to focus my lessons on universal themes rather than tribal-specific messages. I selected stories and songs to highlight these themes and focused on the nobility of the human spirit. When I played flute in these lessons, I chose melodically simple yet compelling songs to share with the kids. I would teach a prayer song, playing a few notes of the melody, sing it to the children, then share a translation of its words. I taught them to sing these songs, piece by piece. In later years, I incorporated sign language to the words of the songs. When possible, I gave the children flutes and had them teach each other songs— any song of their choice, from *Happy Birthday* to a superhero theme song. I discovered that by making the lessons interactive and kinesthetically involved, kids learned better and retained more.

Even in those early presentations, I shared the hoop dance. When I did the dance for new audiences, a special power kicked in—the power of unity I had witnessed in my dreams of Arlo. When my lifelong brother / friend Dallas Chief Eagle suggested I include other people in the circle of my dance, I began to do so and experienced that unity to an even higher degree. Whether in small workshops or all-school assemblies, I gave the children from one to three hoops each, sometimes providing them the opportunity to make and decorate their own hoops. I helped them practice the designs of butterflies, stars, and birds with the hoops, and I repeated the same basic lesson Arlo gave me. The children would come out of their shells, and the audience loved watching them. Then, I would put on a recording, and the children and I would dance together, to show that the only way we could go forward was in unity.

Before I shared the hoop dance with them, I explained to the kids that the hoop dance is a prayer that represents unity and oneness. I said, "The Lakota people, when they pray, orient themselves to the four directions and pray to all of creation within those directions. When we pray, we're not only praying for ourselves, but we're praying for the whole of creation. We all have a place in the universe. We all have a purpose. In a circle, like this hoop, there is no second row—no one has a back seat. We all have a place and have to fulfill our role as best we can."

Every presentation and workshop was a form of self-therapy, a reaffirmation of my original inspiration, an answer to my prayers, and the ongoing fulfillment of my lifelong quest for meaning. Every workshop I did was a fantastic learning experience, and I loved traveling to different communities and meeting new people. Today, grown men and women continue to approach me and share how I touched their lives when I had visited their schools years ago. I feel affirmed knowing that the power of the arts influenced their spirits when they were children.

In 1989, I traveled to a school in Eureka, South Dakota—a town neighboring Wakpala that was known for its homogeneity, cleanliness, and beauty. There, I observed students engaged in an assignment to create pictures portraying their town in the past and future. To depict the past, they drew the predictable scenes of covered wagons and sod houses, European pioneers breaking virgin soil with horse-pulled plows, and the building of their community.

Besides these pictures were the portraits depicting the future. The art I saw frightened me. Many of the children portrayed a world broken—cracked like an egg, attacked by missiles, covered by a big mushroom cloud. No doubt they saw such images on national television. They drew a collapsing economy, nations battling against other nations, and horrors unfolding throughout the world. Their art reflected destruction and chaos.

As I drove out of that town, I perceived the neat homes with pretty flowerbeds and perfectly trimmed lawns as a facade. If these children did not have hope, then what was the point? Was not the purpose of the collaboration between the family, schools, and community to prepare the youth for the future, to give them a foundation from which to spring forth, to instill hope and a sense of destiny in our future generations? Having an outer perfect image and an inner sense of doom is similar to having an empty shell, a movie set with no depth that can be struck down in seconds. This experience affirmed my conviction to use the arts as a means to infuse meaning and hope.

Along with participating in residencies, I continued to travel and perform within and outside of the United States. In April of 1981, I flew to Australia for a meeting of the World Council of Indigenous People. This body gathered representatives from Indigenous populations around the world, including the Sami of Scandinavia, the Maori of New Zealand, and numerous North American tribes. The Aboriginal people of Australia hosted the conference, which was fitting as they had retained much of their culture and language despite great oppression.

An electric spirit pervaded this whole gathering of Indigenous people organizing on a global level and bringing together the dispersed kindreds of the human family. Much of the gathering of the Word Council of Indigenous People focused around our shared history and values. We explored how we, as the different tribes of the world, could support each other in our efforts to protect our lands and safeguard our social, cultural, political, and spiritual rights. We affirmed our commitment to safeguard the spiritual values and practices of our ancestors reflected in prayers, dances, and ceremonies.

Tribes were given the chance to share their own unique cultural expressions, and this opportunity generated much joy and respect among the attendees. Artistic sharing was central to creating a unifying spirit at the conference. I had the bounty of sharing the flute tradition. Billy Briton, a Cree from Manitoba, provided the wonderful opportunity for me to see the electric power of the hoop dance to galvanize and inspire audiences.

The Australian Aboriginals shared a powerful, traditional musical selection and dance. The Aboriginal performers played the Digeridoo, which invokes dream-time, held by the Aboriginal people as a primordial matrix from which all of creation emerges. This matrix is the true unifying force in this world and resides in the consciousness of God alone. Witnessing this dance, I saw the power of the traditional arts to pull all people into the primordial heart of the sacred, the dream-time of universal consciousness and oneness. This consciousness also propelled the vocal composition that accompanied the dance.

From this gathering, I began to understand that the primary point of unity among Indigenous people is spiritual unity. Other group unities can fade away or are limited in scope—unity of language, unity of political parties, unity of ethnicity. Spiritual unity, however, transcends these smaller forms. Music and dance were among the sacred traditions held to create this kind of eternal unity; there was nothing entertainment-based or frivolous about these practices. Art was intrinsic to our societies, and our communities were centered around the well-being of the collective—with special attention to the children—over the well-being of the individual.

After the Council, Bahá'í friends took me to see the House of Worship just outside of Sydney. The nine-sided white stone edifice rose from a hilltop, surrounded by lush vegetation on every side. I felt the same tranquility, dignity, and exaltation I had felt at the House of Worship in Wilmette. Although not as ornate and monumental as the Wilmette House of Worship, the edifice overlooked the natural grandeur and allure of the Australian bush—the perfect ornament to the natural flora of the land down under. Looking out from the sanctuary, I saw only greenery; the cityscape of Sydney seemed to become dissolved in nature.

In the years that followed my trip to Australia, I traveled with the Miccosukee tribe of Florida twice to Madrid and once to Tokyo. We attended large international tourism conventions, where different tourist localities were showcased, and we attracted the interest of travel agencies and government organizations. To promote the Florida community of the Miccosukee, tribal artists, including myself, were invited to perform our own music and dance. I played flute music and performed the hoop dance.

While I loved exploring the countries we visited, I was less impressed with the conventions, which sensationalized Indian art forms. The way diverse cultures were marginalized, exoticized, and reduced to vicarious Disneyesque ride experiences revolted me. The convention as a means to provide visitors meaningful interaction with the people and culture of the Miccosukee did not show much promise.

I brought my daughter, Kim, with me to Spain in 1982. As soon as I was finished with my scheduled presentations, Kim and I toured Madrid. We saw master flamenco artists perform their dance. They executed their movements with speed, precision, and perfect rhythm. We visited the zoo in Madrid and saw European bison, rare creatures that were hunted almost to extinction. She and I offered a prayer in front of its habitat. As we sang the buffalo song, one of the bison perked up and walked towards us, listening with intrigue.

This was the first international trip that I took with one of my children. Traveling gave Kim and me quality time together, outside of the tensions of the home. From then on, whenever I traveled in the country or abroad and I was able, I took one of my children with me.

In March of 1982, I had my largest performance yet at the John F. Kennedy Center for the Performing Arts. I danced for *Night of the First American*, a gala showcasing Indigenous performers from across the United States. Phil Lucas, a Choctaw Indian and Bahá'í, was one of the producers for this event, and he asked me to hoop dance.

I walked into the huge main hall, where the towering ceilings and dazzling lights were awe-inspiring. I noticed that my name was listed on the program between Wayne Newton and Sammy Davis Junior. Also on the program were Vincent Price and Martin Sheen. I had never performed at such a high-profile event or at such a prominent performing arts venue.

At the beginning of my dance, I stood under the intense lights on the massive stage—a contrast to the outdoor grounds or school gymnasiums where I usually performed. A full audience extended out in front of the stage. The Porcupine Singers from Pine Ridge had come out to sing for me before my performance. At the end of my performance, I received a standing ovation, the only one among all the other celebrities. Perhaps this was because the hoop dance was unusual and members of the audience had not experienced traditional songs and dance.

Regardless of the reason, I felt awkward and out of place. For me, the pinnacle of my career has never been performances such as this one—however special they are. I prefer to share the dance at the grassroots level at schools such as Red Scaffold, Upper Cut Meat, and Milk's Camp. I treasure time with children, in small communities in remote areas all over the world.

That same March, my daughter Waniya was born in Wagner, South Dakota. My friend and mentor Grandpa Joe Rock Boy, had once described for me the sudden transition from winter snow into springtime, calling it "Waniya," which means "breath of life." Spring's beauty was ushered in by the breath of the Holy Spirit, bringing and sustaining life. "Ni" in Lakota means "breath."

The night Waniya was born, there had been a huge blizzard. But the next morning, the weather transformed; it was sunny, warm, and breezy. When I drove back to the hospital that morning, I heard a choir of songbirds and meadowlarks singing in harmony. Waniya had come into the world and had brought spring along with her.

At the hospital, in the room adjacent to ours, an elder woman had died at the same time Waniya was born. That morning, the woman's family, weeping with happiness, visited my wife and met Waniya. They expressed their sincere tenderness for this new baby, whom they saw as an incarnation of their grandmother. The blizzard, the new spring day, and this birth and death—all of these happenings were quite mystical.

I had mixed feelings after Waniya's birth. I knew that my marriage was ending and that her mother and I could not continue on together; for this, I felt sad for this new baby. But I felt she had a great destiny before her, as we all do. It gave me a renewed sense of commitment to do the best I could do with my life and work.

The autumn after Waniya's birth, I left my studies for a doctoral degree for a position at Standing Rock College. A good friend of mine had offered me a grant for a position in developing curriculum for teaching Lakota culture. I was not too interested in a full-time teaching position, but I felt impelled by the desire to create a consistent livelihood.

This grant allowed me to immerse myself in Lakota literature and culture. One accomplishment of this research was obtaining recordings made in 1911 of Lakota traditional singers. Ethnomusicologist Frances Densmore had come to Standing Rock during this time and, under the direction of Lakota informants, had made recordings on a wax cylinder of six hundred songs associated with the teachings of the White Buffalo Calf Maiden and the diverse range of musical genres covering the spectrum of Lakota musical expression. She had then gone on to visit tribes throughout the country and make recordings of their traditional music.

I had encountered Densmore's book, *Teton Sioux Music*, as a graduate student in Vermillion. Now at Standing Rock College, I submitted a formal request to the Library of Congress for transcription and access to the wax cylinder recordings. When my colleague and I received the newly-transcribed recordings on cassette, we found them unusable. The sounds recorded were distorted beyond any familiar Lakota music. Yet after listening to the recordings, we heard the female singer do a tremelo call *(uŋgnáǧičala hotȟúŋ / the cry of the screech owl),* done for the praise of a loved one, but this call was off-speed. We realized that perhaps the recordings were all set on the incorrect speed.

With the help of a local sound studio, we were able to engineer the songs to their correct speed. Listening to them again, we now heard the cadence and clear vocals of the beautiful traditional songs, as well as the dialogue between the singers before and after each performance. These recordings, which had not been heard for seventy years, now were accessible to all the different tribes Densmore had visited in North America.

Though we had great success with the transcriptions of these traditional songs, and went on to develop curriculum about Lakota culture, my grant at the college never included a component for the implementation of this curriculum. Whatever we created was never utilized, and after that year, I went on to work at a short-term position as an assistant principal of a local elementary school from the fall of 1983 through the spring semester of 1984.

This was my last full-time job. So much had been percolating at that time, and I had been traveling for workshops, performances, and residencies. I felt inexorably drawn to these activities, to this new calling. I longed for the independence and creativity these activities provided.

Logic had always told me that I needed a full-time job. I feared that I could never earn a legitimate livelihood from working as an artist. But with every passing year, I began to see the pieces of my life shift and show signs that my life was moving in a new direction. I knew I needed to earn a livelihood, but it dawned on me that perhaps I could provide better for myself and my family doing freelance work than I ever could working full time. Every day, I was contacted with new opportunities to share this art. I had unique skills to offer, and the demand was higher than I could have known.

In the summer of 1984, I was accepted to the Chautauqua tour, a movement bringing artists, educators, entertainers, and scholars to present on and discuss cultural and social issues. I would tour one week in two communities in Kansas, Nebraska, South Dakota, and North Dakota—a total of eight weeks around the country—and perform a character sketch of my great-grandfather that included his experiences with being exiled from his homeland and coming to the Dakota territory, as well as stories and songs from his time.

This was the impetus I needed to take the leap of faith required to leave my full-time job. I moved to a freelance lifestyle from that point on, and I have never looked back.

10

I met Lauretta King, something of a patron saint to me, in the 1980s. She served on the Continental Board of Counselors, an appointed international body whose members work for the propagation and protection of the Bahá'í Faith. She was deeply invested in her work, and she diffused the divine fragrances to edify everyone she met. She promoted learning in order to improve human character, and she was detached from material things. Her conduct, manners, deeds and words reflected her love for and healthy fear of God.

A member of the Tlingit tribe from Southeastern Alaska, Lauretta had aided in the planning and execution of the Continental Indigenous Council Fire, where she and I first met. Since that time, with characteristic faith and confidence, Lauretta continued to accompany me in many of my efforts as a new Bahá'í. Though I still saw myself as a stay-at-home type, Lauretta created many opportunities for me to travel to Bahá'í communities across the United States and abroad to share the Teachings of Bahá'u'lláh and to support the development of communities. Initially, I perceived Lauretta's cajoling as annoying, but I am grateful now for her persistence; her influence transformed my life.

In 1984 and 1986, Lauretta arranged for me to tour Alaska to meet with Bahá'í communities in cities and villages there. The Bahá'ís of each locality arranged for me to perform in nearby schools and community centers. In October of 1984, I traveled through coastal cities in Alaska, from Nome and Kotzebue to the northern city of Barrow. I toured through more cities in February of 1986, including Juneau, Anchorage, Metlakatla, and Dillingham.

During my time in Alaska, my hosts showed me great hospitality and kindness. In Nome, an elder invited me for a traditional Eskimo meal of raw, frozen walrus and polar bear meats, sliced thin and dipped in seal oil, with frozen greens on the side. For dessert, I was treated to frozen berries blended with fat to make an ice cream. Whenever I stayed with the friends in their homes, we prayed together and shared readings in our own Indigenous languages. One of the local Bahá'ís, Fletcher Bennett, who also served on the Board of Counselors, accompanied me from village to village. A pilot, Fletcher flew me in his small four-seater plane throughout the Alaskan regions.

Artistic exchange was another part of my travels; as I shared the hoop dance and performed the flute, I encountered local art forms. When I toured Alaskan schools, students often performed motion dances, which were traditional to the high Arctic, Inuit, and Yupik area. In these dances, the dancers pantomimed synchronized activities such as berry-picking or a seal hunt to the beat of hide drums. Familiar with this form of motion dance, I was pleasantly reminded of the many hours I had spent with Paul Tiulana, the founding father of the revival of Eskimo music and dance, at the Welcome Center in Anchorage. Folk arts like motion dancing reflect the human spirit's desire to create order, harmony, and beauty. Passed down through generations, these arts become part of our heritage, influenced by the spirits of our ancestors from the heavenly worlds.

While in Anchorage, I was blessed to receive a set of audio recordings of a seminar given by Adib Taherzadeh, a member of the Continental Board of Counselors and author. At the invitation of Counselor Lauretta King, Mr. Taherzadeh had conducted an extensive seminar on the life and teachings of Bahá'u'lláh. Upon my departure, the National Spiritual Assembly of Alaska presented me with a full set of recordings of that seminar. This goldmine of inspiration covered every aspect of the Bahá'í Faith. I still love to listen to these recordings and to read and reread the multivolume set *The Revelation of Bahá'u'lláh* by Adib Taherzadeh. During my long sojourns between gigs over my beloved South Dakota Highways, I became so engrossed in listening that I seemed to pass through wormholes or time warps between venues.

In March, almost immediately following my '86 trip to Alaska, I joined a small group of Bahá'ís from North America and flew down to Colombia to participate in a study of *Reflections on the Life of the Spirit,* the first book of the Ruhi Training Institute. Counselor King had invited each of us to attend the Training Institute. She explained that Ruhi was an exciting advancement in the Bahá'í world. It is a system of education aimed at deepening its participants in the Bahá'í writings while preparing them to carry out acts of service at the grassroots level. The courses of the Training Institute could perhaps be carried out on a global level in the future.

Though I did not quite grasp the implications of this, I was excited. Our training took place at the Instituto Ruhi, a modest facility in Cali nestled in the valley near the Cauca River. The series of courses in the Ruhi Training Institute centered on developing an individual's capacity to serve their community. *Reflections on the Life of the Spirit* focused on developing the spiritual identity of the individual offering service and discovering the "I" in the phrase "I walk a path of service." In our study, we delved into a detailed, methodical study of the Creative Word. We had animated discussions relating to life after death, prayer, and the basic teachings and principles of the Bahá'í Faith. We honed our capacity to share and study prayers with others—a foundational skill for any path of service. I began to see how the material in this first course, though simple, was truly profound; it allowed us, the participants, to become instruments of change within our communities by first learning how to connect others with the Word of God.

The courses of the Training Institute were a well-conceived system, refined and field-tested at the grassroots. I would later realize that this study circle in Cali was the beginning of the spread of the Ruhi Institute all over the world. These courses would be utilized in communities in every continent as means for mobilizing hundreds of thousands of individuals in service to their communities.

At the suggestion of Counselor King, I had brought my performance gear to Colombia with me. After the training, I visited several nearby communities and did performances in schools. I found many parallels with the Indigenous community in Colombia and back home; the native people there had also been marginalized but had resisted the forces of acculturation. It was a truly mestizo culture, more so than anywhere else I had traveled. Nearly everyone I met was of mixed ethnicity.

I did one particularly memorable presentation at the Colegio Bolivar, located on the outskirts of Cali. As I was sharing the significance of the hoop dance with the student body gathered in the auditorium, the deafening whir of choppers interrupted my explanation. Four helicopters burst through the sky above us and landed in a nearby field. Rapid machine gun fire rang outside of the school.

I looked into the stands, where a group of teachers were whispering frantically amongst themselves. "What's going on?" I said into the mic.

One of the teachers at the back held up a piece of paper that read: *Stall while we organize evacuation.*

I nodded. I distinctly recall not being scared; I did not have time. My job was to hold the kids' attention while the staff could organize buses for evacuation. I continued my explanation to the children about the hoop dance as if nothing had happened. When the teachers returned, they guided us outside, where buses were waiting. As I boarded, I realized that I had just held the performance of my lifetime, a life-or-death assignment to prevent mass panic, pandemonium, and chaos.

At the time, political convulsions were wracking the country. A revolutionary group in Colombia was trying to take power, and they had staged a violent coup. When we got back to Cali, I had no trouble returning to the family home where I was staying. The military was too busy squelching insurgents to think about blockades or regulating everyday commutes and traffic. That night, we heard tanks driving through the city and shootouts happening in the streets outside. Out of fear that stray bullets would enter the home, we slept on the floor. This was the height of the revolutionary invasion. A few days later, when the violence settled down, I was able to leave for the United States.

* * *

The July of that same year, after I returned from Colombia, a meeting of the Iqaluit Indigenous Bahá'í Council convened in Baffin Island, with an honored guest: Ruhíyyih Khánum, the wife of Shoghi Effendi. She had been appointed a Hand of the Cause of God by Shoghi Effendi, the Guardian of the Faith, prior to the establishment of the Universal House of Justice, to assist in the propagation and protection of the Faith.

Baffin Island, a special setting for this Council, was an island in the far Northwest close to the Arctic Circle, now known as Nunavit and officially separated from the Northwest Territories. During the summer, the sun never truly set in the island; it shone throughout the day and night. A large group convened that weekend, comprised of members of the local Bahá'í community, as well as Indigenous believers from different provinces of Canada. Recent teaching initiatives had resulted in new declarations, and many of the Bahá'ís gathered were new to the Faith. Much of the conversation during the gathering centered around the illumined spiritual destiny of Native peoples and how the teachings of Bahá'u'lláh could liberate all those who have suffered from oppression and injustices. Numerous traditional activities were held. Kayakers demonstrated the skills of handling a kayak on the open water. I presented the hoop dance as well and developed a cordial rapport with Ruhíyyih Khánum. I believe she found the dance to be inspiring.

During one of the talks Ruhíyyih Khánum gave at the gathering, expert linguist Jacob Partridge gave translations into Inuktitut (the local language of radio, TV, and everyday life), as very few people spoke English. Ruhíyyih Khánum shared details of her numerous travels around the world to meet Indigenous peoples. Whenever she finished a statement, Jacob would speak noticeably longer than she had. Finally, she asked, "How is it, Mr. Partridge, that you seem to be speaking so much longer than I do?"

"Some of the friends have never left their home villages," Jacob replied with humility. "I want them to understand clearly the different places overseas that you are telling us about." Jacob had been doing his best to paint a vivid picture of countries and places the friends at Baffin Island had never even heard about. So many people had never left their home villages, and he wanted them to understand the richness of the stories that Khánum told.

Ruhíyyih Khánum smiled. "Carry on," she said. "I was just curious."

Ruhíyyih Khánum shared information about and stories of Bahá'u'lláh, 'Abdu'l-Bahá, and Shoghi Effendi, and she focused on the importance of teaching native populations. She realized that she was addressing people who may not even know their own history, how they were defeated by white men not because those men were noble and of good character but because they had more material power. She acknowledged that today some white people study the ancient history of Native peoples and admire their accomplishments. The legacy of oppression had left its mark with problems such as poverty, further injustices, lack of education. That is why it was critical to embrace divine teachings. 'Abdu'l-Bahá stated to the Bahá'ís that they must attach great importance to teaching the original inhabitants of North America, for they will become so enlightened through the divine teachings as to illumine the whole earth. She compared this promise of 'Abdu'l-Bahá to a rope put in the hand of one who has fallen into deep water and cannot swim. If that person took hold of the rope, it would pull him or her to safety and have the effect, over time, of saving not only that individual but future generations.

Later that month, Ruhíyyih Khánum traveled to South Dakota. She asked me to serve as a moderator for her presentation at Pine Ridge, where she would be speaking to a group of newly-declared believers. As moderator, I introduced her at this gathering. I felt inadequate, as I knew very little about the station of a Hand of the Cause, but I spoke about our time together at Baffin Island and how friendly and caring she was to all the friends gathered there.

When it was Ruhíyyih Khánum's turn to speak, she offered loving encouragement to the friends who had come. Just as she had in Baffin Island, she shared details of her journeys through Central, South, and North America. She uplifted everyone in attendance by speaking about the special role and destiny of Native people, as envisioned by 'Abdu'l-Bahá.

In late fall of that year, I traveled to London with Waniya and her mother for the Thames River Storytelling Festival. From there, we flew to another storytelling festival just outside of Oslo, Norway. I was thrilled to connect with the Bahá'ís in this region and for the opportunity to visit Bahá'í communities throughout Norway, Sweden, and Finland. I visited with Bahá'ís in Lapland and met with pioneers from the United States who were living there.

I had come to enjoy my busy travel schedule. Though initially, the constant coming and going was a jolt to my system, I found that I loved the challenge of travel. I learned to adapt myself to all sorts of conditions, from the tropics to the arctic to the rainforest. I grew more flexible and patient, and I learned to find contentment when the unexpected happened. Moreover, I gained a glimpse into what it meant to be a world citizen, as I experienced diverse cultures and landscapes and witnessed the undeniable, fundamental oneness of all whom I encountered.

Much of my travel—related to the Faith and otherwise—involved engaging with local Indigenous populations. I felt privileged to discover the interconnectedness between global Indigenous people—to witness the profound similarities in history, in belief, in practices, and in the deep understanding between us, even though we might be from different countries and continents. I felt that it was a glimpse into the unification of mankind, foretold by Bahá'u'lláh

I had a very interesting experience visiting with Sami elders, the Indigenous people of Scandinavia. The Bahá'í International Teaching Center arranged for members of tribal communities throughout the world to have an extended visit to develop stronger bonds of friendship.

One of the interactions I fondly recall is when members of the tribe invited me to join them for a sauna. Inside the small cabin, rocks were heated on a stove. An elder poured watered over the rocks, enveloping the room in steam.

"Would you mind," I asked my friend and translator. "Asking the elders if I can share a prayer and song while we're in the sauna?" My friend turned to the elders and asked them in the Sami language.

The elders began to discuss among themselves. "They want to know why you want to share a prayer," my friend translated.

I shared that back home, when we bring together the four elements— stone, water, fire, and air—we call it iníkağapi, meaning the place where life is created. "In our tradition, when you do this, you also send up a prayer to the Lord of creation."

"What will you pray about?" my friend asked.

I explained that I would pray for all of the people here and that the prayer would also honor our ancestors. I would send a prayer into the four directions, asking that this place be blessed and that those blessings would radiate outward. We would ask the powers of heaven and earth to cleanse and purify us. "The song I hope to sing asks that we are remade and renewed," I said, "and that all is restored to its original sanctity and holiness."

What I shared and the prayer I sang was translated, I noticed the Sami elders became more animated in their discussion. Some began to weep. After a long consultation, my friend turned to me. "The elders are touched by what you have shared." He went on to say that everything I told them matched their ancestral teachings. More than sixty years ago, when these elders were quite young, their grandparents practiced similar prayers to what I had described. They had not heard these teachings for many, many decades.

"Why did they give it up?" I asked.

My friend shared that when the *Southerners,* (the term the Sami use for Scandinavians) arrived, they colonized and imposed their culture and religion upon the Sami. The Southerners ordered them to discontinue their devotional traditions, which they labeled *satanic* and a form of *devil worship.* Those who continued their practices were punished and persecuted. This story was identical to the stories we heard in Indigenous subsistence communities everywhere.

After a couple of weeks in Scandinavia, the hopes of the International Teaching Center—that Indigenous peoples from various parts of the United States and the Sami could share and discover our commonalities— were fulfilled. Close bonds of friendships were indeed forged.

To culminate what had been a year of travels for the Bahá'í Faith, in December I journeyed to New Delhi for the dedication of the Lotus Temple. This event commemorated the completion of the Bahá'í House of Worship on the Indian sub-continent. It was the eighth House of Worship to be constructed. This edifice, a Mashriqu'l-Adhkár, or "dawning place of the mention of God," would be a pivotal point of devotion and service for India, as well as the worldwide Bahá'í community.

The Lotus Temple was ten years in the making. Its construction required the united efforts of thousands of laborers and craftsmen. Many said that building a structure so complex would be impossible in India because of the difficulty of obtaining materials and coordinating logistics within the country's infrastructure. The Bahá'í world eagerly followed the progress of this structure, as year by year, its construction defied the seemingly insurmountable odds that were stacked against it.

Now, to celebrate its opening to the public, tens of thousands of Bahá'ís from around India and the world would gather for several days of artistic presentations, deepenings and talks, and joyous devotion. We would walk through the marvelous gardens and cross the threshold, for the first time, into this edifice of worship and service.

The National Spiritual Assembly of the Bahá'ís of the United States had asked me to serve as one of the representatives from the U.S. Bahá'í community. I had never been to India and felt it was a great blessing to see this country and witness the dedication of this continental Mashriqu'l-Adkhár. Anticipation brimmed inside of me at the thought that I would witness something so truly remarkable.

During my first days in India, my new surroundings shocked me. I had never been to a place like India, with its swarming masses of people and its unbelievable poverty. The city of New Delhi was immense, sprawling. Children approached cars as they curved through crowded roads and begged for money. Men and women in rags slept on the street. New foods—spicy, varied, and delicious—surprised my palate.

A few Bahá'í friends and I hired a car to visit the Taj Mahal before the dedication events. The structure itself was regal and amazing. A marble dome rose from between narrow spires, and designs in crimson, royal blue, and gold adorned every single tile. A tour guide led us through and told us of the history of the immense structure. He shared stories of the ruler who commissioned it, of the enslaved artisans who dedicated their lives to creating ornamentation for this building, and how one story held that their hands were cut off so that they could never replicate the beauty they had created.

What does this place represent? I wondered as I wandered through it. Its beauty was extraordinary but, in my eyes, was marred by the extreme tourism, capitalism, and stories of inhumanity. What a stark contrast I found in the reverence and unity that imbued the Lotus Temple dedication.

To accommodate the scores of Bahá'ís from India who traveled to New Delhi for the Temple dedication, a huge camping village had been set up near the vicinity of the House of Worship. Hundreds—if not thousands—of tents were clustered together, in row after row. People constantly flowed in and out of the camp, and as it was December, the weather was mild, if not chilly, which added to their ease of movement. Several tents held activities for children, while others served food. Though I did not stay at the tent city, I visited often, offering presentations on the hoop dance and classes for the children.

In the days leading up to the main dedication event, the plenary gatherings and activities created a sense of unity, reverence, and joy. They were held at several nearby venues, including the Indira Gandhi Stadium, a massive indoor arena. Artists from around the world offered uplifting performances and presentations, in true celebration of the diversity of the people coming together in one common Faith. Great care had been taken to represent the beautiful arts of every continent. Artistic traditions, reflecting the incredible heritage of arts and crafts from every region of India, were also shared. The Indian vocalists had unique melodies, which resonated particularly with me.

I had been scheduled to contribute to these cultural events and performed the hoop dance and flute in the Indira Gandhi Stadium. This was my largest audience yet; thousands of people filled every row of the stadium. The crowd was enthusiastic and vibrant. Twenty-five years later, when I traveled again to India, I was humbled and touched that many of the Bahá'ís there remembered that performance.

Along with artistic presentations, different speakers elaborated on the significance of the Mashriqu'l-Adkhár and the story of the design and construction of the Lotus Temple. The Temple's architect, Mr. Fariborz Sahba, spoke about the inspiration behind the Lotus Temple. He explained that the lotus flower was a foundational design motif in both Hinduism and Buddhism, as well as numerous other world religions. This flower, he shared, grows from even the most stagnant, foul waters. As it blossoms, it represents purity among degeneration.

The presence of the Hands of the Cause at these plenary gatherings was especially stirring. I met again with Ruhíyyih Khánum, as well as William Sears and Harold Collis Featherstone. The Hands, when they presented, spoke of the significance of the House of Worship (the devotional center) and the Mashriqu'l-Adhkár (the institution as a whole) in the growth and expansion of the Bahá'í Faith. They shared that our collective duty was to love all people and regard them as members of one human family, to celebrate our human diversity, and to teach the Cause of God. In addition, they painted an uplifting vision of the future. The House of Worship, they said, would serve as a devotional center for people of all faiths. The Mashriqu'l-Adhkár would provide social, educational, and health services, such as hospitals, drug dispensaries for the poor, travelers' hospices, and schools for the orphans.

The culminating event, the dedication itself, took place at the heart of the Lotus Temple. Up until that day, not one of us had entered the Temple. When I approached the Temple for the first time that day, along with thousands of other guests, I beheld an edifice unparalleled in its beauty: a lotus flower with white marble petals unfolding from nine sides. Surrounded by nine reflecting pools, the Temple appeared to blossom from the clear water.

On each of the nine sides, nestled beneath the lower petal, nine doors opened into the inner sanctuary. We drew closer to the Temple and passed through these doors into the domed sanctuary, the heart of the Lotus. As I crossed the threshold, I looked upward. Sweeping vaults extended from every side to form a nine-pointed star at the center of the domed ceiling. Slivered rays of natural light shone through thin windows at this center. At its very apex, inscribed on elegant amber tile, was the insignia of the Greatest Name in Arabic: *Ya Bahá'u'l Abhá—O Thou The Glory of the Most Glorious.*

We were quiet, reverent, awestruck. As soon as the Temple filled with people, a large choir gathered at the front of the sanctuary and began to sing beautiful arrangements of the Bahá'í writings in Hindi. This music had been arranged by Ravi Shankar, a prolific Indian musician and composer, especially for the dedication of the Lotus Temple. Readings in many languages as well as prayers for thanksgiving and unity were shared. Every musical piece, every prayer contributed to the heightened reverence and the awareness of the significance of this event. To complete the dedication, Ruhíyyih Khánum spoke, donning a sari and bindi. I felt awash with gratitude to be there. The music, prayers, and talks uplifted my soul. What an incalculable blessing it was for the world to now have this Mashriqu'l-Adhkár. Though I did not know it then, the Lotus Temple would draw millions of visitors in the decades that followed. It would serve as a point of light for the people of India and of the world and would become a center for the glorification of God that offered refuge and peace for all those who entered therein.

11

I met Andres Jachacollo for the first time in 1982 when he came to speak at the nutrition center in Little Eagle. He had come from Bolivia with several others from Panama, Chile, and various parts of Bolivia, as part of the Trail of Light initiative—an effort of the Bahá'í community to reinforce cultural and spiritual connections between the Indigenous people of the Americas. Groups such as Andres' toured throughout Indigenous communities of North and South America and shared their own songs, dances, and stories, while at the same time participating in the traditions of the local Indigenous people. As the main spokesperson of his team, Andres gave presentations on the commonalities among the Indigenous people. I was one of the few Bahá'í in his audience at Little Eagle and was eager to hear his talk.

Though he was short of stature, Andres had a commanding presence. "My dear relatives," he began, beaming out over the crowd. "I have come a long way to see you. I see in the faces of all who have gathered here my own nieces and nephews, my children and grandchildren. Though we have been separated for so long, we are closely related."

"Yet," he continued, "as I look upon you, I see how sad you are. You have suffered greatly in your lives. For generations, your ancestors have suffered and your people have been downtrodden. Your spirits have grown dim."

He paused. "But today—today is a day to rejoice because God has come to lift us up. God has come to restore our dignity and to enable us to become happy. He has come and given us the great task to recreate the world, to bring light, beauty, and happiness to all of mankind. He has

175

given us the task to make the world into a garden. Our ancestors have prayed and hoped for this day to come."

I absorbed his every word, spellbound. I looked around me to see if the others in the audience were as touched by Andres' speech as I was. This man from Bolivia was speaking with such conviction about the experiences of Indigenous people everywhere. His words bore great certitude that the time had come for the redemption of the Indigenous peoples of the Western Hemisphere.

Andres smiled. "Praise be to God that we are here to experience this day and can fulfill our ancestors' dreams. We must now arise and play our part. We must not allow anything to hold us back. We must align ourselves with the most powerful force in creation, the power of God."

Andres was my first introduction to the Trail of Light, an effort rooted in ancient Indigenous spiritual teachings that prophesied the time when the voice of God would return, call out, and summon diverse peoples to reunite. Many who had the privilege to discover and accept the teachings of Bahá'u'lláh believed that His teachings fulfilled these prophecies. After the Continental Indigenous Council Fire, this initiative emerged to foster continued opportunities for cultural and spiritual exchange among Indigenous people across the Western Hemisphere. Participants in the Trail of Light traveled to Indigenous communities of North, South, and Central America. They participated in a cultural and spiritual exchange and shared their own artistic traditions while learning and participating in the traditions of others.

That day I heard Andres speak, I realized the true potency of this movement—the rearranging of the mindset of the different Native peoples to create an understanding and unity not only with the Bahá'ís of different tribes but also within greater Indigenous communities. The true force of this undertaking was a renewing of familial ties, a coming-together that had been foretold for centuries in spiritual teachings from all around the world.

Andres' words impelled me to share what he had done in my community with other communities in the Americas. Soon after I heard him speak, Lauretta King asked me to join a Trail of Light team that would travel to South America. Though I longed to participate in this effort, family priorities kept me from going. Fortunately, several years later, in the summer of

1988, I was asked to travel to Bolivia and Peru with the Trail of Light, and I readily accepted.

In planning for the Trail of Light trip, I made arrangements for my mother to join me. I had sensed for some time that she was interested in the Bahá'í Faith, and as my own home was too small to host Bahá'í gatherings, I often asked my mother if I could host gatherings in her home. She was very supportive and would often sit in on the gatherings I held there.

My mother had spent much of her adult life working in political activism. Though she and her colleagues had achieved victories to improve educational access and cultural preservation for Indigenous people, she abhorred the negativity and divisiveness of politics, with its potential for corruption. Because the Bahá'í teachings offered relief from the political corruption around the world and offered common-sense and progressive teachings, such as the equality of men and women, the eliminations of the extremes of wealth and poverty, and the dismantling of prejudices of all kinds, she was intellectually curious. However, her negative encounters with Christianity had made her cautious when dealing with religion. As a child in Catholic boarding school, my mother disdained the restrictions placed on women within the Church and the persecution of Indigenous culture, including its spiritual practices, within the school. During her career, she had endeavored to create an awareness of and preserve North American Indigenous spiritual heritage, and she had worked tirelessly to dispel the prevailing view of Indigenous culture as satanic. She feared that the Faith was another organized religion that would ultimately oppress Indigenous people.

We had many conversations in which I shared how the Faith affirms Indigenous spirituality. I shared with her the Bahá'í writings, and when I was elected as a delegate to the National Convention, the yearly gathering for the election of the National Spiritual Assembly, my mother attended as my guest. There, she saw how Bahá'ís advocated for justice and the elimination of prejudice. She met individuals such as Dorothy Nelson, a federal judge on the United States Court of Appeals for the Ninth Circuit. Lauretta King and other Indigenous Bahá'ís also left an exemplary impression on my mother.

Though the formal English utilized in the Bahá'í writings initially reminded her of Christian scripture, which she had seen misappropriated for unjust purposes, my mother eventually developed a deep attraction to the writings of the Faith. As an educator and writer, she appreciated the eloquent usage of words. Being the great researcher that she was, she delved into the teachings on social justice and the Administrative Order.

After many months, the possibility that my mother would become a Bahá'í occurred to me, and I began concocting plans to fan the flame of her interest. A trip to Bolivia and Peru would be the perfect opportunity for her to encounter other Indigenous Bahá'í populations. When I invited her to make the trip with me, she readily accepted.

At the start of our journey, we flew into Santa Cruz, Bolivia. We were prepared with a basic itinerary: a tour of cities, towns, and remote villages across Bolivia and Peru, where we would build relationships and participate in cultural exchanges with the Indigenous groups living there. Throughout our tour, we would be accompanied by Sabino Ortega, who served as an Auxiliary Board Member—an assistant to the Counselor, supporting the propagation and protection of the Faith—for that region. Sabino was a prominent, respected Indigenous man, who provided us with Quechua translations. Dr. Eloy Anello, founder of University Nur, served as Counselor for the area and accompanied us throughout Bolivia and served as our Spanish translator. Our team consisted of Jacqueline Left Hand Bull (then Delahunt), Randy Chipps-Dihtidaht from Western Vancouver Island, Phil Lane, Jr., Dakota / Choctaw from Washington State, my mom, and me.

We traveled first to towns near Santa Cruz, in the lowlands east of the Andes Mountains, bordering the Amazon. Many of these villages housed Quechua communities, as well as large refugee communities from remote Amazonian tribes. Prospectors, seeking gold and natural resources, had invaded their homeland in the Amazon. Miners, poachers, and loggers too came to exploit the forest's natural resources. Their tactics were often ruthless and violent, causing whole communities from the Amazon to flee their homes and settle in refugee communities, such as the ones near Santa Cruz. These Indigenous communities went from living off the abundant natural resources of the rainforest to living in poverty.

During our visit to Santa Cruz, we met with the chief of one of these communities. He could not speak Spanish, but his grandson translated for him. He told us how his people had foreseen this catastrophe—the loss of their homeland—for centuries. "It may seem as though we lived in blissful ignorance, but even as we made our homes in the forest, under God's provisions, we anticipated the foreign invasion. Our people's only salvation," he explained, "was to elude Western civilization for as long as possible." They knew that contact with the invaders would surely result in death. Despite his disheveled appearance and impoverished living conditions, he maintained a regal bearing and dignified composure. He was eager to find solutions to his community's desperate plight.

The chief looked around at us sitting there and said, "What had been the prophecy of the past is the reality of our lives." He explained how, as a child, he had heard from his elders the same warning to avoid contact with civilization. He benefited from the cornucopia of resources the Amazon provided them. As he moved into a leadership position in his community, the chief realized that the encroachment of outside civilization was fast approaching and that, to avoid the threat of their community being torn apart by violence, they would have to leave their homeland. He led his people out of their pristine environment, and they started new lives in the lowest margins of society. Now, in their community, his people faced new horrors: substance abuse, prostitution, slavery, and poverty.

"We need to make our way out of this darkness," the chief said. "We must find a new path of salvation."

We thanked him for sharing with us. As representatives of the Bahá'í community, we spoke with him about the Faith and about the Bahá'í children's classes that were being held in his community.

He listened carefully. "I don't know if the Bahá'í Faith is our solution," he said afterward. "But I'm grateful for the positive relations we have with the Bahá'ís." We ended our meeting with this seed of hope: that though challenges overwhelmed his people, we were one outside group with whom they could connect and collaborate. Other community leaders whom we met with were not as hopeful.

After our time in Santa Cruz, we traveled through the Andes Mountains to Sucre, then to La Paz, stopping along the way to visit several villages. We drove through precarious mountain passages—roads that curved around high peaks, with no guardrails and thousand-foot drops. My mother was terrified. With each sharp turn around the mountain, she prayed we would not encounter a vehicle driving in the opposite direction.

Quechua was the only language spoken in many of the places we visited. Just as numerous Romance languages emerged from Latin after the fall of the Roman Empire, Quechua—the language of the Inca Empire—morphed into several mutually unintelligible languages and regional dialects after the fall of the Inca Empire in 1520. Along the Andes of South America, these languages continued to develop after the Inca Empire dispersed. The Inca highway system was the means by which the empire was able to impose its influence and language throughout the region. The Spanish colonization process served to de-civilize the population. It isolated them from each other and relegated them to enslavement and the lower margins of survival. Spanish was the language of the ruling class. Since Spanish colonial power never implemented an educational system for the rural majority, most of the people in the mountains and villages of Bolivia and Peru spoke only their own language. Throughout our travels, we relied on translators to communicate with the people we met.

As Quechua was Sabino's first language, he translated eloquently for us. At each new village, he elaborated at great length to our hosts about the purpose of our visit. He spoke about the spiritual connection between the Indigenous people of the Western hemisphere and how our visit was symbolic of the dawn of a new day, in which the ingathering of diverse people would be realized. We had come to share the spiritual and artistic practices that connected the North American Indigenous people with Indigenous people of South America and to build ties of friendships in order to establish the reality of our unification in the hearts and minds of both peoples.

We connected with the Indigenous people we met through translation and even more powerfully through the language of the spirit, which permeated all of our gatherings. We relished the opportunities to share music and dancing traditions with the Inca descendants and to learn of their culture and history. Just as I shared North American Indigenous flute traditions, I admired the unique Indigenous flute traditions of South America. The primary flute here was a pan pipe, or *sampona* in Quechua, and typically consisted of forty bamboo tubes bound together. In a village we visited, people divided the instrument into individual tubes and gave a tube to each villager. Each person could play one note; together, the community could play a song. One by one, the villagers played the notes of a beautiful melody. I was struck by this—that no one or two outstanding musicians stood out from the crowd. No one was excluded from sharing their music.

This kind of equal, universal participation created a marvelous feeling of unity and inclusion.

In one village, I played flute music for a few community members. As I started to play, I noticed four large black birds overhead, circling closer and closer. They were Andean Condor birds, the largest flying bird on the planet, and they were distinguished by their vast wingspan and the ring of white feathers around their necks. Mountain birds, they soared indefinitely on the updrafts, typically flying so high that they remained out of the sight of the villagers. But as I played on, the condors flew closer. Even the birds, it seemed, connected with us through music.

As we worked our way to Sucre and then on toward La Paz, we entered higher and higher elevations. Sucre was over eight thousand feet above sea level. We stayed there for a few days and were hosted by Bahá'í families. This was our midpoint to La Paz, and staying here helped adjust our bodies to the increasing altitude. The capital of Bolivia, La Paz, was the highest capital city in the world, at almost twelve thousand feet above sea level.

The high elevation challenged our tour group. We could no longer breathe at a normal rate but instead had to reprogram our breathing to accommodate the low oxygen levels and low air pressure. The Indigenous people, we learned, had developed special physical adaptations—including greater lung capacity and a special type of blood consistency—in order to survive the lower levels of oxygen. Unused to the high elevation, I found my mind frequently wandering and my energy levels waning. My heart often raced, and I had to hyperventilate to reoxygenate my system. Fortunately, my mom had made the ultimate sacrifice of abstaining from cigarettes for the entirety of this trip.

In La Paz, I had the pleasure of meeting the Uladihs, an Iranian couple who had been among the initial pioneers to Bolivia and who had taught Andres Jachacollo the Faith. The Uladihs welcomed us to their home for dinner. After I shared that Andres had come to South Dakota as a part of the Trail of Light initiative, the Uladihs told me the story of how they first met Andres and introduced him to the Faith.

When they had first moved to La Paz, the Uladihs had begun trying to share the Bahá'í Faith but had met with little success. They held several public meetings about the Faith, which only a very few interested people attended. Despite the lack of response, the Uladihs persisted. Once, they posted flyers advertising another of their public meetings about the Faith. At the meeting time, no one showed up, but just before they were about to leave, Andres knocked on the door of the meeting room.

"I'm here," he said, "because of what it said on the flyers—that the Voice of God is summoning humanity to His Kingdom." Pleased, the Uladihs invited Andres to return the following week. He promised to return and to bring others to hear this message. That week, Andres spread the word about the Uladihs' meeting to his community. Three thousand people accompanied him to the second meeting to learn about Bahá'u'lláh and the Bahá'í Faith.

The Uladihs explained that Andres had recognized the message of Bahá'u'lláh as a response to the Great Walkers movement of the mid-1800s. The Great Walkers movement was inspired by the runners of the Inca era who had traversed the historic highway system of that empire and had carried messages from the far ends of the continent. The Great Walkers, too, felt they had the responsibility to relay a divine message to the people of South America. They believed that the voice of God would soon resound on earth and would herald a new message for their people, the descendants of the Inca who, for generations, had been subjected to slavery, poverty, and oppression. The Great Walkers traveled across the continent and encouraged people to break the chains of subjugation and to spiritualize themselves so they could recognize the new message for this day. They emphasized the importance of unity among the Native peoples of the continent, as they believed it was the will of God for their region to be unified in order to hear His message.

Many years passed. The Great Walkers continued their work but never received the anticipated divine message. Eventually, many turned to the influence of the sweeping political and military movements of the region. Slowly, the teachings of the Great Walkers began to fade but were not forgotten.

Because of the labor and toil of the Great Walkers, many were ready to respond to the message of the Bahá'í Faith. Nearly all three thousand of the people who attended that meeting, including Andres, accepted the Faith of Bahá'u'lláh. They saw this Message as the one that, for generations, they had been eagerly awaiting. The Great Walkers had prepared the way.

Before them, the Inca had, in creating their road system, begun to connect disparate communities and villages and had laid the foundation for the unification of the people.

From La Paz, we traveled to Lago Titicaca. Like an inland sea, the cobalt waters stretched between green peaks of Bolivia and Peru. Huge boats hauled cargo back and forth across the lake, alongside smaller reed canoes made by Uro Indigenous people. The Uro lived in floating villages, built upon extensive reed rafts. Dozens and dozens of these reed islands drifted close to the shore of the lake. Small reed huts lined the islands. Taking in all these incredible new sights overwhelmed and exhilarated me.

When we were invited to these villages to share meals, I marveled at the variety of unique foods and the horticultural genius of the people who served dozens and dozens of different types of potatoes in every size and shade of purple, orange, pink, and white. The villagers seemingly had infinite ways of preparing the potatoes, my favorite of which was a potato dip with green peanuts and spices. For the first time, I also tried guinea pig, a staple meat in these regions and one I found very delicious.

Because of his connection with the Native communities, Sabino opened extraordinary opportunities for us. As we journeyed into Peru, we visited places and met people a tourist could only dream of meeting. In particular, we attended special traditional gatherings and meetings with leaders of the Indigenous communities. We stopped in local Bahá'í radio stations that broadcast in Native languages, including Aymara and Quechua. These stations provided information and news for the non-Spanish-speaking communities, who were otherwise underserved. These stations also sponsored music festivals in order to promote local culture, music, and dance. In several villages, we also had the opportunity to visit Bahá'í primary and secondary schools, which served the local communities, to learn Quechua songs and dances and teach some of our own.

In Peru, we saw incomprehensible Inca architecture. Boulders that easily weighed several tons were stacked and carved on top of each other, towering several stories in the air. The stones fit together like a jigsaw puzzle. The tourists visiting these sites seemed as small as ants compared to these juggernauts.

During the latter part of our trip, my mother, Jaqueline Left Hand Bull, and I took a break day to explore one of the earth's great treasures. One of my mother's lifelong dreams was to visit the famous lost city of the Incas,

Machu Picchu, first discovered by people of European descent in the early 1900s. One of my fond memories of the day occurred as we rode the tour bus up the mountain and back. Children who had run through the hills to each of the twenty switchbacks chanted and sang good-bye to us at switchback one, switchback two, and switchback three all the way to the twentieth switchback. They received some tips for their energy and performance.

Upon departing the bus, we took in the view of the foothills of the Andes mountains, felt awe gazing at the vast Amazon basin, and began our hike, with Sabino and a group of Quechua Bahá'ís leading us through these hallowed precincts. As we walked, I reflected on how this site represented the unshakeable foundation that our ancestors had laid for us, the future generations, to arise and regain our divine nobility. Our guides paused at the *Intihuatana*, telling us that this was a stone where the Inca held special ceremonies to harness the power of the sun. The stone was considered a point of connection to the spiritual worlds. Right then and there, they offered special prayers and songs for that sacred place This moment was very poignant, and I felt privileged to participate in it. Indeed, throughout the remainder of the tour, we paused often to pray and connect with all the ancestors there.

Of all the villages we visited in Bolivia and Peru, the small mountain community of Miskipampa held a significant place in my heart, especially for the profound impact its people had on my mother. Miskipampa means *sweet plain* in Quechua. A clear spring ran close to the village situated on the flatlands in the mountains. The people of Miskipampa supported themselves by growing numerous strains of potato and corn and by raising domesticated animals, large rodents, llamas, and alpacas. Many of these families were members of the Bahá'í Faith. Though they were considered to be among the poorest Indigenous people materially, we regarded them as unbelievably wealthy because of the spirit of cooperation and love that pervaded their village.

We arrived in Miskipampa after midnight. The road only went part way up the mountain; we had to leave our car and walk the rest of the way. We walked for many minutes with only the stars for light; no electricity or modern conveniences guiding our way. Ahead, we saw small flickering lights. As we drew closer, we realized that the people of Miskipampa had lined the pathway leading to their village. Candles glowed from within the paper bags they held. We walked along this path of light, grateful to have left the darkness and brimming with anticipation for what lay ahead.

At the entrance of the village, we passed under an archway of woven branches. The entire village had arisen and come out to greet us at this early hour. The entire land was filled with the light of the brilliant flames of the candles they held. I was moved beyond words by their hospitality. My travel companions and I had entered a community of spiritual connection and unity. The moment we walked beneath that archway, we transitioned from being strangers to relatives of Miskipampa.

Each of the village members, as we approached them, looked in our eyes with the utmost tenderness and embraced us. They placed their left cheek on our right cheek and then their right cheek on our left. "Alláh'u'abhá," they said. This greeting, used among the Bahá'ís of the world, means "God is most Glorious" in Arabic. We walked from village member to village member. Each person embraced us as family and lovingly greeted us with "Alláh'u'abhá."

My mother, who did not yet consider herself a Bahá'í, began to reciprocate the loving greeting back to our hosts. "Alláh'u'abhá," she replied after each embrace. "Alláh'u'abhá." At the end of this long procession, this warm and phenomenal welcome, her association with the pure-hearted people of Miskipampa opened her own heart and mind more completely to the teachings of Bahá'u'lláh. That night, she gave her heart to Bahá'u'lláh, even though her official declaration occurred upon our return to the United States.

12

In Fall of 1989, a year after my tour with Trial of Light, I was asked to join Ruhíyyih Khánum on a tour through China for a goodwill visit that would take her from rural villages to the offices of government leaders. My daughter, Kim, and I would accompany her, along with several others. We would have the opportunity to share presentations of music and hoop dance at these different venues. Though I did not believe I had much to contribute, I was honored to have been asked to join this tour.

The year prior to the tour with Ruhíyyih Khánum, I had traveled extensively around the United States, Mexico, Panama, Scandinavia, and the Soviet Union to visit Bahá'í communities and participate in teaching efforts, especially among Indigenous populations. In January of 1989, my mother, Jacqueline Left Hand Bull, and I traveled throughout Yucatan, from Merida to Muna. Prior to our visit, the local Bahá'ís had engaged in extensive mass-teaching efforts that led to huge enrollments in the Mayan villages in this area. We visited these villages, where we visited these kind, eager souls and deepened their understanding of the history and teachings of the Bahá'í Faith.

While we were there, we visited Chichen Itza and Tikal, two of the archeological sites of the Maya civilization. In Chichen Itza, I saw the representation of the Lord of Dawn. This stone carving of a face with intricate designs radiating around it paralleled petroglyphs I had seen in Wakpala. I found it fascinating that similar images could be shared by Indigenous people from South America to the Plains States.

Shortly after our return from Mexico, I flew out to the western mountains of Panama to attend the inauguration of a new Bahá'í Center as a representative of the North American Bahá'í community. There, I was eager to learn about the Ngäbe people who had lived in that region for centuries. As part of their colonization of Panama in the sixteenth century, the Spanish carried out numerous campaigns to exterminate Indigenous people. To survive this onslaught, some Indigenous groups fled to the jungle, others went to the islands, while the Ngäbe sought refuge in the mountains.

Back home in the United States, I joined Fuad Akhtar-Khavari in his teaching work with Native communities. Born in Iran and having immigrated to the United States as a young man, Fuad was undeterred in his efforts to work with Indigenous people. He organized a trip for us to visit Native communities in Oklahoma, to meet with the prominent leaders of different tribes, and to share the Peace Statement written by the Universal House of Justice with them.

Around that time, I was shocked to be elected to the National Spiritual Assembly of the Bahá'ís of the United States. I had spent much of my time visiting Bahá'í communities around the world; this change would bring me closer to the Bahá'ís of my home country.

In July of that year, my son Ohiyes'a and I went together to Stockholm; from there, we journeyed through the northernmost parts of Norway and Finland to visit various Sami communities. We would then travel with some of the Sami friends to Murmansk, Russia, for the first major Bahá'í proclamation event in that country and for a reunion of the Indigenous people of that region. The Sami native lands expanded from Norway, Sweden, and Finland up through a small corner of far northeastern Russia; however, due to the tense political situation in the Soviet Union, the Sami living in Scandinavia had been unable to visit their kin who lived in the Soviet Union, until now.

We had been given a large collection of holy writings that had been newly translated into Russian, including The Hidden Words, *Gleanings from the Writings of Bahá'u'lláh*, and The Kitáb-i-Íqán. We drove on a road built during World War II that stretched from Finland into Russia, which had been blockaded for decades but was recently opened. At the border, our car was stopped by a Russian patrol guard, who attempted to confiscate the Bahá'í literature that we were bringing over. Thankfully, Paul Semenoff

of Dukabor heritage—a persecuted religious group of Russian origin—
spoke fluent Russian, even though he had lived in Canada most of his
life. At the time of our trip, he served on the Board of Counselors for this
region,and he persuaded the border guard to let us take a sampling of each
text into Russia. The guard confiscated the rest of the books but permitted
us to take a few copies of the texts and make our way toward Murmansk.
As we drove along a derelict gravel road, we noticed guard towers lining our
path. Inside them, Russian officials armed with machine guns loomed over
us. Every square inch was under strict surveillance, and it left us with an
ominous feeling about going into this country.

Murmansk was a stark place, comprised of austere, dark, concrete-block
buildings, with everything uniform. The festival we had come for, however,
was a joyous contrast to the bleak atmosphere of the city. Sami people who
had been separated for generations reunited. Tribal people from around the
region were in attendance, which led to a beautiful cultural exchange. People of all ethnicities living in Murmansk came out to learn about the Bahá'í
Faith. There, in a public square, we shared the writings of Bahá'u'lláh for
the first time. Though we had only few copies of each text, a contingent
of Russians volunteered to transcribe these holy works and immediately
began copying the Hidden Words—that concise, yet potent volume—in
their own hand. I had never seen so clearly people thirsting for religious
truth. Eighty people enrolled in the Bahá'í Faith on the spot, so drawn were
they to these writings.

This experience left a significant impression in my mind, with vivid
memories that I have held onto for decades. My son, on the other hand,
was not left with the same positive impression. He disliked the Soviet Union
because of the plain food, the borscht, and the stale bread and cheese. He
struggled to get to sleep each night because the sun did not ever truly set.
I rotated taking my children on trips with me. Since the trip to the Soviet
Union left such a negative impression on him, the next time Ohiyes'a's turn
came up—a two-month trip to Asia and the Pacific Islands—he turned it
down, saying he did not trust me after Russia. Kim happily took the trip
in his stead and reported to him afterward that he missed the "trip of a
lifetime."

When we returned to Finland from Murmansk, we encountered the
same guard at the border and discovered that he had read the copies of the

Bahá'í writings that we had left behind. "These writings are so beautiful," he told Paul with great animation. "Our people have been in the dark for so many years. These writings are like pure light—they are exactly what our country needs!"

In September of 1989, Kim and I flew to Hong Kong. There, we met Ruhíyyih Khánum; Violette Nakhjavani, her frequent travel companion; and Farzam Kamalibadi, a Persian man who had been living in China for many years and would serve as our translator, especially in the rural areas where few people spoke English. We visited with the Bahá'í community, a well-established and active group of believers. The prospect of hosting Ruhíyyih Khánum was a great honor for them, as she was the last member of the holy family and a Hand of the Cause. When we attended community events, she was lovingly received and admired for her regal bearing and commanding presence.

After a few short days in Hong Kong, we traveled by train to Guangzhou, our first major stop in mainland China, as Hong Kong was not considered a part of the mainland. Unlike the megacities and metropolis of China today, Guangzhou was part of the old China. Compared to the sea of bicyclists that traversed the roads, only a few motorized vehicles drove down the streets. No skyscrapers dotted the horizon, though much construction was underway, still carried out through wheelbarrows, shovels, and picks.

From there, we journeyed to Zhongxing, Chengdu, and Gui Zhou, along with several other cities and villages near each locality. We traveled mostly by air across long distances and took minivans, trains, and boats for shorter trips. In each place, I loved sampling the local cuisines and discovered that Ruhíyyih Khánum also enjoyed it. We visited numerous markets where she tried the food and purchased beautiful art objects— statues, enamelware, porcelain, paintings, and musical instruments. Years later, when I went on pilgrimage and visited the house of 'Abdu'lláh Pashá, I noticed much décor from China. Certain objects looked familiar. I did not ask, but I felt certain some of the art had been purchased by Ruhíyyih Khánum on our tour.

During our travels through mainland China, Ruhíyyih Khánum was scheduled to meet with political and government officials. Because I accompanied her to these meetings, I noticed how she employed tact, diplomacy, composure, and finesse as these high-ranking officials vied for her. Like an air traffic controller guiding aircraft through the atmosphere at hundreds of miles per hour, she enabled the planes to take off and land safely and prevented them from colliding.

At the beginning of each meeting, she usually explained that her visit was a courtesy call and that she had come from the World Center of the Bahá'í Faith to visit the Bahá'ís of this country. We were an apolitical and nonpartisan people, well-wishers of the government and obedient to its laws, she shared. She spoke with them about China's heritage, history, and the great role destined for China in the future world civilization. She emphasized that China's significance was not based on politics or power but rather on the spiritual destiny of the land and its people.

Many of the officials we met with held lavish banquets in Ruhíyyih Khánum's honor. Thirty-course meals were served, with ornate dishes served on rotating platters at the center of the tables. Ruhíyyih Khánum enjoyed the local cuisine and the fine dishes served, but she did not hesitate in showing her irritation at the amount of waste produced at these events. So much uneaten food and cutlery that had been used only once was thrown away after these dinners.

She chided her hosts: "All this food is going to waste! And all these disposable chopsticks! Surely you can reuse these."

The powerful men turned sheepish at her remarks.

I smiled to myself whenever this happened; waste was a pet peeve of mine as well.

As we left the cities of China and traveled to rural villages and towns, I witnessed Ruhíyyih Khánum's dignity, humility and kindness in her dealings with Indigenous and minority peoples. "[During her travels] she rarely missed the opportunity to validate people in far-flung and remote places whom few had heard of and whose simple actions none might ever know," wrote Violette years later in *A Tribute to Amatu'l-Bahá Ruhíyyih Khánum*.* In all my travels throughout the world, no matter how remote or how difficult a place was to reach, I would undoubtedly discover that Ruhíyyih Khánum had been there before me. She sacrificed luxury and personal comfort to spend time among the dispossessed, the marginalized, the downtrodden,

---

* Violette Nakhjavani, *A Tribute to Amatu'l-Bahá Ruhíyyih Khánum*, p. 213.

the Indigenous, and the minority peoples of the world. She championed those that the world had scorned. Shortly before my mother passed away, she had the distinct honor of representing the American Bahá'í community at the funeral of Ruhíyyih Khánum in Haifa, Israel. I remember my mother had lamented after the funeral: *Who will represent the Indigenous people now that Khánum is gone?*

I was grateful to personally observe how Ruhíyyih Khánum made a point to spend much of her time in rural villages and towns. The Han, the majority group in China and the world's largest ethnic group, had conquered and colonized the minority populations in the rural villages and towns. One in five people on the planet are Han, and nearly ninety-two percent of people in China are Han.* Tens of millions of Han live in surrounding countries throughout the world. The "Hanification" of the rural populations, along with the development of large cities in China in the twentieth century, homogenized many elements of culture, including dress and language, and relegated traditional practices to the margins.

We visited the villages of the Miao and Buyi people and learned about their cultural way of life. Ruhíyyih Khánum observed how the people lived, the intricacies of their artwork, the designs of their clothing and architecture, and their music and dance. She held meetings with different village councils to share with them, in her own inimitable way, the Bahá'í Faith and the promise of the Revelation of Bahá'u'lláh to their community life. She was very much in tune with the people themselves and met them with abiding love and compassion. I saw how admired she was by all whom she met, whether they were the mothers, farmers, or village leaders, and how, in turn, she demonstrated great respect for each individual.

The lifestyle of the minority communities differed greatly from the culture we experienced in China's cities. These rural communities were distinctive because of their communal lifestyle. Each clan or kinship relation had their own longhouse. In Guiyong and Yunan, I noticed how distinctive these structures—beautifully constructed from wood—were. Longhouses also served as community centers, where the people gathered for their devotional practices, meetings, and special events. Terraces were built

---

* Amanda Lilly, A Guide to China's Ethnic Groups, Washington Post, July 8, 2009, http://www.washingtonpost.com.

along the mountainside for harvesting grains. In the Buyi community, we saw farmers plowing their fields with oxen. The dead were buried on the hilltops, with little houses over the graves.

In one of the remote villages, as a group of locals were walking with us along a path, we stumbled across what many might consider the largest, ugliest, and dirtiest pig, in the middle of the road, blocking our way. Some of the people in the group even shrieked and recoiled at the sight of the pig. Ruhíyyih Khánum, however, continued toward the pig, picking a bouquet of wildflowers as she approached him. As dirty as he was, the pig was beautiful in his own way. He had strength and power—a fine specimen representing his species. Flowers in hand, Ruhíyyih Khánum addressed the pig with tenderness. "Don't pay attention to the others; they are just startled. We're here visiting your village and aren't trying to disturb you. I can see that you're a proud, good pig." She offered the pig the flowers.

The combination of the kindness of her voice and the taste of the flowers caused the pig to relax. It let out a big sigh, then wandered away, allowing us to pass. The incident made me laugh; I was impressed by Ruhíyyih Khánum's ability to connect with all creatures great and small.

In other villages outside of Chengdu, we were given a tour through a local monastery. Displayed in the sanctuary were hundreds of miniature figurines representing the apostles of Buddhism. These figurines depicted a diverse range of human physical features—they were tall, short, bald, obese, emaciated. Some of the figures were deformed, hunchbacked, or missing eyes or legs. They were every conceivable shape and size. Yet all were saints.

Struck by the different characteristics of the figurines, I wondered if the diversity of human physical types mirrored humankind's diversity of spiritual strengths and weaknesses. The divine revelation of Buddha— and later, Bahá'u'lláh—required that each of us bring forth our unique qualities and virtues. Every person has a place, a unique contribution. To this day, whenever I catch myself thinking that a person should be acting differently, I remember these sculptures and that God has created us all for different purposes.

Throughout the tour in China, as Ruhíyyih Khánum met with community leaders, Kim and I gave different presentations of traditional dance and music. Bahá'ís in each locality arranged for us to perform in schools and different community organizations. As much of the population spoke no English, I limited my explanations of the hoop designs and dance. Farzam helped translate what little explanation I gave; he quickly learned the nuances of our presentation and could eloquently express the themes of the dance. I always hoped that our dance and music, however, transcended words and touched the spirits of those present.

Kim and I often performed as part of a cultural exchange; as we shared dance and music, local performing artists also shared presentations of traditional music and dance. The performers wore colorful traditional outfits of silk and satin, embellished with fine embroidery. They shared their arts with great pride, and I was in awe of their talent.

Each day in China was a barrage of fantastic experiences. Even the simplest activities took on added significance for me on this trip. Every morning, just before dawn, I went for a walk in whatever province or town we were visiting. In the cities, I often saw people gathered for tai chi in the park, even in that early hour. As we traveled toward the southern interior, I enjoyed gazing at the mountains, with their dark, rocky summits shrouded in mist.

On one walk, as the sun rose, I saw an eagle high above soar from out of the peaks. The eagle skimmed the skies toward our hotel. It approached the building and circled round it—once, twice, then a third and fourth time. As I watched the majestic bird, a thought struck me: Ruhíyyih <u>Kh</u>ánum was inside this hotel. The bird made its circles in adoration, circumambulating the spot where this significant figure rested. After its fourth arc round the hotel, it flew back to the mountains whence it came. A watercolor depiction of the same mountains behind the hotel caught my attention when I traveled to Haifa, Israel for my pilgrimage. While visiting the home of 'Abdu'lláh Páshá and noticing familiar Chinese art, the painting caught my eye. I drew closer to look at it and saw, positioned right next to the painting, a golden statue of an eagle.

13

My next visit to China in March of 2014 was organized by Arts Midwest, an arts advocacy organization that fosters artistic exchange and collaboration. They brought artists from around the world to tour in the Midwest and often arranged for Midwestern artists to perform abroad. During my tour in China, I performed the hoop dance at venues that were many and varied—grade schools, university classes, festivals, parks, and villages. I engaged with local artists and specifically visited underserved and minority Chinese populations in the Yunan Province.*

We first visited Kunming, the "City of Eternal Spring," the capital of the Yunnan Province. Three million people of diverse ethnicities inhabited this city—making it a small city in China. Not a cloud dotted the bright sky on my first morning there. On my morning walk, I passed through several busy roadways, with cars honking and zipping every which way. This was a stark contrast to my 1989 visit to China—at the time of my tour with Khánum, I had seen oceans of bicyclists and pedestrians flooding the streets, but I had noticed few automobiles. Still, twenty-five years later, the air of Kunming was fresh and sharp, especially in contrast to Beijing and Shanghai.

---

* There were over fifty minority groups in China, and they ranged in population from a handful of people to tens of millions. This was still tiny in comparison to the majority group, the Hans, which comprised nearly 20% of the world's population.

Walking allowed me to more fully explore Kunming and understand the people. I enjoyed discovering this small, beautiful city with its wide avenues, green public spaces, and rich sense of community life. At the foot of our hotel, a huge park with a promenade encircled the central lake. Families walked amidst the greenery and threw bread to the swarming gulls. Elders sat at chess tables. Large groups practiced tai chi exercises in sync.

The diversity of the people gathered there surprised me. Though I saw many people of Han ethnicity, I also spotted individuals from many different Chinese ethnic groups, as well as foreigners from India, the Middle East, and Europe. As a result, I blended in more during this particular trip than I had during the tour with Khánum when people had stopped to stare at my height, which was average in North America but heads and shoulders above the Chinese masses. For this trip, however, my braid was my only distinguishing feature.*

My second tour in China coincided with the nineteen-day Bahá'í fast. Held in early March, this fast was one of my favorite devotional practices. It required those of mature age and good health to abstain from food and drink between the hours of sunrise to sunset, for nineteen consecutive days. 'Abdu'l-Bahá, son of Bahá'u'lláh, wrote, "This material fast is an outer token of the spiritual fast; it is a symbol of self-restraint, the withholding of oneself from all appetites of self, taking on the characteristics of the spirit, being carried away by the breathings of heaven and catching fire from the love of God."** When I first learned about the Bahá'í Faith, I began to observe the fast and found joy in the discipline and awe in its potential to spiritualize the individual and transform communities.

The long distance and duration of my travel—not to mention the intense physical activity of performing—offered me exemption from the fast, but it was hard to imagine forgoing fasting. Though I was slightly disappointed that this trip coincided with the dates of my fasting, my sense of humor kicked in. I imagined that when I died, God might question

---

* The Lakota people first encountered Chinese people during the construction of the transcontinental railroad in the 1860s. The Chinese workers all wore their hair in a single braid down their backs; thus the Lakota gave the Chinese the name *Phečhókaŋ Háŋska*, or "Long Center Braid People."

** 'Abdu'l-Bahá, *Selections from the Writings of 'Abdu'l-Bahá*, no. 35.2.

me—*You mean, you fasted in the wilderness for four days and nights without food or water—and you've observed the four consecutive days and nights of the Sundance, but you can't fast from sunup to sundown because you traveled to dance in China? You, go to hell!*

The thought made me laugh and inspired me to participate in the fast for some of my stay in China, starting with the next day for a meeting at the Kunming College of Professional Arts. This college served national minorities, mostly from the Yunnan province. It offered courses in literature, creative writing, and visual and performing arts, with specific focus on the forms of expression originating from Yunnan. I went with two others who were part of the tour organized by Arts Midwest—Monica Raphael, an Ojibwe master traditional artist; and Edmond Nevaquaya, her partner and a gifted flute player, dancer, singer, and storyteller—a friend I had known since the late 1970s.*

After meeting the director of the college, we visited a textile design class, which taught young people to create the regalia of various regional ethnic groups. The instructors, who were master traditional artists, taught their students how to craft each regalia, as well as the history and symbolism behind the colors and design.

The three of us gave our presentations to the students. Monica kept the students spellbound with her eloquent explanations of Indigenous North American regalia-making and demonstrations of beadwork designs and quillwork. And Edmond had never looked so sharp; his dance regalia included applique beadwork. Monica, an expert at applique work, made sure that his regalia was perfect and not a bead was out of place.

The director prepared a huge banquet—a thirty-course affair—for us. Before the dinner, I slipped away to finish making fifteen incomplete flutes I had brought especially for this event. That evening, we performed alongside an incredibly talented young sister / brother duo from the local Yi tribe that had taken their traditional folk music to a mainstream popular

---

* I remember seeing Edmund around South Dakota at various powwows during the 1970s. He sat with the elder singers and revealed his vocal virtuosity. During these occasions, I also became well-acquainted with his father, the world-famous Comanche artist, historian, and flute player, Doc Tate Nevaquaya.

culture audience. Since it was all about folk arts, we did our part to represent North America. I have always believed that one can learn volumes about a culture through their traditional arts, and the Yi music and dance performances bore eloquent testimony to their values of gender equality, unity, harmony, and beauty.

We went on to visit many Yi communities in the south and west of Kunming. We toured through mountainside villages, past clustered adobe homes. Hilltop cemeteries surrounded each of the villages, and although cremation was more common among the majority in China, the Yi chose to bury their deceased. As we visited the villages, I could feel the reverence the Yi held for their ancestors. The tour here made me grateful to know another side of China—one that differed vastly from the uniformity and urbanization I found in the larger cities.

This tour in China gave me the opportunity to visit the Great Wall for the first time. My fascination with the Wall stretched back to my early childhood memories, and its allure was rekindled when I first saw it on a cold, twenty-degree morning. I forced my way through a melee of vendors jostling for sales opportunities, as I had no interest in purchasing physical souvenirs. Instead, I wanted the spiritual souvenir, to carve the memory of the Great Wall as an indelible neural pathway on my soul.

After paying the entry fee, I wound my way up the mountain to meet the Wall face-to-face. I began traversing the Wall toward the easternmost allowable access point. As I looked at the grey stones underfoot, I remembered how every stone would have been hand-chiseled and transported by foot from great distances to the top of this steep mountain.

I remembered how, on one leg of the tour I had made with Ruhíyyih Khánum to a rural community, a temporary road closure had halted our trip, and when I had left our car, I had witnessed a multitude of workers moving, chiseling, and positioning rocks to lay a roadway foundation. They had been using only picks, shovels and wheelbarrows, and I had been stunned that their sheer human strength could change the shape of the landscape.

Now, at the Wall, I found myself once again humbled by how, a millennia ago, this massive Wall could have been built over the mountain peaks by human power alone. The Wall stood as an enduring symbol to the force of humankind's will and strength. Despite the cold, visitors swarmed the

Wall, speaking languages I recognized from some of my travels. I could hear Scandinavian, Germanic, Slavic, and Romance languages blending with Semitic, Korean, and North African tongues. "Gunaydin," I greeted a group conversing in Turkish—a simple *good morning*.

Later on, I overheard visitors of Chinese descent conversing in English with Australian, British, Singaporean, and Canadian accents. Out of curiosity, I struck up a few conversations and learned that many of them had come to the Wall as an essential part of reconnecting with their roots. They were brimming with excitement and awe to be here. I imagined they could tap into the spirit of their ancestors through this edifice and reconnect with the toil and dedication of their distant relatives.

Even I could sense the ancestral presence in this place over the course of my long hike. It reminded me of my daily jogs around the mile-long periphery of an ancient Arikara village site that sits across from my home on Standing Rock. After a mile or two, I would always be able to feel the history, the laughter of children, the cadence of conversation, the smell of roast bison and boiled turnips, and the prayers chanted across this formerly prosperous and cherished land.

The history of the Wall, however, did not feel as joyous. I could sense the strain and toil of countless hours spent constructing this edifice and the indomitable effort of thousands of people to work in the most trying conditions.

During my tour of the Wall, I ran into an English-speaking Chinese guide, who pointed me to a wall tower at high summit and exclaimed that whoever reached that summit could claim to be a hero.

"Here's my chance," I thought. "To go from Zero to Hero!"

With my sights set on this point, I climbed up, past the reconstructed and well-maintained part of the wall, past the crowds of tourists. I went well beyond the point that most had gone, to a part of the Wall that had been reclaimed by nature. Dense brush and foliage covered the top of the stone. I tread carefully, lest a loose rock cause me to plummet over the precipice.

I fell short of my mark by about one hundred meters. Perhaps, if I had been a few years younger, I could have maneuvered through the thick brush and the loose rubble; however, my path had grown dangerous, and after climbing up over thousands of steps, sharp pains were shooting into my left knee. I carefully hiked back down the tower to the main part of the Wall, then I splurged and caught the cable car back down to the base of the mountain and the parking lot below.

14

In the early nineties, I traveled with my mother, my daughter Kim, and other Indigenous North American Bahá'ís to Yakutsk, Siberia; there we visited the Sakha Republic, an Indigenous region located on the Lena River of northeast Siberia.

My dear friend, Lauretta King, had encouraged me to go on this trip. With the collapse of the Iron Curtain had come new opportunities for the Indigenous peoples of North America and Siberians to unite. She emphasized that both the Indigenous North Americans and the Indigenous Siberians had similar strong spiritual foundations. "The consultation that will emerge from these two peoples coming together," she told me, "will release incredible spiritual forces." These forces, she shared, could inspire individuals and entire communities to contribute to the establishment of a peaceful global civilization. Because of her words, my mother, and Kim and I were eager to meet and interact with the Sakha people.

For this trip, Mom packed an entire suitcase of nonperishable food items: cans of oysters and sardines, crackers, dried fruit, and an abundance of other dehydrated and powdered foods. I considered it rather strange that she was bringing along so much food. I always loved to try different local cuisines and was hoping to try the food in Siberia, though I said nothing to my mother at the time.

When we arrived in Yakutsk, I realized the value of my mother's foresight. The infrastructure in Siberia had disintegrated with the collapse of the Soviet regime. Because of this, the transportation networks had shut down, and supply routes from outside the region had stopped. When I went to a local grocery to buy bread, I found myself in a line that extended out of the shop and down the street. By the time I reached the store, nothing was left. I walked back from the store thinking that perhaps my mother had staved off our starvation on this particular trip.

Not only was food in short supply during the Soviet collapse, but the lack of supply, workers, and infrastructure had put to the test the skills of pilots, as well as the anxieties of passengers. While traveling by air to visit a few remote areas of Siberia, I noticed a particular pattern when preparing to land. With no security or ground crew waiting below to ensure our plane's safe landing, the pilots had to circle the landing field several times to make sure it was clear for landing. In these more remote areas, they especially wanted to avoid moose or abandoned cars sometimes left in the landing fields. Despite the state-mandated atheism after the Soviet collapse, rural Siberian air travel served to bring a newfound prayerful attitude among all the passengers. As the pilot attempted landing, no one spoke; everyone seemed unified in silent prayer for our survival. And after every successful landing, we remained motionless in total and reverent silence, grateful for our lives as we waited for the pilot to dismiss us.

How did the locals survive? I wondered. Over the course of our stay, I learned that many grew their own food. During the spring, when it was still cold and frigid, they planted tomato, cucumber, and other vegetable seeds in indoor window pots. When the seeds had grown into plants, the locals transported the plants to greenhouses, then moved the plants outdoors once the brief summer hit. Of course, they always worried about the effect of the colder months on the plants; during the upcoming fall and winter, temperatures could sink to eighty below zero.

Though the food shortage resulted in a twenty-pound weight loss for me, I had a wonderful time visiting various regions and developing new friendships among the Indigenous communities there.

Around the time of our visit, North American Bahá'ís had been asked to pioneer to many of these remote areas in Siberia. Indigenous and non-Indigenous Bahá'ís from around the world had settled here. These included Jonathan and Audrey Reynolds, who had first brought the Bahá'í Faith to Standing Rock. They had left their former post in Alaska and moved to Kamchatka, along with several other Inuit and Tlingit friends. These Bahá'ís had developed rich friendships among the Siberian residents through devotional gatherings and study classes. They found that the locals wanted to learn about the Teachings of Bahá'u'lláh and that this desire led many to become Bahá'ís. Thus in our travels, we visited many robust Bahá'í communities comprised of primarily Indigenous Siberian believers. We found that they were studying courses of the Ruhi Institute, and we joined them for many devotional gatherings.

The Sakha people, with their strong artistic heritage, had incredible musical and spiritual traditions. At various schools and community gatherings, we witnessed numerous round dance performances, similar to the Native dances performed on the prairies in the United States. One of the round dances impressed me because of its participatory nature. Everyone, including us guests, held hands and danced in a big circle, and we sang in a rhythmic call and response.

We also participated in myriad devotional practices involving a center pole; people offered orations and prayers around this pole. Carvings and decorations on the upper, middle, and lower segments of the pole represented the world below, this world, and the heavenly world above. The pole, to the Sakha, represented the center of creation and the connection between the Creator and mankind. It symbolized a holy point, a portal through which the people could connect to the divine. I knew of similar practices in other cultures around the world. The Lakota equivalent to this universal archetype representing the axis mundi, and the earthly presence of the divine, is *čháŋ wakȟáŋ / sacred tree.*

In one of the festivals we attended, we were meant to enjoy a display of fireworks, perhaps intended to impress the highest officials of the Sakha community in attendance. Unfortunately, though it was evening, no one could see the elaborate display of fireworks against the sun, which still shone bright. This was, after all, the "land of the midnight sun." Much was left to our imaginations instead.

We found great hospitality and kindness amongst the people of Siberia. Though they possessed few material means, the Sakha shared their music, arts, and cultural wealth. Local shamans offered their extensive knowledge of traditional medicines willingly. Out in those village areas, we enjoyed the natural foods—the wild game, berries, and roots—alongside the people. I received numerous books as gifts—books about the flowers and gemstones of the area. Flipping through those books, I recalled Bahá'u'lláh's injunction to "regard man as a mine rich in gems of inestimable value" and felt a deep sense that the true flowers and gems of that area were the Sakha themselves.*

My tours through the Sakha communities were not without the occasional peril. Once, I traveled with a small group of Bahá'ís to a remote reindeer-herding village to visit a family that wanted to learn about the Faith. On our way, we reached a river crossing. From the backseat of the jeep, I could see that the bridge had been completely immersed by the rapids; torrential rain from the mountains must have caused the river to wash over our path. The driver and the woman in the passenger seat, our host on this journey to her home Evenk village, debated what to do in animated Russian. They reached an agreement, and the driver began to reverse our vehicle. *Okay,* I thought, *we're going to turn back.*

Instead, the driver hit the accelerator. We sped off the riverbank. For a moment, we were suspended in the air over the water. Then we hit the water with a tremendous splash close to the opposite shore but not yet touching it. The driver punched the accelerator as the car began to drift downstream. Cold water seeped over my feet, rising to my shins and then knees. Before the waters could carry us away, we felt the jeep's wheels catch the solid riverbed. I sank back into my seat, my heart still pounding.

We turned to watch the van behind us—the van with several of our friends, not to mention all our luggage—attempt the same leap. The driver reversed, accelerated, and flew through the air. The van did not make it to the other side. Instead, it landed smack in the middle of the moving waters. We watched in horror as the river pulled the van downstream, stopped only by large boulders in the middle of the river.

The passengers crawled out of a side window and climbed onto the roof of the van. The van teetered on the boulders and looked as if it would be swept away at any moment. Our friends, though wet and shivering, remained calm. We scrambled from our jeep and found a cable, which we tossed out to our friends. Using the cable to keep afloat, they plunged into the rapids. When they made it safely ashore, we started a fire. Our driver

---

* Bahá'u'lláh, *Gleanings from the Writings of Bahá'u'lláh*, no. 122.1.

set off to go look for another vehicle that could pull the van out of the river. The rest of us could do nothing except warm ourselves by the fire and wait for him to return. A couple of the ladies could speak English, so we shared jokes back and forth to distract ourselves from the crisis. Our sense of humor helped pass the time.

After several hours, our driver found an old tractor upriver, which he hotwired, drove back to us, and used to lug the van into shallow water. The van was so completely filled with water that as it was pulled toward the shore, the water pressure from inside blew out the windows, and all of our luggage went flying into the river. We dove into the icy water to retrieve our luggage and set everything to dry by the fire. We were disappointed to not visit the family, and although we never learned what happened to them, we were relieved to have survived our river adventure and to have lived to tell the tale.

As Lauretta had promised, throughout our travels in Siberia, I found striking parallels between the history and traditions of the Native community there and the Indigenous people of North America. I engaged in conversations with many Sakha people about the shared history of colonization and the cultural similarities. I discovered that, on both sides of the international dateline, a parallel process had taken place: Western Europe had colonized the Indigenous people of North America, just as Eastern Europe had colonized Siberia. The colonizers on both sides had attempted to acculturate the Native peoples. Both communities had been exploited for their resources, and the logging and diamond industries in Siberia had fueled the Soviet economy and jeopardized the rights of the people.

Yet, despite the forces of colonization, similar to their North American counterparts, the Indigenous Siberians had retained many of their cultural and devotional traditions. Isolation had helped them in this; even during the cultural repression of the Soviet era, their cultural traits had survived because they lived in such remote areas. For example, their language had remained free of the outside influence of other languages. The people still revered the creation of the natural world as holy and sacred, and they still held themselves to be the stewards of creation—the same standard to which we Indigenous people in North America held ourselves. The Siberian people also expressed themselves through poetry, dance, and music, just as we did in North America. This form of expression was essential for the survival of both communities because it allowed them to preserve their special connection to the heavens through that inalienable, intrinsic human impulse: the arts.

* * *

In the early nineties, I made several trips to Mongolia for a similar purpose: to make connections with Indigenous and rural Mongolians, especially those who had recently come into contact with the Bahá'í Faith.

On one occasion, I journeyed with a group of Bahá'ís from Ulaanbaatar to visit nomadic communities across the country. Once we left the city, we had no paved roads to mark our way; we drove instead across the steppe, the grasslands of the country. After several hours of driving, we came across a cluster of *gers*—round, white canvas huts where Mongolians lived. Our driver stopped at some distance from the community. As we approached the nearest ger, I saw a round face peeking through the door flap. A few minutes later, the whole family spilled out of the ger with their faces beaming and arms waving us inside.

We walked inside the round structure and were promptly offered milk tea. Mutton sizzled on a wok at the center of the ger. We were offered plates of mutton, along with freshly-cut noodles flavored with the wild onions that grew across the steppe. I knew that Mongolia had also suffered a critical food shortage and was touched by the way this family gave so abundantly of what they had.

As our visit continued, I again realized the deep connection between the culture here and my home culture. As guests, we adhered to certain etiquette, even upon entering the ger. When we entered the structure, we turned left—just as I would have done when entering a thípi back in the Plains—and the men sat on one side of the ger, while the women sat on another. As with the thípi back home, the door to the ger faced east, to greet the rising sun. I noticed, too, positioned opposite to the entrance of the ger, a Buddhist shrine had been constructed—at the same location as the čhatkú, the seat of honor in a thípi. Even the landscape mirrored the Dakotas—we were at a similar latitude and climate, after all—and when I looked out the ger to the grasslands and mountain peaks, I felt as though I were home.

I discovered yet another striking similarity when we left our host's home: the practice of the red line. In the North American prairie tribes, a family will paint a red line about a foot wide all around the base. Effectively, this line is a red hoop touching the ground of their thipi, and it indicates that anyone who approaches the family's home is welcome to enter and receive hospitality. Families choose to practice this custom in honor of a deceased relative or an honored child or simply to celebrate a special family occasion. When we left the ger, our translator pointed to a red line at the entrance. "This line indicates the spirit of generosity and hospitality observed in the home," he told us and continued to explain that the line was often drawn when a family wanted to honor a relative or commemorate a departed soul. I was amazed. Every detail and practice was so parallel that I concluded that our two tribal communities on opposite sides of the world were on the same heavenly wavelength.

Buddhist chants ceremonially open Nadam, the Mongolian national celebration. Fortunate to attend such a devotional Nadam opening, we arrived when the chants were in full swing. At least fifty monks were intoning melodic prayers. The power of the music enveloped us and carried us to sublime heights. Curious to know more about the meaning behind the lyrics, I asked our translator to please brief us on the translation.

"I don't know," she replied.

"Why don't you know?" I asked, still curious.

"It's not Mongolian language."

"What language is it?"

"I don't know," she responded.

Just then, a monk walked past us.

"Can you ask him?" I asked the translator, and she did.

"I don't know," he answered.

Exasperated, I had her ask him; who *does* know? He gestured to an ancient monk seated at the far end of the line of chanters. Now I was on a quest. We patiently waited until the end of the liturgy of chants and approached the ancient monk and posed our question.

He responded, "I don't know." He went on to explain that after the mass conversion of the Mongols to Tibetan Buddhism, an active corridor of commerce and spiritual sharing, called the silk road, sprang up between Mongolia and Tibet, and a class of Mongol devotees to Tibetan Buddhist practices arose. This union flourished for many centuries. Then the Soviets imposed their special brand of atheism and orchestrated a wholesale slaughter of the senior Buddhist practitioners. This tragedy severed ties of the Mongols to the matrix of their faith and destroyed much of their vital spiritual heritage. The elder shared that individuals such as himself had managed to salvage what was left within their collective memory, but much of the meaning of the Tibetan lyrics had been lost.

Prior to my trip, I had heard incredible stories of the emerging Bahá'í community in Mongolia. I learned that an entire village had declared themselves Bahá'ís after one of their members had brought some samples from the Bahá'í writings back to the people. Though no other Bahá'ís had visited this village, they had established their own community and were holding prayer gatherings, classes for children, and study circles. Upon my arrival in Mongolia, I was thankful for the opportunity to visit such communities, to hear firsthand from the friends about their belief in the Bahá'í Faith, to bring them additional material from the writings, and to encourage them.

On another trip, Kim and I had the great privilege of meeting the first Mongolian Bahá'í, known as Ina. She invited us to visit her in her small concrete-block apartment complex. When we arrived to the unit she shared with her husband, she greeted us warmly and offered us a meal of mutton and flour noodles. As we sat down, I asked Ina how she discovered the Bahá'í Faith.

"My husband is my eighth husband," she began. "I have been married eight times and have never been divorced."

Immediately, I knew that this would be an interesting story.

"I was born in Western Mongolia among the Shaman people." Because of their geographic isolation, the Shamans had evaded the mass conversion into Tibetan Buddhism orchestrated by Altan Khan, and thus they retained their ancestral spiritual heritage.

When Ina was a child, perhaps around four years of age, her elderly grandparents sat her down. Sensing that their days on this earth were limited, they wanted to speak about her future. "They told me that I was destined to experience horrendous suffering but that I would also witness the coming of a great message, promised to our people by the divine beings of old. I would be the first of my people to find this light," Ina told us. This was part of a prophetic tradition from Ina's ancestral heritage. "'We have been praying for you,' my grandparents told me, 'and after we depart from this world, we will continue to guide you to this great discovery.'"

Ina recalled that afterward her grandmother took two rocks, placed them on either side of Ina's right ear lobe and pressed them together, hard enough to draw blood. Ina cried out in pain. "My grandmother apologized, saying that she wanted only to be sure that I would never forget this moment and what they had told me."

Years later, Mongolia was overtaken by the Soviet government and suffered the imposition of Stalin's brutal policies, including the suppression of spirituality. Individuals who rebelled were arrested and sent to eastern Siberia. Ina was among the first to be exiled and was treated very harshly in her banishment.

"Did you resent the Russians for this harsh treatment?" I asked.

Ina shook her head. "I loved the Russian people."

During her exile, Ina became fluent in Russian. She met other exiles— great poets, philosophers, and visionaries who possessed a shared dream for a great future for their people. People such as herself, who thought outside the box, represented a significant threat to the despotic forces bent on squelching resistance from thinking, awakened souls. Despite the darkness, the genocide, and the oppression, they too believed that future generations would witness the miracles promised by their ancestors.

The reasons Ina married several times during her exile was because all of her husbands suffered death in forced labor camps. They were each commissioned as highway workers for the Magadan Road, a road that stretched from Yakutsk to Magadan—nearly two thousand kilometers.

"It was said that for every hundred kilometers built of this road, one million lives were lost," Ina explained. The Soviets did not provide sufficient food and shelter when the winter set in. As a result, many workers froze and starved in one of the coldest inhabited regions on our planet. This was how Ina lost her beloved husbands.

Miraculously, Ina survived. She returned to the workforce and to ordinary life in Mongolia. Propaganda surrounded her. The Soviet regime had extinguished the spirit of the people. Ina felt as though she had entered a lightless tunnel with no end in sight.

"Every year, I went deeper into this rut," she said. "I found little purpose in my life. I grew more distant from the teachings of my ancestors and all but forgot the prophecy of my grandparents."

One day, years after her return, as Ina trudged across the main square in Ulaanbataar, she heard music and saw that a large crowd had gathered. She felt herself drawn to the source of the upbeat melodies. She pushed to the center of the crowd and discovered a young musical group from Peru. "I was carried away by the spirit of their performance," she remembered. "Such joy was there. I felt as though I were young and in the presence of my grandparents again. I knew it was their spirits that enabled me to be present for this moment."

The youth in this musical group, El Viento Canta / Song of the Wind came from devout Bahá'í families in Peru. They used traditional instruments, like most Andean performers. One such instrument was the sampona, or the pan-pipe, which was independently developed in both the Western Hemisphere and Eastern Hemisphere long before Columbus. They also used a vertical flute called the quena, which achieved a three to four octave range, and a small guitar-like instrument, the charango. These instruments combined to create beautiful vocalizations and a spirited, stirring genre of music, so infectious that like most Andean music transcended many cultural barriers.

People everywhere were attracted to the blended sound and cultural mixing of the music. The Andeans may have pioneered the phenomenon of musical fusion, which has truly enveloped the globe. In recent decades, music groups such as the Rolling Stones have taken inspiration from the Mississippi Delta blues. Technology—social media and Youtube, for instance—now serves to unite us, allowing different cultures to meet, mix, and form new genres of expression. We now have greater access to diverse music genres than ever before. Musicians from around the world can collaborate with ease. Artists from different parts can contribute to the same song—a phenomenon that is gaining momentum. The fusion of different cultures and the collaboration between artists from different parts of the globe is truly a testament to the fact that the human spirit transcends limitations of geography, race, gender, and even time and space.

I learned that the youth in El Viento Canta had served at the Bahá'í World Center, where they had formed El Viento Canta and honed their musicianship. When the former Soviet bloc countries opened up, El Viento Canta was asked to tour in these areas and share the Bahá'í Faith. Through their musical talent and radiant spirits, they opened many regions to the teachings of Bahá'u'lláh, including Ulaanbaatar and neighboring parts of Siberia.

After El Viento Canta's performance, the crowd dispersed, and Ina approached the performers. She related to us, "I asked them, 'Why are you here? What message are you trying to share?'"

The members of El Viento Canta were reluctant to tell Ina about the Bahá'í Faith, as governing officials had forbidden them from openly mentioning the Faith while in Mongolia. Ina persisted in English, a language she had also learned in exile. She remembered that her grandparents had told her she would recognize the new message through the joy and illumination of the message-bearers. She knew the members of El Viento Canta had the message her grandparents had assured her of many years back. She did not let up until they divulged the information she was seeking. As a result, she became the first Mongolian Bahá'í.

What a blessing it was to sit with Ina, as she reflected on what led her to the divine message for today. These instances from her life could easily appear as disparate threads, but when examined together, they revealed an intricate tapestry. Hearing Ina's story led me to reflect on how the seemingly disparate threads of my life had intertwined to lead me to the Bahá'í Faith. For both Ina and I, reading and meditating on the Bahá'í writings enabled us to understand our past. The Word was the foundation, the matrix, from which everything fell into place, and all my different stories and experiences could be filtered through its lens. This process had allowed the Truth, the Sun of Reality, to become manifest in both my life and Ina's.

15

When my mother gave me our family pipe, in those early days of my youth, I set out on a quest to understand its significance. The practices with the pipe reinforce our connection to the divine, and this connection is vital for making choices about one's personal, family, and vocational life. Its mystical significance exceeds that of a mere reminder or symbol. Fully comprehending the pipe is as challenging as fully comprehending God, yet to know and love God is our purpose in life, and finding one's path is a holy and eternal process, linked to our love of God.

My understanding of my own path had advanced significantly since that time in my life. I had found and accepted the Bahá'í Faith, I had been given the hoop dance by Arlo, and I had begun to realize my purpose of educating others through sharing traditional arts. I was still learning, however, about the history and deep meaning of the pipe.

The pipe was brought to the Lakota people by the White Buffalo Calf Maiden. The Maiden appeared on behalf of Grandfather, Tȟuŋkášila, to the Lakota people, at a time when the Lakota did not have a written language. She conveyed to the Lakota their connection to the Grandfather through the sacred, physical token of the pipe.

The bowl of the pipe is made of a red fine-grained stone, a sedimentary mineral known as catlinite found in southwestern Minnesota. This catlinite is thought to be the remnant of holy souls of the past. Long ago, according to Lakota tradition, the Creator sent a flood to cleanse and purify the world. During the flood, a few faithful souls fled to a high point to pray that whatever was holy and heavenly in their hearts would be preserved.

Hearing their prayer, the Great Spirit sent a holy being in the form of an eagle to rescue the sole survivor of this deluge—a young woman. Together, the eagle and the woman flew over the flooded earth until they reached the topmost branch of the Tree of Life. There, they alighted and remained in safety until the flood waters receded.

As the waters dried, land at the base of the Tree appeared and spread out, becoming verdant, fragrant, abundant, and renewed. From the eagle and the woman descended the human race. The eagle is a metaphor for a holy soul or divine being. The Tree of Life represents the link between heaven and earth. These descendants eventually dispersed and spread out around the world. The oral tradition is silent after the dispersal of the descendants of the eagle and the woman. One can surmise that the eagle is symbolic of a noble heavenly being (male) and the woman is symbolic of the matrix of life (female). From the metaphorical eagle and woman descended the human race. The human race, in turn, dispersed and diffused throughout the earth.

How did the human race recreate and disperse? It was foretold that some-day these descendants would come together and see each other but would not recognize each other. We can see with the current state of conflict, conflagration, polarization, and disunity, that this is indeed true. It was also foretold that someday a generation would appear that would be able to open their eyes and recognize the spirit of the eagle within themselves and each other. This new generation would recognize their shared nobility and ability to activate their wings of knowledge, love, and understanding. They would lift humanity up to achieve its true destiny—the attainment of unity and *wólakȟota*—*peace*. Then, the people would truly fulfill their rebirth and redemption, a process that started with the few holy souls pray-ing for salvation in the midst of that great flood. It is believed that the remains of those steadfast few percolated in the earth after the flood and formed the deep red catlinite of the pipe.* The remains of the infidels, it is also believed, became the quartzite mineral, which serves to protect and shield the soft catlinite.

---

* Catlinite is named after the famous painter George Catlin, an adventurer who first described and painted the Pipestone Quarry to Euro-Americans.

In Lakota devotional practices, the pipe is used to invoke and transport someone into the divine presence. It recalls that mythical time and the sacred moments when the people were in the presence of the White Buffalo Calf Maiden and were experiencing their nascence in the shade of the Tree of Life. This image brings to mind one of the Hidden Words of Bahá'u'lláh:

O My Friends! Have ye forgotten that true and radiant morn, when in those hallowed and blessed surroundings ye were all gathered in My presence beneath the shade of the tree of life, which is planted in the all-glorious paradise? Awestruck ye listened as I gave utterance to these three most holy words: O friends! Prefer not your will to Mine, never desire that which I have not desired for you, and approach Me not with lifeless hearts, defiled with wordly desires and cravings. Would ye but sanctify your souls, ye would at this present hour recall that place and those surroundings, and the truth of My utterance should be made evident unto all of you.*

During many ceremonies, such as the Sundance and sweat lodges, the pipe is often loaded with tobacco at the commencement and is also smoked by the participants. Every ceremony honoring the White Buffalo Calf Maiden requires the use of the pipe to consecrate the ceremony. The loading and smoking of the pipe summons the presence of the divine.

Tobacco originated in the Western Hemisphere. Prior to 1492, tobacco was unknown in other parts of the world. A generic story about tobacco occurs in many tribal communities. Each community tells a variation of this story. The Creator put certain gifts down on the earth but withheld other gifts. One time, the eagle was flying up above the world and noticed that a certain gift was being withheld. The All-Knowing Creator had observed that the eagle had witnessed this and commissioned the eagle to fly back down and convene a gathering of all the creatures to consult on and decide who would receive this gift on behalf of all of creation. The eagle obliged, and when the creatures gathered together, they all began

---

* Bahá'u'lláh, The Hidden Words, Persian no. 19.

to brag about themselves and about all the gifts and powers they had that would qualify them as the recipients of this gift. The dog boasted about his ability to smell. The owl expanded on his gift of seeing in the dark. The deer could run and escape danger quickly. The swallow could swoop and dart hither and fro. They went on and on and engaged in heated arguments about who should receive the gift.

A mole intervened and said, "Hey, Hey. Wait, we all have these beautiful, fantastic gifts, but there is one among us who is really pitiful, who really doesn't have anything, whose gifts are nothing compared to us, one who doesn't have sharp teeth, one who can't see very well, can't hear sounds miles away, can't even smell the way we do. He has no fur, no claws with which to dig, and no wings with which to fly. This creature can't move quickly, can't go far, and can't run fast. It's pitiful in every way." As this creature was being described, all of the animals slowly came to a state of consensus.

The Creator, observing from on high, called out, "Hey, my grandchildren, well done, well done. I am in agreement with you. So it shall be that humans, the two-legged ones, shall receive this gift on behalf of all of creation. Whenever they use this gift in prayer, with consideration for the well-being of all of creation and all the past hopes and dreams of the ancestors; when they use it in consideration of how their decisions will affect the well-being of future generations, even up to seven generations ahead; when they use this gift and the incense of it wafts up to My heavenly kingdom, I shall be well-pleased and I shall grant that prayer. Thus it shall be."

According to the story, human beings, the two-leggeds, received the gift of tobacco as part of a Covenant between human beings and the Creator. For thousands of years, tobacco was used for special occasions and always to accompany a state of prayer and mindfulness. Whenever tobacco was used in this way, the Covenant was being invoked. If one checks the records of the Europeans when they met with the Indigenous people, one finds that the Indians would always kindle a fire at the outset of every meeting, then they would pray and consult. After they achieved unity of vision on their consultation, they separated some of the embers from that fire and placed the tobacco on those embers. The prayer and that incense wafted out in the four directions, symbolically covered all of creation, and slowly rose up into the heavenly realms. The Creator would thereby know that this great law, this great Covenant, this remembrance, was being acknowledged and cherished.

The prophecy went on to say that people would forget these heavenly teachings and would abuse this gift and become unmindful of its meaning. When this happened, the source of life and blessings would then become the cause of destruction. So it is that today tens of millions of people are dying of the ravages of tobacco abuse. This death and destruction would be a clear sign that the Covenant must be renewed and that God would reestablish the laws that would bind heaven to earth.

In my years as a Bahá'í, I have come to believe that the pipe represents the Covenant between God and man. "This is the changeless Faith of God," Bahá'u'lláh writes, "eternal in the past, eternal in the future."* Bahá'ís believe that the Covenant is a binding agreement between God and humankind. In this Covenant, God will never leave people to themselves; in return, every individual must strive to recognize God's divine Messengers and to steadfastly obey the divine teachings. The Covenant signifies that God will continually send these divine Messengers, Who reveal religious truth for the time they are sent. As part of the Covenant, humanity agrees to turn to the appointed successor of every divine Messenger after His or Her passing.**

In my years as a Bahá'í, I began to recognize the theme of the Covenant in the pipe. The Maiden came to the people as a messenger to link humanity with the Grandfather, and she brought with her the pipe as a token of this eternal connection between God and man. The stem of the pipe, connected to the bowl, represents the Tree of Life becoming rooted in the sacred heart of humanity. Catlinite, comprising the bowl of the pipe, formed because of the reciprocal faithfulness of certain holy souls to their Creator and of the Creator to these souls. I now saw the Grandfather as

---

* Bahá'u'lláh, *Gleanings from the Writings of Bahá'u'lláh*, no. 70.2.

** In the Bahá'í Faith, authority was passed to 'Abdu'l-Bahá after the ascension of Bahá'u'lláh. After the passing of 'Abdu'l-Bahá, authority was passed to Shoghi Effendi, known as the Guardian of the Bahá'í Faith. After the passing of Shoghi Effendi, authority was passed to the Universal House of Justice. The Guardianship and the House of Justice were the twin successors of 'Abdu'l-Bahá.

Bahá'u'lláh. As I made these connections, I began to substitute the word *Covenant* in my mind and heart whenever I sang sacred songs and prayers that mentioned the pipe.

The power of the Covenant became especially crystallized in my heart and mind when I attended the 1992 Bahá'í World Congress in New York City. There, thirty-five thousand Bahá'ís, representing hundreds of countries, territories, and islands from around the world gathered for a four-day Congress commemorating the centenary of the passing of Bahá'u'lláh. Moreover, the Congress paid homage to the inauguration of Bahá'u'lláh's Covenant—the line of succession after Him according to His explicit instructions. During that holy year, 1992, Bahá'ís around the world honored the "world-shaking" importance of these occasions and celebrated the beginning of a new epoch.*

At the time of the World Congress, my career had reached new heights. A cassette recording of my flute playing sold over 350,000 copies. I was surprised to receive the National Heritage Award, the highest recognition for traditional artists in the United States. New opportunities for travel unfolded before me. Performances and workshops took me from Japan to Guam to Knoxville, Tennessee, and around the Dakotas as well. I traveled to Rio de Janeiro for the Earth Summit, a United Nations-sponsored global conference on the environment and development. At that time, I scheduled my own tours, booked my own gigs, and negotiated my own fees—self-managing my career without the Internet, cell phone, or fax machine. When one gig ended, another began. I felt like a human pinball, ricocheting all over the world.

Though the intensity of my schedule did not cause me stress—I adjusted well to the busyness, to new time zones and cultures—I struggled with my family life. I knew my marriage, long on a downward spiral, would soon end. Thankfully, my touring schedule kept me out of the house while still allowing me to spend time with my children.

In the spring of 1991, I was serving as an Auxiliary Board Member, a local assistant to the Continental Board of Counselors, when the Bahá'í

* The Universal House of Justice, *A Wider Horizon: Selected Letters 1983–1992*, 90.

community first received notice of the World Congress. Robert Harris, the Counselor with whom I was working, remarked that he viewed attending this World Congress as analogous to going on pilgrimage. "If humanly possible," he said. "I believe it is our duty to attend." Over the course of that year, Robert and I circulated throughout the Dakotas to encourage others in the Bahá'í community to attend. The more Bahá'ís from the Dakotas who could attend, I hoped, the more abundant the blessings we would all experience.

On the beginning day of the Congress, in November, 1992, all three of my children, their mom, and I arrived in New York City to bright, crisp weather. As we arrived at the Jacob Javits Center, a convention center on the Hudson where the Congress was to be held, volunteers greeted us warmly. As they escorted us into the massive glass building, I felt as if I had witnessed the parting of the Red Sea. The chaos that characterized New York City subsided in the center of that building. Though thousands of people flowed through the spacious venue, there was no sense of freneticism. Volunteers organized and ushered the influx of attendees around the center with great hospitality. An intense joy pervaded the space as friends from near and far reunited. How miraculous that over thirty thousand people could gather together in commemoration and praise.

At the commencement of the World Congress, the chairman of the National Spiritual Assembly read a letter of welcome from President Bush. The Mayor of New York gave a cordial, official welcome. Prayers were offered in myriad languages and in song. Ruhíyyih Khánum spoke to the historic nature of this occasion, which she said marked not only the inauguration of Bahá'u'lláh's Covenant but also the spread of the Bahá'í Faith to all parts of the globe.

Later on, in a roll call of sorts, representatives from each of the tribes and countries who had come to the Congress walked through the aisles of the Javits Center. A stirring drum beat and melody sounded from the orchestra, and a voice from the loudspeakers spoke: *We are from Angola, Algeria, Zambia.*

One by one, Bahá'ís from these countries walked towards the stage. They were wearing their national dress and bearing radiant smiles. Young and old, dark and fair, these men and women donned colorful headdresses, tunics, intricate lace collars, and thick woven vests. The faces of some were adorned with traditional paints. Still others wore Western-style dress, plain T-shirts, blazers, and suits. *We are the Poles, the Greenlanders, the Pakistanis, the Bank Islanders, the Maori. We are the Lakota, the Arapahoe. We are from the Bahamas, Scotland, Argentina, Belize.*

The representatives gathered at the main stage. We in the audience could see a vibrant display of people who had responded to the clarion call of Bahá'u'lláh from every background, race, and nationality. *We are the people of the world.* The audience rose in an unhesitating standing ovation. The individuals on stage twined hands, no longer strangers but brethren in a common faith and purpose.

Seeing these diverse people fill every corner of that stage was, as the Universal House of Justice promised, "an affirmation of the efficacy of . . . the world-redeeming, world-revolutionizing purpose" of this Faith. Spellbound, I sat in awe and gratitude to witness what I believed was the fulfillment of prophecy. We were representatives of the generation who would appear, the generation who would recognize the spirit of the eagle within ourselves and others, the generation who would perceive our shared nobility, the generation who would discover our ability to activate our wings that would carry us to divine heights of understanding and love.

While the beginning of the Congress marked the centenary of the inauguration of 'Abdu'l-Bahá as the Center of the Covenant, the subsequent days of the Congress explored His station and role. In 1892, upon the passing of His father, 'Abdu'l-Bahá was appointed as Bahá'u'lláh's successor and head of the Faith in the will of Bahá'u'lláh, the Kitáb-i-'Ahd. 'Abdu'l-Bahá was authorized by Bahá'u'lláh to interpret the Bahá'í writings and was declared the "perfect exemplar" of the teachings and spirit of the Faith.

'Abdu'l-Bahá had visited New York City in 1912, where He elucidated His role as the Center of the Covenant. He had declared New York to be the City of the Covenant, which made our commemoration especially significant.

Sessions centered around the life and ministry of 'Abdu'l-Bahá and His time in the United States. One plenary gathering featured dramatizations of the experiences of early North American Bahá'ís who knew 'Abdu'l-Bahá during His time in the United States. Phillip Hinton, a Bahá'í and friend from Australia, offered a dramatization of the experience of Howard McNutt, a Bahá'í who initially doubted then found great faith in 'Abdu'l-

Bahá's station. A talented actor, Philip utilized his speaking voice the way musicians use their instruments. In another session, people who had met 'Abdu'l-Bahá during His tour in the United States spoke of their recollections of Him—especially His pure warmth and kindness, which etched itself in their memories all these decades later.

Throughout the days and evenings of the Congress, breakout sessions featured different artistic and cultural presentations. During these sessions, I often had the opportunity to reunite with friends from my tours in Africa, China, Bolivia, and Peru. I attended as many theater and musical presentations as I could and presented and participated in panel discussions as well. On one memorable evening, alongside gifted Aboriginal and Pacific Islander artists, I performed the hoop dance as a part of a large gala celebrating Indigenous artistic expressions from around the world.

The most notable session for me featured a man named Juan Bejarano from the Guaymi tribe in Panama. His humble posture and sense of devotion exemplified the words of 'Abdu'l-Bahá—that if Native peoples received education and were properly guided, they would become so enlightened through the divine teachings that the whole world would become illumined.*

"Good morning, dear Bahá'í sisters and brothers," Juan addressed the audience, "Alláh'u'Abhá. It is a privilege for the Guaymi people to receive the beautiful message of Bahá'u'lláh, and at this time, I take this opportunity to address you. The most important thing I have to tell you is that the Guaymi People have embraced the Cause of Bahá'u'lláh and want to be obedient to His Teachings. That is why we want to be faithful to the administrative institutions of the Bahá'í Faith, the Local Spiritual Assemblies, the National Spiritual Assembly, and the Universal House of Justice—God's infallible institution. With their guidance, social economic development projects are being established, such as Bahá'í Radio, the Guaymi Cultural Center, and the Schools for the Education of Children. With the institutions' guidance, we are developing deepening programs, literacy programs, women's conferences, native councils, teaching projects, and others. Through these programs, we have been achieving a transforma-

---

* 'Abdu'l-Bahá, *Tablets of the Divine Plan*, p. 33.

tive effect in the area, to help balance the quality of the spiritual life of the Guaymi people. These positive examples demonstrate that, little by little, we are coming to understand the Covenant of Bahá'u'lláh and are trying to serve Him. What more can this humble people do, but be the instrument of Bahá'u'lláh? Thank you very much."

As I listened to this presentation, I felt some envy. This tribe had experienced true progress—and I longed for the same changes to occur in my home community and throughout the tribes of North America.

As the World Congress came to a close, I felt as though the experience had been such an incredible affirmation of faith. The spirit of Bahá'u'lláh had moved us all to be there, and there we had seen the power of the Covenant to unify the seemingly disparate people of the world. Those four days were nothing short of miraculous.

However, it was one thing to get together and experience that joy—to sing kumbaya, so to speak—but I knew that after the Congress, the rubber had to hit the road. Bahá'ís would have to work to marshal the energy and momentum from the Congress into constructive change.

The close collaboration between Bahá'ís of global Indigenous backgrounds continued after the Congress in my home area of the Dakotas. A group of Aboriginals visited many reservation communities and shared traditional music and dance from their home in Yirrkala. Already, they had had the privilege of representing Australia and its people at the World Congress; now this blessing extended to the tour in the Midwest. The people of the Dakotas, too, were touched by their visit—that these individuals had come so far to interact with the remote communities here.

During their visit to Bemidji, Minnesota, the tour group was invited to speak on a local radio station. "What brings you to Northern Minnesota?" the radio announcer asked.

"The spirit of Bahá'u'lláh," one of the Yirrkala men answered. "It picked us up and brought us over here."

Also during their visit to Bemidji, the men of the tour group saw snow for the first time. I drove them to a huge lake, frozen over and covered by snow. Pick up trucks had parked over the frozen lake and ice houses had been constructed by local fishermen. When I told them that this was a frozen lake, the men had immediate doubts. "No," they said. "Surely this is not a lake." To prove that it was, I parked the car, got out, and walked across the ice to one of the huts. A fishermen let us in and demonstrated to the incredulous Aboriginal men from Northern Territory in Australia how he fished from his hut. Only then did the men begin to believe that this was, indeed, a frozen body of water.

In the decade that followed, I would witness the true impact of the Congress. In these years, the Bahá'í community began to systematize and sustain our efforts to better the world. Bahá'ís in localities around the world would work shoulder-to-shoulder with people of diverse faiths and backgrounds to contribute to the spiritual and material progress of their communities. At the grassroots level, Bahá'ís and their collaborators would work to advance the education of children and adolescents, reinforce constructive dynamics within the family unit, build friendships and dissolve prejudice amongst community members, create spaces for collective devotion, and establish shared patterns of community life.

16

Ever aware of the rampant injustices that existed in the world around her, my mother dedicated her life and career to achieving justice for the Indigenous people of North America and of the world. Her Lakota name—Tȟawáčhiŋ Wašté Wíŋ—reflected this purpose.

In 1969, when she was forty-one years old, she received her name. Her name-giver, Amos Dog Eagle, received the name Tȟawáčhiŋ Wašté Wíŋ through prayer and meditation. The first word, *Tȟawáčhiŋ*, refers to a person's thoughts and consciousness; together, the three words of her name mean *to have a good conscience*. This name signifies one who is aware of the reality of things and cannot sit idly by, but rather seeks to bring compassion and justice to the world.

My mother aimed to demonstrate the meaning of her name in everything she did. This was challenging. Because of the nature of her work as an activist, she faced numerous obstacles, resistance, opposition, setbacks, and defeats. While many might succumb to expressing outrage in the face of such obstacles, she instead aimed to live up to the high calling of her name. She strove to bring understanding and compassion to her interactions with her family, community members, and even those who did not understand her. Her keen sense of social justice drove her to work for the betterment of the world starting at the local level.

At the Welcome Center in Alaska, where her activism began, she honed a radar-like ability to perceive the needs of the Indigenous community. She created the center to help Indigenous people who had moved to Anchorage from villages adjust to urban life. The services provided helped people find housing, work, and healthcare. Determining that the greatest need of the community was education, she utilized her capacities to create educational opportunities. Her steadfast commitment to service enabled her to learn so much.

Mom left Alaska in 1969 after accepting a position with the Western Interstate Commission for Higher Education in Boulder, Colorado. Here, she focused on developing tribal colleges. Ever practical, my mother knew that nothing could be done for these colleges without material means, so she sought opportunities for funding. She developed an incredible network of connections in Washington, D.C. She forged an alliance with Leonard Garment, a New Yorker, arts advocate, public servant, and attorney serving as Special Counsel to the Nixon administration. Mr. Garment helped to push through the Indian Post-Secondary Education Act, authored by my mom, to give a budget to support existing tribal colleges.

Mom continued to write and work with the policy makers of Washington to implement legislation. She worked on the Freedom of Religion Act, which legitimized Indigenous rights to worship and protected sacred lands and burial grounds. She also collaborated on the Indian Child Welfare Act, which provided support and social services to the children of various tribes. Having previously taught English at UCLA, Mom wrote with a silver pen, which aided her greatly when it came to writing legislation and grant proposals.

Among Indigenous communities, the tribe has more inherent sovereignty than the state; unsurprisingly, collaborating with people from the tribe brought about the most effective change within the tribe. As she continued to work with policymakers in Washington, Mom also joined forces with tribes to formulate educational policies. She drafted legislation for tribal constitutions to develop schools and education departments on reservations. In particular, she aided tribes to formulate policies regarding tribal languages that required that teachers have basic proficiency in the tribal language. Efforts such as these contributed to the revitalization of Indigenous languages.

Activism suited my mother. She moved forward without hesitation to achieve justice. Systematic action allowed her to create and sustain momentum and inspire others to crusade with her. Though determined, she faced difficulties in her quest for progress. Mom built and then lost consensus, and conflict and red tape slowed down some of her numerous efforts. She persevered through the various attempts to stifle proposed change, however, and through these difficulties, she realized one of the Bahá'í teachings—that instead of working within old systems, she could make more progress building new systems.

Because of her activism, educational policy work, and development of tribal colleges, Mom went on to receive the MacArthur Genius Award in 1991—a prize for those who have demonstrated "extraordinary originality and dedication in their creative pursuits and a marked capacity for self-direction."* The significant financial award allowed Mom to continue her work in the areas of language, cultural, and sacred site preservation.

In 1993, my mom was elected to serve on the National Spiritual Assembly of the Bahá'ís of the United States. In 1995, she joined other National Assembly members such as Juana Conrad, Dorothy Nelson, and James Nelson to represent the National Spiritual Assembly at the United Nations Conference on Women held in Beijing, China. Jacqueline Left Hand Bull, another Bahá'í, also traveled with them. Mom was elected to chair the session on Indigenous people at the conference. Her service in this capacity required her to revise the propositions that were made before they were voted on. She had the capacity to edit in such a way as to transform the rather accusative proposals to positive and proactive ones. Her presence caught the attention of the Dalai Lama, who invited both her and Jacqueline Left Hand Bull to meet with him. Receiving a present from him at the end of that two-hour session was significant and meaningful to her.

My mother lived in Wakpala for nearly twenty years. She was a trusted member of the community and was relied upon by many for her sage advice and wisdom. Her regal bearing commanded respect. She took time to advise those facing challenges, and she had a sixth sense of what people needed. Her home was a center of attraction. Visitors sought her wisdom, her company, and her cooking.

Wherever Mom went, she earned this same respect. In Bismarck, she always stayed at a particular hotel. Years later, when I visited, staff mem-

---

* About MacArthur's Fellows Program, MacArthur Foundation, http://www. macfound.org.

bers shared their fond memories. Mom had always treated them with great courtesy, listened to their life stories, remembered their children's names, and offered great advice. She also tipped them well. They admired the great love she demonstrated for everyone.

A large part of my children's upbringing was spending time with Mom. In the midst of my tumultuous first marriage, my kids found refuge with their grandmother. Mom doted on them. She cooked delicious meals. She offered comfort and penetrating insight to their woes. Waniya once wrote a poem about her grandmother's hands—how her hands were very soft, how she could make the most delicious foods, how she could solve any problem with those hands.

Mom spearheaded numerous community endeavors. She provided creative thought and continuous effort for various initiatives. One year, when she served on the powwow committee in Wakpala, the progressive governor of South Dakota, George Michelson, declared a year of "reconciliation." Mom and I planned several events to bring White and Indian people together. We coordinated a reconciliation run; youth from the reservation ran to a bridge that crossed the Missouri River, and the White youth living on the other side met them in the middle of the bridge. The youth from the reservation escorted the White youth from Mobridge, as a gesture of hospitality, back to the powwow grounds for prayers. Mom also hosted a devotional gathering for different religious leaders to come together to pray for unity and to share a meal together. Even before she became a Bahá'í, she was opening her home for me to host fireside gatherings, where community members deepened on spiritual themes inspired by Bahá'í teachings.

I learned much from my mother, as a part of her everyday discourse, about sharing the teachings of the Bahá'í Faith in the most natural way. Teaching as a part of her everyday life was a manifestation of her generosity and magnanimity. Without any airs and in numerous settings, whether in a public talk or on a visit to a friend's home, she mentioned Bahá'u'lláh and shared passages from The Hidden Words. Her favorite point of conversation was progressive revelation—that God has revealed Himself to mankind throughout time in the form of spiritual teachers who have brought to us religious laws and teachings suited for the time in which we live. She loved the quote "Unto the cities of all nations He hath sent His Messengers, Whom He hath commissioned to announce unto men tidings of the

Paradise of His good pleasure, and to draw them nigh unto the Haven of abiding security, the Seat of eternal holiness and transcendent glory."*

I believe this particular passage resonated with her because of her own spiritual journey. Though instructed in Catholicism as a youth, she felt distant from God. Acquainting herself with the spiritual underpinnings of Indigenous people and serving her community through activism had readied her heart for the Word of God. Mom admired the response of Sitting Bull when he was asked to abandon his Indigenous spiritual beliefs: "It's not necessary for an eagle to become a crow."** What he was implying was that humans are born to be ascendant beings; we should not forfeit our progress towards nobility and give up that which is higher for that which is lower. The principle of progressive revelation, that God reveals Himself throughout time as mankind matures, is mirrored in the spiritual progress of my mother's own spiritual journey. After years of seeking the truth, my mom joined me on a visit to the village of Miskipampa. There, she met Indigenous people who accepted Bahá'u'lláh's revelation within their own cultural and linguistic context. Deeply moved and inspired by the people of that village, my mother made the decision to embrace the Bahá'í Faith as her own faith.

Though robust and active throughout most of her life, my mother was physically and emotionally devastated after the death of her grandson, my nephew, in a car accident. This loss compromised her normally strong immune system, and she succumbed to a virulent diabetic condition. Her limbs, especially her feet, became necrotic toward the end, and she could barely walk. She still attended meetings and fulfilled her duty on the National Spiritual Assembly and remained active in the community. However, her heart and soul were wounded, and this took a deep toll on her body.

In 2001 my mother attended a spiritual retreat, organized by Gary Kimble, a dear friend, on the San Carlos Apache Reservation in Arizona. Because of her significant health challenges, I volunteered to accompany

---

* Bahá'u'lláh, *Gleanings from the Writings of Bahá'u'lláh*, no. 76.1.

** Charles A. Eastman, "Sitting Bull—Lakota Chief and Holy Man, Legends of America," http://www.legendsofamerica.com.

her on this trip. Upon leaving her house in Wakpala, she paused and looked back at her home and the landscape she so cherished. Her home was built on a peninsula overlooking the confluence of the Grand River and the Missouri River. The view, both of the water and of the land on the other side, stretched out as far as one could see. Mom joked that she suffered from "horizon deprivation" when she traveled. Her heart yearned for the freedom of this unrestrained landscape that also bore the sacred history of the ancestors. Mom soaked in the view for a minute more, a farewell of sorts to her beloved homeland.

We landed at Sky Harbor Airport in Phoenix, rented a car, and drove a couple of hours into the mountains to the Apache Reservation. After the loss of so much of her mobility, traveling again brought her joy. I felt uplifted to see her regain some dynamism. We reached the reservation, and I felt even more uplifted to observe Mom's increasing levels of contentment. Spending time with her friends was just the remedy she needed.

During one of the sessions, Mom began to feel lightheaded, and her stomach bothered her. I drove her to the health clinic serving San Carlos. Upon discovering her blood pressure was dangerously low, the doctor ordered an air ambulance. A helicopter arrived and whisked her away to Maricopa County Hospital in Phoenix. I returned to the hotel room, collected her belongings, and drove to Phoenix, my heart heavy and afraid.

When I arrived, she was in the emergency room, heavily medicated, with a tracheotomy that had been put in place. Within hours, her condition worsened and doctors performed surgery to place a stent in her heart. When I was allowed in her room, her condition continued to deteriorate, and she fell into a coma. As often as I could, I remained in her room. I talked to her. I sang prayer songs. I believed that her spirit could sense me, even though she was not conscious.

After my sister flew in to join us, the doctors conveyed to us that our mom had no chance of survival unless her legs were amputated above the knee. We made the difficult decision to consent to the surgery. Though the operation was successful and Mom woke from the coma, she was traumatized by the loss of her legs. She began therapy, which we hoped would help her learn to manage, both physically and emotionally. Days and weeks passed, and her spirits did brighten. When awake, though she could not speak, she pointed this way and that and used hands and facial gestures to communicate. Once, she held up two fingers to her lips, a coy smile planted there. Confused, I asked, "What do you want, Mom?" She lifted her two fingers again. I still did not understand, so I handed her a pencil and paper. She drew a picture of an arrow and pointed to her box of cigarettes. We both laughed.

My mother asked me to return to South Dakota and gave me detailed directions to retrieve a small box. A year before I was born, my mother had given birth to a stillborn daughter. My sister's remains had been cremated, and my mother had always kept the remains with her in a box. My mother was relieved when I returned to Arizona with my sister's remains.

On October 20th, 2001, the day Bahá'ís commemorate the birth of the Báb, I visited Mom. She waved good-bye as I left the room. A few hours later, I got the call that she had slipped back into a coma and was brain-dead. Back at the hospital, my sister and I made the joint decision to disconnect our mother from life support.

We buried my mother at Camelback Cemetery in Paradise Valley, a suburb of Phoenix. A desert cemetery, cacti, sand, and stone adorned the land. The funeral brought together Bahá'ís from the area, members of the National Spiritual Assembly, and all of my mother's family, so beloved to her, her children and grandchildren, nieces and nephews, and great-grandchildren. Later, we held memorial events on the reservation—a pow-wow, children's games, and a spirit run, all in my mother's name.

The funeral service aired live on the Standing Rock radio station that my mother had helped establish. Joe Brown Thunder, a clergyman from South Dakota, offered a prayer in Lakota, as a representation of my mother's work with language preservation. My nephew sang a song composed by his recently deceased brother, the one whose tragic death had shaken my mother. Singers from Standing Rock sang for the procession of the casket to the gravesite. These songs came from pre-reservation days and spoke to the temporality of life. They signified how now was the time for the living to arise, to make their mark on the world for our lives move as swiftly as a shadow over the prairies.

After mom had passed, the design of the headstone came to me during one of my runs. I worked with a Bahá'í designer to create the image. A motif of the Ojibwe people—floral designs on the side of the stone—represented the everlasting spring, the spring that autumn can never overtake, the spring that blooms in every heart. A Lakota design of seventy-two feathers represented each year of my mother's life. At the center of the headstone, a morning star design radiated. I also made the decision to engrave a line of the long obligatory prayer revealed by Bahá'u'lláh on the headstone in Lakota. While my mother was in the hospital, she had read the prayer—a prayer that requires genuflections and motions, which she was unable to do—every day. I had wondered about this and realized that her spirit was longing for movement.

The spring following my mother's death, I returned to Phoenix for the dedication of her headstone. I brought sage from Wakpala and a brilliant red earth paint for the dedication. We equipped four children with the vermillion paint, and using the sage for paintbrushes, they ceremoniously clad the tombstone in a cloak of crimson—God's color—thus making it heavenly and related to the eternal. I then inscribed the line I had chosen from the long obligatory prayer, *"Maȟpiya na Makȟa Wokuŋze kiŋ oyas'iŋ kiŋ Nitȟawa, O Wamakȟognaka Itȟaŋčhaŋ / The Kingdoms of Earth and Heaven are Thine, O Lord of the Worlds."**

After my mother died, Janet Rubenstein, the assistant to the Secretary of the National Spiritual Assembly of the Bahá'ís of the United States, called me to share a dream she had had of my mother. In the dream, Janet observed my mother as a radiant and luminous being, physically restored to her robust and powerful self. In the dream, two young people embraced my mother. One was my mother's grandson. Janet knew about him and how his loss had affected Mom. Janet was not sure about the other young person. She described her as a young woman who was about my age and looked like me. I knew this was my stillborn sister, welcoming my mother to the next world.

I also wondered about my mom's dogs. She had several dogs at the time of her death. Though they weren't old or sick, each of these dogs died within a few short months of her passing. I recalled how a Bahá'í friend had once spoken to my mother about the afterlife. When he mentioned the teaching that only the human reality has an eternal soul, Mom was concerned. She

---

* Bahá'u'lláh, in *Bahá'í Prayers*, p. 16.

lamented that she wouldn't have the close-knit bond with her dogs when she died. "Oh, don't worry," he exclaimed and showed her a quotation that indicated God would provide everything the soul required for progress in the next world. This assuaged Mom's concern, as she truly felt that the canine companionship would be essential for her soul's progress.

Four years after her passing, in 2005, my mother was posthumously inducted into the National Women's Hall of Fame, the country's oldest not-for-profit membership organization dedicated to celebrating the achievements of women. The national organization was founded in 1969 in Seneca Falls, New York, the birthplace of the American Women's Rights Movement. All inductees are nominated and then scored by a panel of judges on the basis of the significance, value, and lasting impact of their accomplishments. My mom shares this honor with Susan B. Anthony, Rachel Carson, Maya Angelou, Hillary Rodham Clinton, and many other leaders from various disciplines and backgrounds.

I recently dreamed that I was standing in my mother's kitchen, alone. I heard the sounds of a car pulling up to the house. Suddenly, my mother burst through the door, robust and joyous, wearing her long coat and carrying a suitcase. She walked through the dining room and into her room. She passed by me matter-of-factly, with no great acknowledgement, as if we'd never been apart. I was paralyzed with shock. *She's alive,* I thought, and I began to weep.

Upon waking, I realized how the dream represented the reality of my mother in the next world. She is always with us. Walking through the door of her home, she did not need to reunite with me—because we have always been together. I thought of the passage from the writings of Bahá'u'lláh, referring to the spiritual world: "Behold it is closer to you than your life-vein!"*

---

* Bahá'u'lláh, *Gleanings from the Writings of Bahá'u'lláh,* no. 153.5.

17

By this time, I was no longer married, and after being single for a number of years, I felt ready to search for a potential life partner and create a successful marriage. A friend of mine suggested that I check out a Web site called "Two Doves." I checked out their Web site and decided to try out a three-month subscription. I lost interest because I did not find any connections. About a year or so later, motivated to try again, I registered for another three months. Every once in a while, I explored various profiles, personal information, and some photos. Again, I decided to let it go because much of the Bahá'í population resides in urban areas. As a rural kind of person, I doubted that few people would sacrifice their urban lifestyle to live in Wakpala. At the end of the three months, with an hour to go on my subscription, I took one last look. That's when I saw my future wife's profile. I sent her a smile icon. I checked back a few minutes later, the last couple of minutes to go, and saw that she was not online anymore. "That's the end of that," I thought.

Ceylan, like me, had signed up for "Two Doves" upon the recommendation and then the insistence of her friends. Like me, she only occasionally checked the notifications, and when she received the smile I sent, she sent back a friendly and unassuming message. Since my subscription had run out at that point, however, I did not receive her message. Fortunately, I had sent her my Facebook address, and we began to communicate back and forth. I knew nothing about Ceylan except her description on "Two Doves." For her part, she knew that I was an American Indian hoop dancer but had never been to a performance. She remembered taking part in a small portion of the Spirit Run where Native American Bahá'í youth ran from the West Coast to the East Coast, and she remembered hearing that I had something to do with that run. But other than that, we did not really know each other. We soon discovered areas of compatibility, however. As independent people, we both valued autonomy, and we appreciated a simplistic and healthy life, without a lot of concern for materialistic trappings.

Ceylan originally came from Turkey and a Sunni Muslim culture, and her story of coming to the United States impressed me. While growing up, she had demonstrated talent in the arts, especially music. She had mastered the traditional dances of Turkey, had a pitch-perfect singing voice, and played the guitar and piano. Encouraged to focus on her academic work, she ranked second in Turkey academically and possessed a mastery of all subject matter. Because of her academic excellence, she was offered a scholarship to study in the United States, and she earned a degree in psychology at the University of Maryland in College Park. From there, she went to Indiana University in Bloomington, where she earned her doctorate in neuroscience. She then completed five years of post-doctoral studies at the University of Michigan with a focus on mental health research. When we met, she was well into her professional work as an assistant professor in neuroscience research at Florida Atlantic University. There, she studied addiction neuroscience early in her career, set up a neuroscience lab, and was named researcher of the year at FAU.

While studying at Indiana University, she came across a magazine that caught her attention because people representing various nations of the world were featured on the cover. She obtained the magazine, a magazine about the Bahá'í world. She began attending firesides every Friday, and in a short period of time she had become a Bahá'í and had accepted the teachings of Bahá'u'lláh. The reason, she believes, that it took such a short period of time between her learning about the Bahá'í Faith and accepting it was because her heart had been attracted to the diversity of the human family captured in the cover of the Bahá'í magazine. Two teachings, in addition to the unification of our beautifully diverse human family, especially attracted her—the agreement of science and religion and the equality of men and women. Ceylan had grown up in a Muslim household that valued the education of girls. Though not all family members believed women needed education since they were going to get married, Ceylan's father had valued the education of girls and had made sure that both his daughters received a high quality education.

Years later, on a visit to Turkey, Ceylan had discovered a Bahá'í book in her grandfather's library and had felt an interesting confirmation in her choice to become a Bahá'í. She was descended from a long line of educators. An educational inspector who traveled all over Turkey to inspect the curriculum at elementary schools, her father had collected many books in his travels and had a large library. Discovering that book felt to her as if she had come full circle.

After a short period of writing each other, I asked Ceylan for her phone number so we could chat. During our early exchanges, Ceylan could not say much because she had contracted the swine flu and was so ill she had lost her voice and was barely able to move. I was ready to proceed with investigating her character using the list of questions provided by the Two Doves Web site for that very purpose. I navigated through the list of questions and managed to carry the conversation. I shared some ideas and many passages from the Bahá'í writings. According to Ceylan, I also cracked unending jokes that caused her to smile.

When she regained her voice, she contributed heartily to our conversations. We discovered similarities and differences in our personalities, communication styles, and financial management. Sharing our personal history helped us learn about each other's families, the challenges we had faced, and the successes we had experienced. We discussed our thoughts on having and raising children. The deep exploration of these questions facilitated our learning about one another in important ways.

After a couple of months and hours and hours of talking, I invited Ceylan to meet me in Washington, D.C., where I was scheduled to perform at the Museum of the American Indian at the Smithsonian on the mall. Washington, D.C., seemed to be a good halfway point between South Dakota and Florida. I picked Ceylan up at Reagan National Airport that early October day we first met. She was one of the last people to get off the plane.

Right then and there, when I saw her, I felt something intuitively. I sensed that we were going to be a good couple. Over the next few days, we spent time together. She saw me perform for the first time and loves to recall that what she remembers most about that day was that I was ecstatic, smiling the whole time, and putting my arm around her wherever we went. She claims that my generally positive attitude is amped up to the nth degree when I am being romantic.

Our relationship progressed quickly without either one of us pushing the other. We met online in September, in person in October, and by November we sensed that marriage was the next step and that it was part of our destiny. Ceylan is the only Bahá'í in her family and the only person in her family on this side of the Atlantic Ocean. Bahá'ís must receive approval from parents in order to get married, and because her mother was our last living parent, we traveled to Turkey to receive her mother's consent. Her mother was surprised about this particular Bahá'í law but offered her consent.

We were married on January 15, 2010 in Florida, and the wedding ceremony was showered with the love from Ceylan's local Bahá'í community. Ceylan attended a Bahá'í choir regularly, which had created a catalyst for community-building. Deep spiritual bonds were formed through the choir's selfless service and the heartfelt interaction that occurred before, during, and after the choir practices, performances, and devotionals. Jeanette Contant-Galitello and her husband Christopher organized the choir and attracted many people representing various nationalities and races. Jeanette (stage name Kiskadee) came from a cross-cultural musical family. Her mother was a native of Guyana, and her father was a native of Trinidad. A composer, producer, and arranger, she moved from England to South Florida with her husband. They generously opened their home to host a variety of events, and their spirit of fellowship drew Ceylan in. She loved their warm hearts and the creative environment they created.

When we received consent from Ceylan's mom for marriage, we announced this at the choir to friends. Jeanette and Christopher offered their home for the intimate wedding ceremony we had in mind. Every single choir member helped with some aspect of the wedding: the baking of the two-dove themed cake with four colors of the hoop, the flower decorations, the program printing, the food, the music, the make-up of the bride, the setting up of the sound system, and the arranging for a DJ. Today, Ceylan always declares that this was the best party of her life. We both could not believe how our small and intimate wedding came together with everyone pitching in so naturally.

The wedding program itself reflected the diversity we hold close to our hearts. Sonny Nevaquaya, one of my Comanche friends, offered a sage blessing to start the ceremony. Ceylan's coworkers shared Hindu prayers. A Cameroonian musical dedication, a Guyanese musical offering, and original music from Kiskadee inspired everyone in attendance. We also included Bahá'í prayers, selections from The Hidden Words, and readings from Ella Cara Deloria about family. To conclude the ceremony, we exchanged our wedding vows, rings, and then were draped with a Lakota Morningstar Quilt.

When we reflect on the wedding, our hearts fill with gratitude that we were wedded in the bosom of a loving community and that our wedding was an act and product of a community-building process. We also included prayers and passages on gender equality, a critical component to a healthy marriage and world. 'Abdu'l-Bahá wrote that "The world of humanity has two wings—one is women and the other men. Not until both wings are equally developed can the bird fly. Should one wing remain weak, flight is impossible."* Success and prosperity are dependent on the realization of equality. Like most couples today who believe in gender equality as the ideal, we made the commitment to work towards advancing this teaching from God in our marriage.

Bahá'u'lláh has upheld and restored the sanctity of marriage, a foundational institution of society. Unity begins in the family. Communities and the world will not achieve unity until and unless family unity is created. As an individual, I realize that I have few memories of healthy marriages. My parents had a dysfunctional marriage. My first marriage did not survive. So many of us, including me, are learning what marriage as an institution means. The divorce rate ranges between forty to fifty per cent in the United States. Since the required Bahá'í wedding vow is "We will all verily abide by the Will of God," a rather mysterious, striking, and profound vow, reading the writings on marriage is critically important.** The word *abide* means to have constancy, never deviating from the will of God, which is the Word of God. Reading the writings morning and night and studying the writings

---

* 'Abdu'l-Bahá, *Selections from the Writings of 'Abdu'l-Bahá*, no. 227.18.
** Bahá'u'lláh, in *Bahá'í Prayers*, p. 115.

on marriage can aid us in experiencing God's will as a natural state of being both inside and outside the institution of marriage. I continue to study the Bahá'í writings on marriage and strive to translate into action what I read.

* * *

Just a couple of months later, we started our first Bahá'í fast together. During the fast, however, Ceylan realized she was pregnant. Naturally, she stopped fasting. We were excited to prepare for the arrival of our child. In the months to come, we found a house in Delray Beach, Florida, continued on with our busy work schedules, with mine including a lot of travel. By the second trimester in August, our pace intensified, especially for Ceylan. Since I was traveling and performing, Ceylan finished organizing our home to prepare for our new baby girl, on top of meeting numerous work deadlines.

I returned to Florida in late October to prepare for our daughter's birth. We had decided to name our daughter after my late mother, Unci Patricia Ann Locke. Her first name would be Patricia. We decided on Ȟupáhu for her middle name. Ȟupáhu means *wings* in Lakota. The áhu part of Ȟupáhu is a Turkish word that means *gazelle*. Ceylan's first name is also a poetic way of saying gazelle.

On November 16, Ceylan was working hard on finishing up a manuscript when her water broke. Her doctor suggested that she take a few hours to rest at home and then come to the hospital when the contractions began. We set the alarm for a few hours later and slept the entire few hours. When we woke, we were surprised that there were still no contractions, no pain, no movement, nothing. Being the man of eternal calm, according to Ceylan, I made coffee for myself and gathered a tea concoction with the medicinal plant I had brought specifically for Ceylan's labor in case she had any difficulties. I had learned about this childbirth medicine from my mom's aunt, Margaret One Bull, or Nakíwizipi Wíŋ, the daughter of Chief One Bull. Margaret had learned a lot of her medicine from her mother, and she was a midwife for many decades around the Little Eagle and Wakpala area. She had delivered over a hundred children and used a variety of medicinal plants for all aspects of midwifery. She also knew how to stimulate lactation for nursing mothers.

In the early 1970s, Margaret had shown me this medicine called *wíŋyaŋ tȟa-pȟežúta,* a woman's medicine, which is a form of sage. I had used it during the birth of my oldest daughter, Kimimila. The information Margaret imparted required what is called *wóȟeyaka.* This word is not directly translated into English; it is a symbolic payment that one gives in recognition of the lineage of the knowledge. The knowledge that she imparted was not from her as an individual but instead came down from the spirit world into this world. This is the right of God, and this knowledge and practice is not for the material world. It is something that is given over to the next world for the perpetuation and continuity of divine blessings. The person who is the recipient of the knowledge will receive it and use it in a way that is commensurate with the divine source.

In September, a couple of months before Patricia's birth, while visiting my home and family in Standing Rock, I sensed Ceylan might require this medicine. My Grand-Aunt, my mom's Aunt Margaret, had told me that I would need to keep the medicine in a very clean place and that I must harvest it standing downwind of the plant. Standing downwind accentuates the idea of the plant remaining uncontaminated. One morning, the thought occurred to me that I needed to find that medicine. I said some prayers and headed out for my morning run on the prairie near my house. I spotted the perfect plant growing near the edge of a huge ant hill. What the ants do is mound up the dirt and pebbles around the entrance of their den and pick out all the vegetation around the circumference of their hill. There, at the edge of that ant circle, completely denuded of vegetation, I saw the perfect plant growing. The plant had formed big seedpods, indicating that this was a mature plant and at the peak of potency for medicinal purposes.

I ran back and asked my granddaughter Waníkiya to join me. We walked out to the ant hill, where the plant was growing. Waníkiya offered up some tobacco, and we used sage incense for purification. We prayed and asked if we could use this gift from God's creation—use the power of and strength of this holy medicine to assist in the appearance of a new soul and to benefit a new life coming into the world. We thanked the ants there for watching out and being the stewards and trustees of that special plant that was unique in its shape and form and its degree of efficacy in terms of potency. We then sang a prayer for the day and the gift of the plant.

Standing downwind of the plant, my granddaughter, leaving the root in the ground, harvested the medicinal portion of the plant. Later, I packaged the plant in such a way that I could transport it.

In October, I returned to our home in Florida. Six weeks later, on November 16, Ceylan's water broke at eleven in the evening. Ceylan called the doctor and the doula. Since Ceylan had no contractions, the doctor suggested she go to bed and get some sleep before labor intensified. We anticipated a couple of hours of sleep but slept through the whole night. The alarm woke us at six in the morning. Ceylan was still not having any contractions. To prepare the plant, I boiled the water, placed the medicinal yellow part of the plant in the water, and let it steep for over twenty minutes. Then I poured the contents into a jar. We tucked it in Ceylan's bags and left the house for the hospital.

We met Ceylan's doula, who also arrived at the hospital at the same time we did. The doctor examined her and reported that she had not dilated at all. After a few hours of no progress, the doctor informed us that she would attach an IV drip to Ceylan to artificially dilate her. She emphasized the process would be very slow and that she did not expect the birth to happen any time soon. Her plan was to leave the hospital, make her rounds at other hospitals, and return later. She left to give directions to the attending nurse.

When everybody left the room, I administered the medicinal tea I had made earlier that morning. Ceylan chugged down the drink and declared that it tasted awful. Concerned about her ability to dilate and Patricia's health, she walked around the hospital room with the doula who helped her get into positions that could stimulate contractions.

Very soon, Ceylan called out to the nurse that the baby was coming. She literally felt as if an internal door had opened and that her insides were falling through that door. The nurse, reluctant to disturb the doctor over a possible false alarm, assured Ceylan the birth would not be happening any time soon. But Ceylan insisted. The nurse shuffled out of the room to call the doctor, came back, and ordered Ceylan to avoid pushing until another doctor arrived. Thankfully, a doctor entered the room within minutes, and Patty was born.

I whispered into our newborn's ears a prayer that I later learned was not an authenticated prayer. Nonetheless, the words are beautiful and I'm happy that I shared them with my new daughter. "Áwičhakheya, Wakȟáŋ Tȟáŋka u nišÍ čha yahíhuŋni! Tuwá Thehílapi na Iháktapi čha iwóyaglakiŋkte na ilágyayiŋkte čha yahínaphe!" This translates to "Verily, thou hast come by the command of God! Thou hast appeared to speak of Him and thou hast been created to serve Him Who is the Dear, the Beloved!"*

Then I cut her umbilical cord and laid our new baby on Ceylan's chest. Patricia's big brown eyes were wide, and she began scanning her surroundings, checking out her new parents and everything around her.

For the next several months, I did not schedule presentations so that I could remain with Ceylan and Patricia every day. Ceylan adapted to motherhood and quickly became an expert in taking care of Patricia. Patricia was blessed to have such an attentive, loving, and diligent mother.

At her first check-up, the doctor stated that her heartbeat was remarkable, pronounced, and powerful. He also mentioned there was some risk that could result in a birth defect. But I sensed her strength would carry her through. She had a zest for life that could not be defeated. That is why we gave her the Lakota name—Čhaŋlkíyapi Wíŋ, which translates to *They use her for a heart*. Her name signifies that she is a child that is so loved by the people that she will inspire people to do magnanimous things on her behalf. The love for the child will extend out to humanity, and it will be a love that transcends barriers. This child therefore has a capacity for compassion and love that unites and attracts others.

Right from the beginning, Patricia possessed an exuberant spirit, a zeal for life, and remarkable creativity. Even before she could sit up, she enjoyed listening to music. As a toddler, her love for music grew, and she loved to sing and memorize nursery rhymes and princess songs; she was able to come up with an original song for almost any occasion. She sang about the stars coming out at night, the wheels on the bus, and Humpty Dumpty. When she could stand on her own, she started dancing to all kinds of music. One of her favorite activities was to watch YouTube videos of powwow dancing. Together, we practiced new choreography.

Today, we share a love for the outdoors. Patricia, like me, prefers the outdoors to the indoors. We often spend time at the park or boardwalk and enjoy many outdoor adventures together. I admire her natural tendency

---

* Quoted from *Star of the West*, vol. XXIII, no. 3, June 1932, p. 71.

towards inclusivity. She loves to include all of her "friends"—all of the little kids she meets at the park or school or wherever we go.

18

One of the greatest rewards of my career has been and continues to be connecting with Indigenous communities around the world. Through the great privilege of interacting with and exploring commonalities between our cultures, I have discovered numerous themes that unite us; in particular, I continue to observe a shared sense of stewardship for the natural world and all of creation among Indigenous people.

During one of many tours to Polynesia and Micronesia, I shared with the Indigenous Bahá'ís there that as Indigenous people, we have much to offer humanity in terms of our experience with elements of the natural world that appear as metaphors in the Bahá'í writings. In particular, we have rich experience with the divine springtime and the ocean.

For Bahá'ís, our understanding of the divine springtime is this: that God will, through various divine Educators specifically chosen by Him, renew the spiritual teachings of old and provide humanity with new teachings to advance civilization. Each world religion goes through the seasons; the divine springtime is the return of the Day of God, the Dispensations of old made new after a long winter.

Where I come from, Standing Rock, the metaphor of the divine springtime comes to life. During the long, deep winter, snow blankets the earth, ground blizzards white out the air, and temperatures plunge to thirty below zero. After those intense months come and go, we appreciate the signs of spring. The earth gradually thaws, and buds shoot up from the earth. These signs of new life fill us with a sense of home. The days grow longer. The prairies green and fill with wildflowers. The trills and warbles of returning birds provide fresh music to the ears. The metaphor of the divine springtime takes on added meaning for those of us who experience the four seasons, because we experience winter's desolation and await the promise of spring. One might say that our knowledge of spring is a relative understanding based on the intensity of one's experience with winter; the harsher the winter, the more revitalizing the spring.

The metaphor of the ocean also provides the Polynesian and Micronesian Bahá'ís, who have lived on and navigated the oceans for centuries, with rich insights into the writings that can enlighten those of us who don't have these same insights. Easter Islanders, who inhabit a tiny pinprick of an island, shared with me that before their ancestors set sail in canoes from Tahiti, they dreamed that an island of their own was out there, somewhere in the ocean. Their vision propelled them to set out to find their own island. Armed with mystical knowledge and deeply-rooted navigational skills, they could read the oceans well and connected with the waters. They found their island. The story of how the Easter Islanders found their homeland parallels, to me, the spiritual journeys of many individuals who were led by dreams, visions, or a deep spiritual conviction to new teachings. These individuals trusted this mystical sense and their navigational skills and began their search with the faith that they would find the truth.

In my travels to New Zealand, Marshall Islands, and Hawaii, I have been struck by how the Bahá'ís there have numerous spiritual experiences connected to the ocean. One time, while at the Bahá'í Center in the Marshall Islands, I was sitting at the back of the Bahá'í Center for a Feast. While enjoying the beautiful music, chorus, and prayers, I glanced off to the side to watch the tropical breeze playing in the palm leaves. I noticed an elder woman walking slowly by the Bahá'í Center. She then turned and walked by again, pausing to gaze with rapt attention at the activities in the Center. I pointed her out to Dr. Korean, a Marshallese gentleman and member of the National Spiritual Assembly, who happened to be sitting next to me. He promptly jumped up to invite her in.

Crying and overjoyed, she confided to him that her husband, who had recently died, came to her in a dream. She was on a boat that was rapidly sinking. "Get off the boat," he told her.

"What boat should I go on?" she asked.

"Get on the ark," he responded. "You'll know it because of the people on the ark."

"How will I recognize them?"

"By the radiance of their faces. Get up now. Go out and find the ark."

The woman leapt out of bed and began walking. When she walked past the Bahá'í Center, she felt something stir within her. She walked back and forth, listening to the prayers and the music, and knew this was the ark to which her husband had directed her.

Though I treasure sharing more stories of the numerous travels I have been blessed to take, I will share one last highlight of my career—a trip to Edirne, Turkey, historically known as Adrianople, that I took in the late 1990s. Bahá'u'lláh had been exiled in Edirne for five years, from 1863 to 1868.

Prior to this trip, which included performances throughout Greece, I had contacted the Bahá'í National Center in Istanbul. The staff there arranged with the mayor of Edirne for an ensemble of performers and I to share our art at a plaza in front of the largest mosque in the city. This mosque was especially significant: Bahá'u'lláh Himself had prayed there every day during His time in the city.

When we arrived in Edirne, we were greeted by the mayor himself. Though the mayor was not a Bahá'í and could not speak any English, he welcomed us by opening his arms wide and announcing: "Edirne! Bahá'u'lláh! City!"

When we arrived, I was awestruck by the beauty of the plaza and the mosque, as well as the size of the crowd—some eight thousand people had gathered to watch us perform. We performed alongside Roma (gypsy) performers. The large Roma troupe excelled in their synchronized folk dances, while our ensemble offered various traditional dance and music, including the flute music and hoop dance.

Sharing the hoop dance next to that special mosque was a deeply spiritual experience for me. All the people in the audience were descendants, I imagined, of people who had encountered Bahá'u'lláh on a daily basis.

Prior to this trip, I had intellectually understood the significance of Bahá'u'lláh's time in Edirne. Government authorities threatened by His increasing popularity did everything in their power to extinguish the flame of this new Revelation and exiled and imprisoned Bahá'u'lláh throughout His adult life. The journey from Constantinople to Edirne was perilous. Bahá'u'lláh and His family traveled twelve days by foot in mid-winter, and the family fell ill and suffered greatly. In Edirne, despite His status as an exile, Bahá'u'lláh's reputation grew. Though He had already announced to His followers that He was sent by God to bring teachings for a new day, He publicly made His mission clear. He wrote letters to rulers of the world proclaiming His station, and He urged these leaders to establish peace, to eschew war, and to establish a global commonwealth dedicated to justice and disarmament.

I knew about Bahá'u'lláh's time in Edirne, but to experience being in a place associated so closely with the life of Bahá'u'lláh filled me with the kind of wonderment we see in children first experiencing the world. There, at the foot of the mosque where he prayed, I was filled with a heightened sense of presence. I was dancing on sacred ground. Awe filled my entire being when I later entered the mosque and prostrated myself. I attempted to etch into my heart the feelings of being there. My prayers were buoyed by my gratitude—I could not have asked God for more.

When I consider this trip and many others, I am able to frame the challenges and obstacles I have experienced during the course of my career in a perspective that enables me to focus less on the stumbling blocks and more on the stepping stones of advancement. Like anyone in any profession, I have experienced tests and difficulties along my path. I hope that I have grown from them. I have had various managers through the course of my career, and some have opened new doors for traveling, receiving grants and fellowships, and collaborating with other artists. However, other people I have worked with have had me believing the doors to my career were closing, that my opportunity to serve had come and gone, that I was getting too old to perform. I am grateful for my current manager, who has given me opportunities to perform with regularity and to serve in the way I was meant to serve.

Despite some of the obstacles, setbacks, and tests I have faced and continue to face, I am grateful that my career has allowed me to promote both Indigenous themes and even more importantly universal themes that serve the entire world.

There is much discussion in our Bahá'í communities on developing coherent lives that integrate personal, professional, and community spheres. We do not have one set of values for our profession and another set for our family. We do not reserve our beliefs solely for attending a devotional meeting and then forget them when we leave the meeting. Rather, we are challenged to weave our beliefs into every area of our life.

We are living in propitious times, especially in regards to our role as proponents of an ever-advancing civilization and creators of a unified world. I feel blessed to promote "world citizenship" through my travels, presentations, and performances. Ostensibly, people think I give presentations on Indigenous culture, and I would not want to correct them, but my intent is to affirm universal themes. Folk arts by definition reflect the salient qualities of a culture—qualities that withstand the test of time and speak to the universality and the nobility of the human spirit. I always hope that my audiences walk away uplifted by something that I affirmed within them as human beings.

The revelation of Bahá'u'lláh shines a light upon one's heritage and identifies the aspects that are universal and that touch the hearts of all who see, hear, and witness this revelation. The revelation enabled me to identify universal aspects and themes of Lakota culture, heritage, and language, and this is exclusively what I aim to present. For example, God has established a Covenant with humankind. He has progressively revealed Himself through the appearance of holy souls who bring spiritual teachings to aid in the development of the people. The White Buffalo Calf Maiden, I believe, was the holy soul who brought God's teachings to the Lakota. Many of the teachings I share with audiences around the world transcend cultural and tribal sensitivity. People of all backgrounds recognize and celebrate that we are all legitimate co-heirs to our shared heritage of humankind.

One such teaching and theme is servitude. If we want to present our lives at the end of our journey as a gift to God, the truest gift to bring is one of servitude. Why spend our days accumulating knowledge, if God is already the All-Knowing? Why spend our days accumulating riches, if God is the All-Possessing? The best gift we can offer God is the one the Recipient does not have, and that gift is to live a life of acquiring virtues through service to the greater good. During presentations, I often share the meaning of the eagle staff. The feathers on the staff represent virtues. If we look at ourselves as eagles born into this world, the only way our virtues become activated is when we use these virtues in service to God's creation, to all of humanity. Then and only then can we soar.

Like the eagle staff, the hoops also have symbolic significance. When I do hoop dance presentations at schools, I end each presentation the same way. With the final beat of the drum, I pick up the sphere made of many hoops—the world design—that I make at the end of every dance. I hold

249

it up to the children. "This represents the world." I hold it straight over my head, then bring it down and peer through it. I walk towards the kids. They are quiet, intent. I say, "This is my crystal ball, and I can see the future. The future is not out there." I move to look at all of them. "The future is right here, right now."

I place the globe down. "The future requires that we all work together in this circle. In a circle, there is no corner. No place to hide, no dark place to flee to. There's no back row. We all have a front row seat. We have a place in this circle, and no one can be excluded. I pick the globe up again. We all have strengths. If one of us gets left out. . ." I pull a hoop from the globe, and the whole thing collapses.

Then, I pick up the hoops and form them into a long chain. "Only together can we create patterns of unity." Setting the chain down, I walk the line of hoops on the ground. "Only together can we progress." I lift the chain of hoops from the center point, forming a bridge, with each side touching the ground. "Only together can we overcome obstacles and go beyond all the strife and hatred and wars. We must cross that bridge together."

I hold the hoops up like a ladder. "Only together can we climb the mountain of knowledge." I turn to the children and ask them, "When we get to the top of the mountain, what do we do?" I take the hoops and make wings and pretend to fly away. "We have no choice but to soar on the wings of knowledge. As we're soaring together, what do we see?" I make another globe. I toss it up in the air and catch it.

"Remember: every eagle needs a nest, a place of security and safety." I crouch inside of the circle. "We need a place to break out of our shells." I stand up. "We need a place where we can stand in this world, open our eyes to all the beauty, wonder, and magic." I extend my arms outward.

"We need a place from which we can launch our flight into the new day."

PART IV

INÁŽIŊ
(TO ARISE)

Though I have enjoyed and benefited from an early morning discipline everywhere I have traveled, I prefer running at home in Wakpala. The wisps of wind in the buffalo grass, the crunch of snow on the prairies, the faint crackle of sprouting plants in the spring, and the intonation of the meadowlarks and occasional mockingbird exhilarate my soul. They remind me that though we exist in a material world, we are spiritual beings.

My early morning practice involves running three, four, or more laps of a mile-long path that circles an ancient village site. Centuries ago, the members of this community perished from the relentless onslaught of introduced diseases. Measles, smallpox, influenza, and even the common cold devastated a population that had been sealed off from the rest of humanity for tens of thousands of years and that was lacking the necessary immunities to protect them from these diseases. The souls who passed away winged their way upward to the eternal realm. Their sacredness continues to permeate the soil that nurtures the plants, just as it encases their tombs. Their physical presence may be absent, but their spirits endure.

As I run, I feel the wind's rush against my face and see wind ripple through the grass. I focus on the intake and outtake of my own breath. The word *breath* in Lakota is the same Lakota word as *life*. Its root is *ni*, which refers to the collective life of all of creation. I ponder White Buffalo Calf Maiden's song:

Niyáŋ tȟaŋíŋyaŋ with visible breath
mawáni ye I am walking
oyáte waŋ this nation (this Buffalo Nation)

imáwani I walk toward
na and
ho'tȟaŋíŋyaŋ my voice is heard
mawáni ye I am walking
niyáŋ tȟaŋíŋyaŋ with visible breath
mawáni ye I am walking
walúta waŋ this scarlet relic
awáu we (for it) I am bringing

The White Buffalo Calf Maiden sang this song as she approached the camp of people awaiting her teachings. On her back, she carried a bundle containing the pipe. *With visible breath,* she repeated, *I am walking.* This breath is the breath of the Holy Spirit wafted over the world when the Voice of God resounds. With each new religious Dispensation, Divine Teachers, Manifestations of God, appear in human form and revive mankind with new spiritual teachings. Their influence is similar to the coming of spring after a long winter. The songbirds soar upon this breath of spring and stir up all of creation with their song.

The breath of the White Buffalo Calf Maiden transformed the hearts and minds of the people. Her teachings caused a disparate body of individuals to unite and gain in strength. From her teachings, these different people became a nation. This Message was sacred, as symbolized in the bundle the Maiden carried: the scarlet, holy relic of the pipe, or walúta. *Walúta* translates to "something red, ancient, and sacred" and is a reference to God's Covenant. In this instance it refers to the first *čhaŋnúŋpa / pipe.*

Continuing to run, I glance at a notecard that I had selected from a stack at home to carry with me. I had previously written passages from the Bahá'í writings on each card. As I run, I repeat the passage of my daily pick. The words replace the mindless chatter of my brain. I consider each word and phrase. This practice of mine allows me to more deeply ponder and memorize the Word of God—to find clarity and possible solutions to the challenges I face.

On this run, I ponder a favorite prayer for children, an allegorical prayer, about heavenly influences in the rearing of children: "O God! Educate these children. These children are the plants of Thine orchard, the flowers of Thy meadow, the roses of Thy garden. Let Thy rain fall upon them; let the Sun of Reality shine upon them with Thy love. Let Thy breeze refresh them in order that they may be trained, grow and develop, and appear in the utmost beauty. Thou art the Giver. Thou art the Compassionate."*

Often, I recall my days as an elementary school teacher. In the long winter months, when outdoor play was deemed unsafe, the children often drew pictures inside during recess. Many drew similar pictures of idyllic summer scenes. A strip of green lined the bottom of the page; blue shades filled the top half. A happy-face sun beamed from the upper right-hand corner. Squiggly-lined birds and clouds moved across the top of the page, while colorful flowers sprouted from the bottom center. The central motif would be a colorful flower, house, or tree (the same scene found on every refrigerator, office cubicle, or living room of every family with small children around the world).

I often looked outside to the contrasting white-out blizzard conditions and then back to these illustrations. "What inspired your beautiful drawing?" I would ask the children. "Where is this?"

The kids would always give me a puzzled expression, then, ignoring my question, would continue drawing.

As I read the prayer and run, I reflect that these children are drawing self-portraits—illustrations of their pure inner condition. Children, like flowers in God's meadow, have the potential to adorn the world with beauty. They need the sun of reality shining upon them with love and a gentle rain from the clouds to grow. This they must receive not only from God but from their caregivers. All the way to and beyond early adulthood, they require loving education from their parents, family, and community to release their true potential.

However, releasing one's potentialities in a historically oppressed and isolated region, such as Standing Rock, presents obstacles.

Reservations were created throughout the 1800s by the federal government. The government enforced solemn and often illegal treaties in which vast tracts of Indigenous lands were exchanged for miniscule submarginal lands. Certain guarantees of education, health, and other services were to be provided in perpetuity by the federal government to prevent land

---

* 'Abdu'l-Bahá, in *Bahá'í Prayers*, p. 28.

boundaries and rights disputes between Whites and Natives. The Federal Trust Doctrine declared the government the trustee of Indian affairs—and thus the legal owner and manager of the land. This and subsequent acts and treaties involved the relocation of tribal communities. The government expressed intentions to provide housing, employment, and basic infrastructure but has continually fallen short on those promises.

Standing Rock, an approximate 3500-square-mile reservation located in both South and North Dakota, suffered what scholar Vine Deloria, Jr. called "the single most destructive act ever perpetrated on any tribe by the United States," the Pick-Sloan Act.* It pains me to consider and write about this historical atrocity committed against my tribal community.

The Pick-Sloan Flood Control Act of 1944 authorized the construction of over fifty dams in the Missouri River, its tributaries, and other connecting rivers. History books may describe how these efforts controlled flooding, provided water for irrigation and municipalities, generated power throughout some of the central states, and even provided great watersport fun for nearby residents. But the devastating cost to the tribal people remains largely unwritten.

Thousands of residents of Standing Rock who lived along the Missouri were relocated against their wishes to areas that could not accommodate their subsistence lifestyle. After millennia of living communally along the river and relying on the water for fish and fertile land for game, timber, and agriculture, the once-stable community was moved to lands that could not sustain its way of life. The new town sites had no infrastructure—no roads, water systems, schools, or community facilities. The government provided individual land allotments with small shacks for the people to live in.

The people resisted, but they had no recourse. Prior to the relocation, the tribal communities were independent. Suddenly, they could not grow their own food or care for livestock. They were now placed in the humiliating position of dependency on the government that removed them from their homes in the first place.

---

* Peter Capossela, *Impacts of the Army Corps of Engineers' Pick-Sloan Program on the Indian Tribes of the Missouri River Basin,* Journal of Environmental Law & Litigation, Volume 30 Number 1, 157 (March 2015).

The federal government made other direct efforts to force assimilation upon American Indians; "Indian Termination" shaped the laws and policy of the government between the 1940s and 1960s. The Indian Relocation Act of 1965 pushed American Indians to leave reservations and relocate to urban centers; it dissolved federal recognition of tribal communities and ended financial support for hospitals, schools, and other services on the reservations. Though some moving and accommodation expenses were covered and basic vocational training provided, nothing could have prepared the Indigenous relocatees for the culture shock, discrimination, and isolation they faced outside of their reservation communities. Most of the Indigenous population secured only low-paying jobs that did not cover the cost of urban living. The Indigenous people were lonely and disconnected from the close-knit communities to which they were accustomed. Teachers of Indigenous children used a Eurocentric curriculum, and the children endured implicit and explicit bias from teachers and administrators. This unjust treatment manifested itself in poor educational outcomes.

Prior to the Relocation Act, the creation of boarding schools devastated American Indian populations. Children were forcibly taken from their families and placed in these schools. Designed to eradicate Native American language, culture, and religious practices, these schools had the stated goal of "kill the Indian to save the man." Indigenous children were indoctrinated in Christianity and other practices of the dominant culture. They performed hard labor. They were given Western names. They lost their homes, their families and communities, and they were severed from their heritage and cultural identities. Scholars have explored the effects of five generations of this widespread atrocity and affirm that up to half of the students in these boarding schools did not survive. They became casualties to alcoholism and suicide; they transmitted the abuse they experienced down through the generations.

"It's not necessary for an eagle to become a crow." This was Sitting Bull's response when asked to assimilate and acculturate. The idea was that we are all born to soar, to use the wings of knowledge, love, and spirit to reunite with our heavenly origin. I do not think that Sitting Bull had anything against or intended to put down crows. But their nature is to squabble and fight over roadkill and other forms of carrion and to make a cacophonous racket in the process. He was emphasizing that we need to claim and live our birthright. The Lakota had formerly lived as eagles. They had handled their own material and spiritual affairs, and they had taken pride in their thriving communities and vibrant culture.

However, the Lakota have been forced to live as crows for generations. One treaty after another relocated entire populations, placed community land in the hands of the government, and stripped the community of its resources. Longstanding patterns of destabilizing the Indian way of life have prevented entire communities from making material strides and realizing their spiritual prosperity. The legacy of oppression persists.

Today, the poorest counties in the country, as identified by the census bureau, are here in South Dakota. According to the Pew Research Center in 2014, the poverty rate is a little over forty-three percent—almost triple the national average. The enormous unemployment rate on the reservation has had a devastating effect. Too many Indigenous people living in these counties struggle to meet their basic needs for food, healthcare, and housing.

The poor economy on the reservations has resulted in few businesses opening doors there. The nearest city with shopping malls and full-service grocery stores is in Aberdeen, South Dakota, over one hundred miles away from my home in Wakpala. The scarcity of grocery stores on the reservation, along with the lack of access to transportation, causes most residents to purchase overpriced, unhealthy food at convenience stores. Though historically tribal members relied on the land to provide their food and basic needs, forced relocations made the subsistence lifestyle impossible and stripped a tribe of the ability to provide for itself. The lack of access to real food contributes to high rates of obesity and diabetes.

Proper health care, necessary to deal with these problems, is lacking, and few physicians are willing to serve in remote and impoverished areas. Four full-time doctors staff a clinic in McLaughlin and a small hospital in Fort Yates, where they struggle to meet the needs of approximately ten thousand people. When residents seek treatment, they wait hours and hours to be seen. However, most do not seek healthcare and dental treatment or follow basic hygienic practices. In a state of resignation, many can't imagine the possibility of changing their poor health or lifestyle.

How does one undo the effects of discrimination when discrimination and inequality still persists? How does one handle the feelings of powerlessness? Depression and suicide rates are high among the Indigenous population. Many turn to alcohol, which exacerbates the high depression rates. In some tribes, nearly eighty-five percent of the population struggles with alcohol dependency, which has become an epidemic.

The insurmountable challenges of poverty also lead to relationship problems—with oneself, one's spouse, one's children, one's extended family, and one's friends. Parents, for several generations, have lost sight of what it means to parent. For decades, social service agencies have removed Indian children from homes deemed unsuitable and have placed them in the foster care system, often away from the reservation, their extended family, and their cultural roots. Biological parents are not guided to resources they need for transformation. This lack of guidance continues the destruction of the family unit started in the era of boarding schools.

Rather than being seen as continued victims of discrimination and oppression, members of my tribal community are often viewed as incapable of providing for themselves. A lack of understanding of the causes for the poverty and social ills on the reservation harms the spirit of an entire group of people, and they lose sense of their own inherent nobility.

Standing Rock serves as a homeland to many Indigenous people. Both the most capable and blessed reside with the downtrodden here. They are drawn to the land of our ancestors. Interestingly, the trend for towns surrounding the reservations is depopulation; these areas have become ghost towns, with abandoned schools and few young people.

The reservations, however, are experiencing rapid population growth. The median age is around eighteen. The growing population of young people make it ripe for transformation. All parts of a community must rise up—the institutions and the individuals—for change to occur. But, when institutions continually deny the legacy of inequality and continue to perpetuate unjust practices, how can a population find the necessary hope to transform?

The revitalization of our community and taking charge of our spiritual and material destiny are pressing concerns among the people of Standing Rock. Education is a strong focus; efforts to revive and strengthen tribal colleges such as Sitting Bull College are underway. The food sovereignty movement, involving Indigenous-driven efforts to embrace traditional ways of producing food, continues to grow on the reservations. This global movement has brought numerous tribal communities back to implementing traditional methods of growing food, of increasing the knowledge and use of traditional plants, of promoting nutritious diets, of restoring cultural food practices, and of serving as stewards of the natural world.

A cultural renaissance is also underway. The Lakota community went from almost no use of our native language to a linguistic cultural shift—a gradual, increased use of our language. I specifically remember many elders praying for the revitalization of our language. Many tribal members have balked about the leadership role nontribal members were and are taking in language renewal. Jan Ulrich, from the Czech Republic, is the linguistic genius behind the development of a comprehensive dictionary of Lakota. He also created a consistent orthography that was based on the pioneering linguistic work of great native Standing Rock linguist and scholar Ella Deloria. He recently completed *Lakota Handbook*, a pedagogically-sequenced workbook of Lakota grammar. I believe that once the prayers of the elders were released, we were not able to control the manner in which they were fulfilled. Ulrich's work proves that the human spirit transcends language, as well as gender, race, and nationality.

In 2016, the Lakota Summer Institute celebrated its tenth year of bringing together fluent Lakota language speakers and second language learners. Many schools on the reservation offer Lakota courses, while one hosts a full-immersion program to inspire a new generation of language learners. Increased use of the language, by both Lakota and non-Lakota learners, creates a vessel for understanding and connecting with Lakota culture and heritage. Some Lakota of my mother's generation put great labor into the language revitalization efforts, and now, decades later, we are beginning to see their efforts bear fruit.

The spiritual importance of language revitalization struck me when I watched a television interview of a Kanza elder whom I had met in his home state of Oklahoma. He was the last fluent native speaker of his language—Kansas. He answered a question about the significance of his birth language by explaining that he was orphaned and raised by his monolingual Kanza grandparents. When forced to attend school at the age of ten, he knew not a word of English. At first he struggled, as did his other monolingual classmates who were Cheyenne, Arapahoe, Pawnee, Otoe, Ioway, Missouri, Ponca, and Kiowa. He and his classmates slowly learned English and began to communicate with each other. He went on to say that he loved learning English because he was then able to make acquaintances with White people, as well as Black and Brown people. He emphasized to the interviewer that he used English to talk to people, but when he wanted to talk to God, he had to use His language. The logic may have been lost on a few viewers, but essentially he was saying that God gave us a native tongue so that we may unloose it in praise of Him! This was what we must reclaim!

Great American Indian leaders of the nineteenth century who emerged at the same time as the Revelation of Bahá'u'lláh—such as Crazy Horse, Black Elk, and Sitting Bull—realized they were living at a time of great spiritual potentiality. They knew they needed to resist material forces. They did not oppose progress; they yearned for divine civilization. They prophesied a time of darkness and despair, followed by a great awakening. After seven generations, they predicted, the people would reconnect with their spiritual reality and develop their spiritual powers.

Black Elk, as a young boy, had a vision. He stood high on a peak, which symbolized the mountain of God. From there, he saw the hoop of the whole world, as well as the sacred hoop of his own people. That hoop was one of many hoops that made one circle as wide as the horizon and as high as the stars. A flowering tree grew in the center of the hoop to shelter all people. Throughout Black Elk's life, he visited *Hiŋháŋ Káǧa Pahá / Owl Maker Peak,* now known as "Black Elk Peak," the highest point between the Rockies and the Alps. This peak is situated in the heart of the Black Hills. When, as an old man, Black Elk returned to Owl Maker Hill, he lamented to see the flowering tree withered. In a feeble and sorrowful voice, he asked the Great Spirit to nourish the root of the Sacred Tree so that it would blossom again and fill with singing birds. In that final prayer, he begged the Great Spirit to help his people return to the Sacred Hoop, the flowering tree, the red road.

Sitting Bull articulated a parallel vision at the Sun Dance in 1876. He had a vision of soldiers with no ears falling headfirst into the Lakota camp—foreshadowing the victory over Custer and the seventh cavalry. Sitting Bull warned his people to not take trophies from the fallen, but in their rage and anger, some of the people did not heed his warning and allowed their lower natures to prevail. Because of their disobedience, Sitting Bull prophesied that six generations would fall into a state of stagnation and torpor. The seventh generation would awaken from this state of semiconsciousness. This generation would arise to fulfill the dreams and visions of the ancestors.

Now, seven generations later, the time has arrived for the rebirth of the flowering tree, for the transformation of Indigenous communities. The revitalization efforts underway are indications of the beginning of the realization of the prophecies of the elders. Sweeping transformation, yet to come and spoken of mostly by elders—has been a part of our community discourse for generations. Only now has this vision of transformation entered the discourse of the youth of this seventh generation.

* * *

When I fly over the Midwest, I see hundreds of lakes and rivers scattered below. Some run clear and translucent, while others appear choked, putrid, and stagnant. Those connected to the ocean have greater flow and movement and appear brighter and cleaner. The purity of the waters depends on the abundant connection to the ocean

The Missouri River winds through the prairies of the Dakotas. The river has sustained life for the animals, plants, and people on its banks for tens of thousands of years. Years ago, during the catastrophic Dust Bowl (1930–36), when the rains quit, tribal people turned to the Missouri as an oasis, a source of bounty and renewal, a life-giver. Because of its glacial origin, the river did not dry up.

Water is a frequent literal and metaphorical reference in numerous religious texts. God in the Old Testament creates floods and parts the Red Sea. The Word of God is also referred to as water in the Bible. The Word, like water, cleanses and purifies the hearts of those who read it. It nourishes and sustains life. In the Bahá'í Faith, laws exist around water. We perform ablutions before obligatory prayers. We are admonished to wash our soiled garments and to bathe, as cleanliness impacts both our physical and spiritual well-being.

The Bahá'í writings also place importance on agricultural and environmental integrity. Arthur Dahl explains in "The Bahá'í Perspective on Water": "The wise management of all the natural resources of the planet, including water, will require a global approach, since water is not a respecter of national boundaries. The use, sharing, protection and management of water need to be governed by spiritual principles of justice and equity, and the fundamental concept of moderation. Decisions on water need to be taken through processes of consultation involving all those concerned or affected."*

The judicious care of water, the most abundant natural resource, which covers about seventy percent of the earth's surface, has become a critical global issue. Water, a fundamental human right, is required to sustain all life on this planet. Yet large corporations continue to commodify this basic human right and charge rates for water service that limit access. Not only is the cost prohibitive, pollution further inhibits access to clean water. This lack of respect for *Uŋčí Makhá*, Grandmother Earth, also results in health problems and disease.

Indigenous people's historic fight for our land extends to water. In recent years, Standing Rock has caught national and global attention for the Standing Rock tribe's protest of the construction of the Dakota Access Pipeline (DAPL). This almost four billion dollar project would construct a pipeline to carry 470,000 barrels of crude oil a day from the fracking fields of western North Dakota to Illinois.

Initially, the pipeline was to be routed north of Bismarck. When residents of Bismarck complained, DAPL rerouted the pipeline construction to run a few yards/meters away from the Standing Rock Reservation reservation border. The revised plans would have caused the pipeline construction to cross illegally-seized treaty lands. The status of these lands had never been resolved in court. Some farmers and ranchers accepted thousands of dollars from state and federal agencies to allow the pipeline to cross their land. While some tribal members were open to this offer, the majority of tribal members objected. Though the pipeline would create jobs and provide income to the local economy, members of the Standing Rock Tribe understood these benefits as temporary and saw greater problems with the con-

---

* Arthur Lyon Dahl, *The Bahá'í Perspective on Water,* Bahá'í Library Online. http://www.bahai-library.com.

struction. They saw the pipeline as a cultural and environmental danger. The pipeline route would cross land where our ancestors once hunted and fished, as well as lands where our ancestors were buried. Moreover, the tribe felt an obligation to protect water. The pipeline would cross underneath the tribe's only water source. An oil spill would devastate the local wildlife and endanger the health of the people living in the surrounding area. A spill would also irrevocably damage the water supply. Cleanup of pipeline spills have only been partially successful in the past and have left tens of thousands of barrels of oil polluting the environment for years.*

The tribe had long been ignored, abused, deceived, and destroyed by dominant powers, and the routing of the pipeline played into these same patterns. The original pathway of the pipeline would have passed through the predominately white, wealthier city of Bismarck; however, when the residents of Bismarck complained, the pipeline was rerouted. When members of the Standing Rock tribal community expressed similar concerns, we were not given the same regard.

With the decision to route the pipeline along the reservation, the young people of Standing Rock arose. Many people of the older generation believed this cause was lost, and they saw this as yet another colonizing beast that couldn't be stopped. But the youth, not wanting to give up, believed the words and actions of the tribe could protect the environment and achieve justice. Igniting a spiritual fire, they advocated for the tribe to engage in peaceful, direct, and nonviolent resistance. *This is in our blood, this is in our history*, the youth shared.

The youth reminded the tribe of our belief that all life is sacred and interrelated, reflecting qualities of the Divine. The physical essence of water has spiritual significance—it is the first medicine, a purifier, a bestower of health. A spill or pipe break could poison the water supply for the entire tribe and numerous other cities that relied on the Missouri River as their water source. How many more examples of environmental harm did we need?

And so what is now known as the Water Protector Movement began—a movement led by Indigenous youth that attracted attention and support

* Stover, "America's Dangerous Pipelines," http://www.biologicaldiversity.org/campaigns/americas_dangerous_pipelines/.

from people all around the world. The youth realized that they were the generation who had been prophesied by the ancestors. They listened for and heard the song of their spirit—so different than the petty calls of materialism and moral laxity—and fueled this growing movement.

In April, 2016, a few youth approached the tribal council for consent to set up a prayer camp to serve as the heart of their peaceful, spiritual advocation for justice and environmental rights. The youth constructed their camp at the mouth of the Cannonball River, a place of pilgrimage for the Mandan. There, they lit a fire that was maintained by the camp, a fire that was not allowed to die out. They prayed and carried forth traditional ceremonies. Alcohol and drug use were prohibited. A profoundly spiritual atmosphere was maintained through prayer and communion with God. Divine principles and selflessness were the core virtues and elements governing the movement. The water protectors relied on consultation, unified action, work done in the spirit of service, and advocating for the best interest of future generations.

As members of numerous tribal communities began to see the Water Protection Movement as fulfillment of the seventh generation prophecy, more joined the efforts. At the annual Long Soldier District Powwow—the largest powwow on the reservation—the Water Protectors took center stage to share their concerns during the Saturday evening grand entry. Within a week the tiny camp of tens exploded to thousands. More camps were set up. Thousands and thousands of thípis and long-houses were set up. The cold spring weather challenged everyone to work together in a spirit of unity to prepare food and lodging and to maintain the fire. Many served the camps by cleaning, cooking, organizing childcare, and even setting up a school environment for the children at the camps.

My wife, all four of my children, and I feel deeply that this movement was just, and each of us has participated in our own way, and as members of the Lakota tribe, in this awakening process. I visited many of these camps. There, I had the privilege of explaining the sacred sites and sharing the songs associated with them. If we did not have our language, our songs, and our oral tradition, what did we have to claim a relationship with these sites? One of the songs I sang went like this: *"Thuŋkášila waŋmáyaŋ ka yo. Makȟá-ta táku wakȟáŋ mayák'upi čha lenáke tȟaŋíŋyaŋ ye čhe tȟaŋíŋyaŋ yaúŋ kte."* This translates roughly as *"Grandfather behold me. All the holiness upon the earth reflects/manifests You(r) reality."* This song is a great expression of the principle that everything in this world is a physical manifestation of a spiritual reality. The creation (both the seen and unseen) is the handiwork of one Creator. Everything in this physical world is a counterpart to something in the unseen realms, and the only way we can access the unseen realms is to meditate, pray, and study this physical counterpart.

Fueled by the spiritual energy of the prayer camps initiated by the Lakota tribe, members of numerous other tribes began to have visions that resulted in inspired action. In early April, a long-distance runner decided to initiate a run to Omaha to deliver a letter to the Army Corp of Engineers. This run attracted other bands on the reservation, and subsequent runs—one all the way to Washington D.C.—were planned. During these runs, an eagle staff, representing the ascendant nature of the human spirit, was carried and transported from individual to individual across the country. The runs represented clarion calls to justice and showed the result of unified action.

Running is a devotional practice throughout the Western Hemisphere in tribal communities. A particular distance is pledged as part of a collective endeavor. The great walkers in Bolivia had a devotional purpose. The movement across the earth propels the prayer. The prayer is not static, and momentum is created by the energy of the collective participants. Throughout the world, numerous walks and runs are held for a cause greater than the participants' completion of a race. The St. Jude's Marathon in Memphis, Tennessee, raises awareness and needed funds for the hospital. Runners raise awareness of cancer, diabetes, heart disease, and more. This particular run, inspired by visions, raised awareness of the Water Protectors Movement and issues of justice.

The movement grew as days turned to months. Schools across the reservation organized trips so students could come to learn about the situation and participate in the protest. Environmental activists and supporters from other tribal and non-tribal communities—including those from Ecuador, the Amazon, and Hawaii—came to show their solidarity with Standing Rock. A group from Arizona performed their songs and prayers. With this surge of activity, I marveled at how a small movement of youth deciding to become champions of their own destiny had empowered so many others to preserve and protect the environment.

As the camps grew in size and support, military personnel, law enforcement officials, and security workers appeared. Bunkers and barracks lined formerly quiet rural roads, and choppers hovered over the prairies. Many believe officials were dusting the prairies with chemicals when so many individuals in the camps became sick.

Over Labor Day weekend of 2016, a deeply disturbing event disrupted the efforts. Employees of DAPL arrived with bulldozers to the sacred grounds. They desecrated the grounds and ancient artifacts, and they upset gravesites. Just days before, members of the tribe had submitted legal papers to protect these sacred sites. Hearing the bulldozers in the distance, water protectors rushed to the scene. When they arrived, authorities unleashed attack dogs and used pepper spray, pressurized cold water, rubber bullets, and tear gas on the peaceful protestors.

To maintain the nonviolent and peaceful aspects of the resistance, the elders reminded the water protectors to remember Sitting Bull's prophecy regarding the tactics of the oppressors to incite negative emotions. The elders reminded the youth that they could not afford to let negative emotions rule. They urged them to maintain the spiritual integrity of the movement and, in so doing, conform to the directives of the ancestors.

Word spread through the news and social media of these aggressive actions, and more people arrived to support the water protectors. Among the supporters to arrive were veterans of combat, joining us, they said, because they had sworn an oath to protect liberty and justice for the citizens of this nation and believed that what had happened was a great injustice. With this wave of support came additional opposition. Opponents described the movement in the foulest possible language and propagated false information.

With the sudden growth, tension emerged in the camps. Once a fairly unknown place, Standing Rock was now on the world stage. To express solidarity with the tribal communities and environmental movement, supporters from around the globe contributed large amounts of funds to maintain the camps. Some came with alternative agendas and goals; the isolated, individual actions of some were publicized widely and exaggerated to question the validity of the Water Protection Movement. All of this attention—both positive and negative—challenged the community.

Different ideas about how to proceed created conflict, and disunity gripped the community. The suffering caused by this internal division was much greater than the obstacles that came from the outside.

Prior to this, one of the elders had a vision of a black snake rising up. This paralleled ancient lore that Monster Beings—with spikes, spines, and horns—had roamed and dominated the earth for countless eons. (If these Monster Beings sound like dinosaurs, they are, and Indigenous people have known about them). The Thunder Beings battled these Monster Beings. (Scientists have determined that it was a meteor that struck on the Yucatan Peninsula that ended the age of the dinosaurs. Whatever it was, it was divine intervention that purged the world of the Monster Beings.) The Thunder Beings relied on God, and the hand of destiny purged the earth of the defilement of the Monster Beings and reduced them to their current form of lizards, snakes, and turtles. The Great Spirit thus cleansed the earth and prepared the world for a new order of existence.

A prophecy existed of a recrudescence of these Monster Beings. Some might interpret this prophecy literally, but from a metaphorical standpoint, the exploration and release of fossil fuels are the recurrence of these beings. Fossil fuels are closely linked with materialism, and their exploration has unlocked monstrosities in the hearts of humanity—greed, ego, and a thirst for power. The pipeline, too, was similar to a black snake sneaking underneath the earth and waters.

The elder's prophecy was right. The Monster Beings had once again asserted ascendency—not through the physical dangers of the pipeline itself, but through the materialism, greed, and aggression of mankind. We must rely on prayer to respond to the injustices that occur when materialism ensnares people. Nonviolence is the only response. We must aid and support the divine forces and must refrain from using violence, which only throws fuel onto the fire. This is true whether materialistic monstrous forces are internal or external. When those forces rise within us, berating ourselves will not serve as a healing and unifying agent. We must rely on prayer, realign ourselves to divine powers, and move forward to work for justice.

In early 2017, an executive order was signed to begin the construction of the Dakota Access Pipeline. To some, it may have seemed as though this movement had come to an end and even failed. However, this sort of thought does not contribute to the transformation of the world. The Water Protector Movement triggered a dynamic spiritual awakening in Standing Rock. It initially brought great unity of thought and action to the tribe. This local issue attracted global support from the masses who believe in protecting the earth's resources. The Water Protectors did not arise to carry out these efforts in order to receive validation from materially driven institutions. Rather, they arose because they felt a divine calling to protect the environment and to seek justice. The spiritual forces unleashed through this movement—unity, consultation, devotion, perseverance in the face of opposition, and service to the greater good—have already released forces that have changed our world.

The movement did not end with the evacuation and bulldozing of the camps, nor with the signing of the executive order. We must realize the path to achieving our goals is not a straight line and that there are setbacks and pitfalls. Dead-ends become curves in the road. Those who persevere will follow that curve, even if storms blind their vision and slow their steps. Faith and surrender are required. Always, we must keep forging ahead.

Though we have far to travel on this path of transformation, though this generation cannot even begin to imagine the vision of a united world, we must do our part. We must contribute to the construction of new systems and must serve those most impacted by the injustices of the old systems.

Those of us who have declared our belief in Bahá'u'lláh as the latest Manifestation of God strive to translate His teachings into action—teachings we believe are sent from God to transform the individual and to advance civilization. Many people today—including Bahá'ís, members of other Faith communities, and individuals of good conscience—have come to embrace Bahá'u'lláh's teachings of love, justice, and unity. The Bahá'í Faith upholds the oneness of humanity, the oneness of religion, and the oneness of God. Bahá'u'lláh taught that we must eliminate prejudices of all kinds—racial, class, gender, ethnic, religious. Religion and science are not in conflict with one another, and education unleashes the gems latent within humankind. We must work to serve our communities, just as we develop our own spiritual qualities. We must utilize our own gifts and capacities in service to the common good. Individuals, communities, and institutions must strive together for humanity's unification, coming to see that indeed: "the earth is one country, and mankind its citizens."*

Mankind's reality at this stage in its development, as the Universal House of Justice states, is far from this vision. Rather than depress and paralyze us, this realization must encourage us to arise and do our part to alleviate the suffering of humanity. Discussing how we can transform the world and create a different order, the Universal House of Justice writes, "We set this objective before the Bahá'í world conscious that it is truly formidable; that a herculean labour will be required; that many sacrifices will have to be made. But faced with the plight of a world that suffers more each day bereft of Bahá'u'lláh's elixir, we cannot, in conscience, ask anything less of His devoted followers."**

On her deathbed, my mother wrote a message, a difficult task due to her declining condition. These words took her nearly an hour to write and required all of her strength. In those final moments, before her soul left this world and winged its way to the next one, she wrote:

> "To the Bahá'í youth of the World,
> We come to you in loving consultation.
> Signed,
> The Locke family"

Why, in her last moments, did my mother choose to address the Bahá'í youth of the world? Who is the "we" in "we come to you in loving consultation?" Why did she write these words?

I ponder these questions. I ponder the Bahá'í youth and their collaborators of all different backgrounds who want to transform the world and work for unity. She appeals to them in a spirit of love and humility. In those words "To the Bahá'í youth of the world," she lays her concerns at the feet of these youth, concerns that the work she had dedicated her life to—achieving justice—is not yet over and that the youth must be the ones to arise to champion the cause of justice.

---

* Bahá'u'lláh, *Gleanings from the Writings of Bahá'u'lláh*, no. 117.1.
** Letter from the Universal House of Justice dated December 29, 2015, ¶20.

My mother knew that youth are at a time of their lives of great potential. They have energy, enthusiasm, and vitality that are unique to this stage of their lives. They are not yet entrenched in the status quo; most are eager to build the world anew. They serve as examples to those younger than themselves. As they begin to establish themselves in their careers, start families, pursue education, serve their communities, and build a foundation for a successful future, they often wonder how they will contribute to the betterment of their communities and how they will leave their mark on the world. They wonder what their purpose in life will be.

I think back to when I was a youth. I longed to find my path, but I often felt lost and purposeless. Though I had university degrees, work, and a family of my own, I felt that I had not yet found my red path. I had not yet created a life where my spiritual values aligned with my day-to-day activities. I did not believe that I was making the world a better place.

Through obedience to the spiritual law of fasting, prayer, and facing my struggles by relying upon God, I found my path. Finding my path was a bounty. Bahá'u'lláh has revealed, "O Son of Man! Noble have I created thee, yet thou hast abased thyself. Rise then unto that for which thou wast created."* As a youth, these words spoke to me deeply. Whenever I read this passage, I think of an airplane. The airplane on the ground moves clumsily, clunkily along the tarmac, and it must generate enormous power to pick up speed. Finally, its wheels lift from the land. It ascends higher and higher, still requiring great power to reach the right elevation where flight becomes smooth. If that power is cut off for just a moment, the plane begins to drop from the sky. Like the plane, we must plug in to divine power and exert all of our energies to arise to the heights where we belong.

My mom then wrote, "*We come to you in loving consultation.*" Is the "we" the ancestral voice of North America? Is it the National Spiritual Assembly, the administrative body for the Bahá'ís of the United States of which my mom served as a member? Is the "we" our family? Perhaps she uses the pronoun "we" rather than "I" because of the importance of working together to achieve justice.

---

* Bahá'u'lláh, The Hidden Words, Arabic no. 22.

My mom well knew the story of the V-shape flight of migratory birds. To preserve energy, migratory birds fly in a V-shaped formation to cut into the wind. The V-shape fosters orientation and communication. When the leading birds become tired, they fall to the back, and other birds assume the lead role. No one bird becomes exhausted; all get their chance at the forefront. When geese fly together, they fly further. If one bird is injured, a couple of birds fall out of formation to remain with their companion.

Knowing that the world beyond was mere breaths away, my mother made her final appeal for unity. Now, we who are left on this earth must strive to transform the "I" so celebrated in our cultures into the collective "We." Living together on our planet and working for its transformation requires loving consultation and collaboration. We must build a home on Mother Earth for all people—before it is time to leave and enter the mystical spiritual realms. We must build the Kingdom of God on earth.

My mother knew sign language and used to sign the Indian version of the twenty-third Psalm. She learned it when she was a young girl and shared it with others often, to great effect:

The Great Father Above is the Shepherd Chief
I am His and with Him, I have not want.
He throws out to me a rope, and the name of the rope is Love.
He draws me, and He draws me,
and He draws me to a place where the grass is green and the water is good.
I eat and lie down satisfied.
Sometime, it may be soon, it may be longer, it may be a long, long time,
The Shepherd Chief will lead me to a place between mountains.
It is dark there, but I will be afraid not.
I will draw back not.
For it is there, between these mountains, that the Shepherd Chief will meet
    me.
Sometimes the Shepherd Chief makes this love rope into a whip.
But afterward He gives me a staff to lean upon.
He puts his hands upon my head, and all the tired is gone.
He spreads before me a table with many good things to eat.
My cup fills until it runs over.
What I tell you is true. I lie not.

For the roads lead to a great Lodge where dwells the Shepherd Chief,
And after I die, I will be with Him forever and ever.

This Psalm is a particularly great synopsis of the Covenant between God and man. It speaks to the prophecy of the day of fulfillment, when man attains the presence of God. The banquet spread before man is a spiritual one, a universal metaphor of spiritual food. This is the spiritual nourishment that enables our eyes to perceive the spiritual reality, our ears to attune to the divine intonations, our hearts to become the receptacles of divine grace, our legs empowered to advance on the path of service. This Psalm speaks to the promise that we will be relieved of the burden of the roles we have taken on in this world—that we will shed the roles of oppressed and oppressor, of enslaved and enslavers—to take on our true spiritual identity.

Whenever I imagine my mom signing this particular Psalm, I envision a great mountain. At the top of the mountain, there is a lodge where God, the Shepherd Chief, lives. All the diverse kindreds of the world traverse different paths leading to the same pinnacle. Previously, in the history of mankind, each people and group made their way separately up this peak; indeed, different religious leaders denounced all those who were not part of their faith. Yet we are now at a point where we see each other on this quest. We are beginning to see that we must scale these heights together to achieve spiritual and material prosperity. We must abandon nationalism, racism, and xenophobia. We must rely on the Divine Messenger for this day to guide us. And once we reach this great summit, we cannot come back. We must launch our flight, eagles as we are, into the New Day.

I realize I have not done enough in my life. If I had to apologize, it would be for not being more thoughtful and diligent about the reality that we are living in a unique time in history. Now humanity is more interconnected and aware than it has ever been. This is the Day of God.

I feel so blessed to see the sunrise every morning, to hear the birds and the north winds in the wintertime. I feel blessed to feel the power of the natural world. My wish for the future generations is that they use our homeland as a beautiful nest from which to raise up enlightened future generations who can love God and serve humanity.

Yes, the Locke family comes to you in loving consultation, whether from the realms above or here on earth. It is our hope that all people, most especially the youth, will reflect on how we can live lives of service to human-ity. May we strive to have vision that embraces the whole world, rather than vision confined to our own selves. May we all work towards creating Bahá'u'lláh's vision of a prosperous and peaceful world. As 'Abdu'l-Bahá has said, "Bahá'u'lláh has drawn the circle of unity, He has made a design for the uniting of all the peoples, and for the gathering of them all under the shelter of the tent of universal unity. This is the work of the Divine Bounty, and we must all strive with heart and soul until we have the reality of unity in our midst, and as we work, so will strength be given unto us."*

* 'Abdu'l-Bahá, *Paris Talks*, no. 15.12.

AFTERWORD BY KIM DOUGLAS

I sat in quiet meditation after saying a few morning prayers and focused on my vision board, a collage that contained images of my faith; my family; and my professional ambitions as a writer, editor, and business leader. A photograph of the Shrine of Bahá'u'lláh was at the center of the board, surrounded by pictures of my husband, daughters, and grandsons. Images of fruits and vegetables, yoga poses, and a bicycle reflected my commitment to a healthy lifestyle. The words "Leadership Teams" were significant to me because my reason for shifting from my work as a professor to developing a franchise was to inspire healthy living and empower individuals, especially women, to break free of cultural norms and personal limitations that hold us back and to step into greatness, to become leaders, and to serve our world in significant ways.

One such leader I admired was Patricia Locke. She was a social justice activist who won a MacArthur grant and was inducted posthumously into the Women's Hall of Fame. I had read about and admired her life's work. She embodied virtues I prayed to more fully develop in myself, so naturally her picture was on my vision board.

As I gazed at the image of Patricia Locke, a woman who exuded dignity and strength, I heard the words, "Help my son, Kevin, write a book about his life."

"Oh my," I thought to myself. "Now there's a vain imagining."

The next morning, in the very same spot I sat every morning, the same words came to me, "Help my son, Kevin, write a book."

By the third day, I was beginning to pay attention. I had had a few mystical experiences in my life. I had also had several unpleasant experiences of not paying attention to what came to me in prayer and meditation because I thought what I was sensing was pure imagination. Then some situations occurred that made me realize I needed to listen and act on what I was hearing in these states of prayer and meditation.

So I was being told to help Kevin Locke write a book.

Hmmm.

I knew who Kevin Locke was, but I was certain he didn't know or remember me, someone who had been merely a face in one of his audiences.

However, the idea of a book written by Kevin Locke was incredibly appealing. Kevin, a member of the Lakota tribe, was not only well-known in our faith community, he was known both nationally and internationally as an accomplished hoop dancer, storyteller, and flutist. My husband and I had taken our children to see Kevin perform a few times. On a different occasion, we had the privilege of picking Kevin up from O'Hare airport and bringing him to the Bahá'í House of Worship in Wilmette for a meeting. I can't even remember exactly when this occurred and what meeting was being held, but I remember feeling honored to meet someone whom I had seen perform and whom I admired.

Since I had done some work with Bahá'í Publishing, I contacted Tim Moore, the general manager at the time, and asked him what he thought about the idea of having Kevin Locke write a book. As a writer, a professor who taught writing, and an editor, I was always thinking of ideas for a new book. I often set aside spare moments during the day for my writing, and because of my love for my faith, I also found myself considering book ideas for Bahá'í Publishing.

Tim liked my idea and suggested I contact Kevin to see if he was interested.

That very night, I reached out to Kevin by phone. I left a message, and he returned the call within a few days. When I proposed the idea, his first response was, "Why would anyone want to read a book about me?"

I was surprised by this question but managed to say something to the effect that his work as a hoop dancer and his service to the Bahá'í Faith would surely be of interest to others.

"I don't want to do anything that is self-serving. I'm really not interested."

Kevin didn't have a lot of time to continue our conversation due to an obligation.

"How about we talk in a few days? In the meantime, why don't we both pray more about the idea?" I suggested.

We set a time to reconnect. I had no idea how I was going to convince Kevin that this was a worthwhile goal. So, I prayed for clarity. I prayed to Patricia Locke. I wish I could say Patricia Locke spoke to me again and provided specific guidance on what I should say to her son, but that didn't happen. The only thing I sensed was to just proceed.

A few days later, I called Kevin back. Kevin was friendly, kind, genuine, and down to earth. He said again that he couldn't see how a book about his life would serve others, and I didn't really know enough about his life to honestly answer that question in a well-developed way. I only had hunches. For example, I thought his cultural knowledge and expertise, his travels, and his Bahá'í service would interest and inspire others. He, on the other hand, wasn't so sure. And then there was another problem.

"Kim, this is nice of you to think of me, but I'm not even a writer. I can't write a book. I'm not sure what would be so interesting about my life to others."

"Well, you are a great speaker, storyteller, and performer. You enrich your audiences. The content of what you share could be put in book form."

"I would need help."

"I could do that. I'm a writer. I've taught writing. I know about writing. What if we had a few conversations where I bring some questions and get to know more about your life? I think more clarity would come for both of us. Would you be open to that?"

He agreed, and this is how we began the process of creating this book, a truly unique and collaborative effort unlike any writing endeavor I have experienced. It has been one of the most rewarding experiences of my life as a writer and editor.

We faced numerous challenges and opportunities while working on *Arising*. The first was how to focus the book. In writing an autobiography or memoir, a clear direction is necessary. Writing about an entire life is impossible, and it doesn't necessarily produce good writing. Since Kevin would only agree to proceed if I could prove to him the book would serve others, I prayed for guidance and began to see possibilities that emerged from our conversations.

One of the challenges Kevin faced as a young adult was a deep sense that he wasn't doing what he was meant to be doing with his life. He had studied, earned degrees, married, and become a father, yet he had also sensed that he had a deeper purpose and mission. He didn't know what it was. During a four-day Lakota fast, Kevin—who was then in his twenties—was reduced to a sense of his nothingness before God. That is precisely when his own "arising" began.

I won't say any more than this because I want you, the reader, to experience Kevin's search for answers and how he was led to utilize his faith, his culture, and his vocation to live a life of service.

Another challenge was that my worldview differs greatly from Kevin's worldview. While we share a common faith, the Bahá'í Faith, I grew up White in America, part of what sociologists refer to as a "dominant" rather than a "minority" culture. Even though I have faced challenges as a female in our society, my ethnicity and class influenced my conditioning and the way I perceive reality. My sincere hope is that my continued commitment to undo the racial conditioning I've inherited has allowed me to work with Kevin in such a way as to honor his worldview and provide the utmost respect for his perspectives. Throughout the writing of the manuscript, I would say to Kevin, "Can you explain this situation more thoroughly? My whiteness is preventing me from fully understanding this situation." My deep desire was to support Kevin to bring to all readers the details and explanations that would help them value Lakota culture. I am grateful for Kevin's patience and willingness to explain, sometimes several times, what is so innately a part of him.

Though the following passage from the Universal House of Justice's December 28, 2010 message concerns the role of the Auxiliary Board members and their assistants, I have been drawn to and continually ponder these words:

Unqualified love free of paternalism will be indispensable if they are to help turn hesitation into courage born of trust in God and transform a yearning for excitement into a commitment to long-term action. Calm determination will be vital as they strive to demonstrate how stumbling blocks can be made stepping stones for progress. And a readiness to listen, with heightened spiritual perception, will be invaluable in identifying obstacles that may prevent some of the friends from appreciating the imperative of unified action. (par. 5)

As I ponder these words upon completion of the book, I find so many concepts apply to our experience. In addressing racism, the most challenging issue in the United States, the Guardian of the Bahá'í Faith, in paragraph 58 of his work *The Advent of Divine Justice,* exhorts white believers to "abandon once for all their usually inherent and at times subconscious sense of superiority, to correct their tendency towards revealing a patronizing attitude." In the commitment to complete this book—not an easy task—and in the process of working side-by-side, facing various challenges, I pray that if I unconsciously revealed any sort of paternalistic attitudes, Kevin forgave me. He is patient and kind, always overlooking faults and shortcomings. He was always more inclined to focus on what I was doing right than to bring up where I fell short. I also hope that, in my endless questioning, God was aiding me to develop a heightened spiritual perception and that Kevin perceived my questions as a deep desire to more fully understand and appreciate his worldview.

Another obstacle we endured was that both Kevin's and my busy work schedules, travels, and family responsibilities kept us from progressing with the book as fast as we had hoped and anticipated. Thankfully, Aleah Khavari joined Kevin and me and brought her youthful energy, talents, and expertise to help us. Aleah and I both shared a particular struggle in working with Kevin. Kevin freely shares in these pages that he is extremely private and an introvert. While he was sharing many interesting aspects of his life, we were finding it rather difficult to sometimes obtain the kind of details we knew were important and that would also make for powerful and interesting reading.

Aleah had the wonderful idea that we all needed to meet. So she left her home in Boston, I left my home in Michigan, and we met up with Kevin in Florida. This weeklong visit with Kevin, his wife Ceylan, and their daughter Patricia allowed us to forge a deeper connection and trust in one another that opened up new possibilities for a closer friendship.

Ceylan's insights and expertise especially helped us bring the last part of the book to fruition.

Last spring, I found myself stalling as the process of completing the book was approaching. For several weeks, when I had time for the work I treasured, I found myself avoiding it and not consciously understanding why. Then it dawned on me. I didn't want the process to end. I treasured the conversations, the writing and rewriting, the additional insights and discoveries, the sparks of creativity and collaboration. I realized, though, that while the process of writing this book was ending, our friendship and collaborative service were just beginning.

My prayer and hope are that we were all hollow reeds that God was able to use, and that He worked through our strengths and weaknesses to create a story that will inspire you to arise and serve humanity with the God-given gifts you have been given. I also pray that the soul of Patricia Locke is well-pleased with the results of the encouragement she gave me several years back. During certain moments, I catch myself thinking that I look forward to meeting her soul when God calls me home, and then I realize I have met her soul—in prayer, in meditation, and through her family. Her legacy endures, and I am humbled, honored, and grateful for that sweet nudge she sent my way and that, through the grace of God, I listened to.

KIM DOUGLAS
Wyoming, MI
November 2017

BIBLIOGRAPHY

Works of Bahá'u'lláh

Gleanings from the Writings of Bahá'u'lláh. Translated by Shoghi Effendi. New ed. Wilmette, IL: Bahá'í Publishing, 2005.

The Hidden Words of Bahá'u'lláh. Translated by Shoghi Effendi. Wilmette, IL: Bahá'í Publishing, 2002.

Works of 'Abdu'l-Bahá

Selections from the Writings of 'Abdu'l-Bahá. Wilmette, IL: Bahá'í Publishing, 2010.

Tablets of the Divine Plan. First pocket-sized edition. Wilmette, IL: Bahá'í Publishing Trust, 1993.

Works of the Universal House of Justice

A Wider Horizon: Selected Letters 1983–1992. Compiled by Paul Lample. Riviera Beach, FL: Palabra Publications, 1992.

Compilations

Bahá'u'lláh, the Báb, and 'Abdu'l-Bahá. *Bahá'í Prayers: A Selection of Prayers Revealed by Bahá'u'lláh, the Báb and 'Abdu'l-Bahá.* Wilmette, IL.: Bahá'í Publishing Trust, 2002.

Bahá'u'lláh, 'Abdu'l-Bahá, Shoghi Effendi, and the Universal House of Justice. *Compilation of Compilations.* Mona Vale: Bahá'í Publications Australia, 1991.

Other Works

Bahá'í International Community, Office of Public Information. *The Prosperity of Humankind*. Wilmette, IL: Bahá'í Publishing Trust, 1995.

Neihardt, John. *Black Elk Speaks: The Complete Edition*. Lincoln, NE: University of Nebraska Press, 2014.

Star of the West: The Bahá'í Magazine. Twenty-five volumes. 1910–1935. Vols. 1–14 RP Oxford: George Ronald, 1978. Complete CD Rom Version: Talisman Educational Software / Special Ideas, 2001.